CW00956908

FATHERCARE

John Griffiths was once Britain's youngest JP and reckons he is now probably, at 63, its oldest single father. He gained a degree in English at Peterhouse, Cambridge. He works from home both as a writer and running a successful independent television production company – Minerva Vision. A former journalist and broadcaster, in 1985 he founded Europe's first satellite Arts Channel which he ran for five years. However, he now regards bringing up his thirteen-year-old daughter, Emily, which he has been doing for the past seven and a half years, as his principal occupation.

A former National President of the Liberal Party, but no longer politically active, he doubts whether any of the parties have paid sufficient attention to the plight of the thousands of men who are single fathers and the many more who would like to be.

"The anecdotal material, in particular, is a valuable contribution to the study of lone fathers"
DR MARTIN RICHARDS
Director Centre for Family Research,
Cambridge University.

"Accessible, easy to read and will be popular with those engaged in or contemplating single fatherhood.
Too often 'single parent' is taken to mean 'single mother'."
JILL PITKEATHLEY
Chief Executive Carers National Association,
author of *Only Child*

OTHER BOOKS BY THE SAME AUTHOR

Non Fiction:

Afghanistan
Modern Iceland
Three Tomorrows
The Science of Winning Squash
Afghanistan: Key to a Continent
Flashpoint Afghanistan
The Third Man
Nimbus

Fiction:

The Survivors
The Queen of Spades

FATHERCARE

A Guide for Single Resident Fathers

John Griffiths

COLT BOOKS
Cambridge

For my children and their mothers with gratitude
for having taught me so much about love

Colt Books Ltd
9 Clarendon Road
Cambridge
CB2 2BH
Tel: 01223 357047
Fax: 01223 365866
First published 1997

ISBN 0 905899 56 3

British Library Cataloguing-in-Publication data:
A catalogue record for this book is available from the
British Library.

Set in Palatino

Printed and bound by Biddles Ltd, Guildford, UK.

CONTENTS

ACKNOWLEDGEMENTS

I am indebted to many for help, information and advice in devising my research and writing my text, but in particular to Dr Martin Richards, head of the Family Studies Centre at Cambridge University for both research guidance and general advice, to Richard Sara, a benefits specialist, who advised me on those aspects of the book and to my editor, Gina Keene. Any errors, however, are mine not theirs. Above all I am grateful to the fifty-two lone fathers who amidst all their other commitments found time to bare their souls and sorrows for the benefit of others in like situations or threatened with them.

NOTE ON REFERENCES:

The letters and numbers in brackets in the text refer either to the research or publication on which an assertion is based and where an idea can be explored further or to the identifying letter of one of the survey subjects. The lone fathers in the survey have been given arbitrary first names in the text itself to preserve their anonymity, but their letter suffix will enable a reader to relate comments to the general information about that subject in the tabulations of research results in Appendix Three at the end of the book. A short bibliography of work I found particularly relevant is given at the end of the book. Each title is preceded by the letter and number by which it is identified in the text. A Q before a reference letter means I have taken a quotation from the work referred to, but not necessarily checked the primary source.
The addresses and telephone numbers of organisations referred to in the text are given in Appendix One. References to tables in the text are by the number of the table in Appendix Three.

INTRODUCTION

PROSPERO: I have done nothing but in care of thee – of thee, my dear one! thee my daughter!

The Tempest Act I Sc II

Prospero was deluding himself. As well as being a loving and protective lone father he was also a man who loved to control. As the play unfolds, he eventually learns to let go, to grant freedom to those he controls, including his only child. If we are honest, it is the same for present day lone fathers (and lone mothers) who have any choice in the matter though the balance is different in different cases. Our motives for taking on the lone parent role are a mixture of altruism and ego-bolstering even though concern for the children is almost always the more important.

Like so many men today I did not want my marriage to end (seventy-five per cent of British divorces are started by wives) but like so many men today I had been blind to the fact that it was about to and done too little to mend it. When Carole left with her (then) lover for what she felt to be good and sufficient reasons I was in a state of shock for a time. A couple of weeks before she left, the satellite Arts Channel I had founded, sunk most of my modest capital in and run for the previous five years, was axed by its majority shareholder. When, less than a month later, I found myself standing with my sons at the funeral of my first wife (whom I had left with three teenagers ten years earlier) I was not only in danger of wallowing in self-pity, but so lacking in self-confidence, about my judgement and much else, that I only had instinct to go on.

A day or so later my five-and-a-half year old daughter, Emily, found me crying – something I did often, but usually in private at this time. She took my hand and said 'cheer up daddy. I'll tell you some jokes'. As she stood in front of me solemnly reciting the riddles of her infant class I did indeed smile, dry my eyes and in pitying her loss began the long process of ceasing to pity myself for mine and to appreciate my good fortune. The very circumstances that had conspired to knock me down now coincided to pick me up again. My daughter needed me. Moreover, needed me as a supportive, loving, practical parent to solace her in her bewildered unhappiness, not as a self-absorbed wreck. Because I no longer had a job I was in a position to provide that support and because I loved her I was determined to do it. Moreover, for both practical and emotional reasons, Carole had not tried to take Emily with her when she moved out. I would not have let her anyway and remember telling my mother-in-law over the phone that Emily would be taken from our home over my, or someone else's, dead body – and I meant it. Looking back, after seven years, I do not honestly know how much my attitude was governed by my own need to keep with me at a time of so much loss the daughter I so loved of the woman I still loved and how much by my firm and genuine belief that Emily would be better off with me than with her mother. I believe the decision has turned out to have been the right one, but whether for the right or the wrong reasons I shall never really know.

In many ways the harder part is that of the parent who does not have the daily care of her (or, more usually, his) children. If lone parenting, the post divorce damage limitation exercise – and that is all it is not some panacea – turns out to have been successful, a large part of the credit must often go to that other parent. It certainly does in our case. Although there have been deep disagreements, and fierce quarrels over what was the best thing for our daughter at different times we always thought and spoke of her as our daughter not my daughter or your daughter. Now disagreements are rare and rational and Carole and I are good friends who turn to each other for advice and help. The guardian of this peace is Emily who will never allow either to say an ill word about the other.

I have given this personal information because I do not believe it is possible for anyone with experience of lone parenthood, for whatever reason, to write a completely objective book about it. But I do not think either that an outsider to this experience, however sympathetic, knowledgeable, objective and well intentioned can fully appreciate all that goes on in the heart and head of a single father or a single mother. For these reasons it seemed only fair to let the reader know at the outset the direction and background from which I approached this task so that they may make whatever allowance for my prejudices their personal experience suggests.

The sociological jargon of divorce talks unhelpfully of 'broken' families as if the damage were inevitably irreparable.

I think it more constructive to think of a 'scattered' or 'dispersed' family, as one would if a husband were working abroad, a wife in hospital long term, a son or daughter away at college or work. A family which has experienced divorce, separation or death is still a family even if they do not all still live under the same roof. Although the circumstances are very different from those in most intact families the best outcome for the children is if they are still thought of as part of a single, dispersed family. But even that constructive attitude does not resolve the central question – who are the children actually to live with?

A father's (or mother's) only justification for keeping the children of his broken relationship is that they need him as their resident parent more than they need their mother and that he will be the better parent at that time. This very first decision of all may be the hardest he has to make – in whose daily care will the children flourish more, or at least suffer less? The question is emphatically not one about which parent the child *loves* most. In the majority of families, intact or dispersed, children love one parent more or less than the other, regardless of gender, from day to day, even from minute to minute, as the tensions and pleasures of family life and child\parent relationships fluctuate. A punishing parent, for example, may be right down the charts at one moment and top of the pops again an hour later as a child either regrets its temporary feeling of hate and overcompensates or some benign action wins its approval. The fundamental thing to remember is that in ninety-five cases out of a hundred, overall a child loves both parents equally if differently.

So few men have the joy and privilege of bringing up their children, of exploring and strengthening the daily bond which is many women's richest reward. As more and more men come to realise what they are missing, so more separating fathers will want to secure that reward for themselves. But before pursuing it every father should consider carefully whether he is conscientiously observing the absolute imperative that 'the interests of the child must come first'. The courts, the Child Support Agency, the welfare services, even the most angry or broken-hearted partner in divorce or separation will endorse that sentiment – in principle. The difficulty arises when the time comes to decide exactly what those interests are. Then the temptation is to fall back on traditional and often child-damaging assumptions. One of the most damaging of these is that unless a child's mother has died or deserted she should automatically be the parent with whom a child lives. Is this always, or even nearly always, in the child's best interest?

Are men really eleven and a half times more likely than women to want to sever their lives from those of their children? Is a mother really eleven and a half times more likely to be a better single parent to a child than its father? Men love their children no less than women do, feel equal heartache and joy, pride and shame as they grow up; make no fewer sacrifices for them, demand no less of them; father, dad, daddy, pa and pop loom as large and necessary in a child's eye and heart as mother, mum, mummy, ma and mom; fathers as much as mothers are the objects of love, are turned to for care and protection as often, are as capable, in most circumstances, of nurturing and bringing up a child as any woman, yet ...

Yet there are only two lone home parent fathers for every twenty-three lone home parent mothers, not because men do not want to pick up the human pieces of their broken relationships, but because society and the law militate most heavily against their doing so. This is the starting point and moving passion behind this book, a wish to help other men achieve and manage the bringing up of the children they have fathered if they wish to and are the fitter parent to do so.

Nobody says to the bereaved widower 'you are a man, and therefore unfit to bring up your children. They must be handed over to the care of some female relative or to the local authority'. So why is it said to divorced and separated fathers? Does bereavement suddenly purge a man of all the many differences and shortcomings that he is otherwise presumed to have as a lone father? When a woman is left by death or desertion to bring up children on her own society expects her to be able to cope, either to scrape by on the pittance provided by the state or to manage the conflicting demands of job and family. A man in the same situation is expected to give up, to hand his children to a female relative, usually his mother, who steps back into the role she gave up when he married. Alternatively it is assumed that a single father should plead his incompetence and ask the Local Authority to look after his children, or that he should remarry. Is there really no other child-benefitting choice?

Child rearing is certainly exhausting, exasperating, distracting and all the other negative things parents complain about, but it is also immensely rewarding in so many ways. That being so why should men not have an equal opportunity with women to choose child care as a way of life just as women now rightly expect equal opportunity and reward in other fields? While some inequalities may still be suffered by women in economic and public life they are much smaller than they were a decade ago. The same cannot be said of the inequalities suffered by men in the private life of the family and in the right to equal care of their children when their parental partnerships end. Nor, I suggest, can this disparity meet the even more important right of children to the equal care of *both* their parents.

It is not easy for men to get themselves taken seriously on the subject of lone fatherhood. To suggest that there are many circumstances in which children's fathers may make better lone parents than their mothers is to breach one of the more deep-seated taboos of the late twentieth century. As professor Dench has pointed out, fathers are either expected to suffer in stoical silence, in which case they may be ignored or, if they voice their feelings, are condemned as unmasculine whingers who may safely be dismissed.

We are all prone to generalise from the particular and I am no exception. It was my own conviction that, for the foreseeable future at least, I was the better parent to bring up our daughter that made me determined to do it. But was it also my own needs, the recognition that I could not survive the double bereavement of losing my wife and my child? How did other men feel about this dilemma? This book is my attempt to answer that question. In taking on this responsibility and carrying it out I made mistakes through ignorance and prejudice, but looking back after seven years feel that, on the whole, I have done a good job as a lone parent father. Surely I am not alone in this? Surely there must be thousands of other single fathers in the same situation, thousands more who would like to have been if they had been given the choice? Most of them would probably also be glad of advice, to be taken or rejected, on how to deal with the multitude of difficulties they must overcome from learning how to make new relationships, if they want them, to getting the knack of ironing a pleated skirt. This book suggests possible solutions to many of these problems.

As well as drawing on personal experience I have also tried to approach the subject scientifically, basing my observations on wide reading and my own research programme. I knew that although my case, like anyone else's, was unique in some particulars, in many others it would be bound to follow a general pattern, so what generalisations could I make by studying a statistically significant number of single fathers and relating those broad conclusions to my own individual experience? I decided to find out by carrying out a survey as professionally as I could with my limited resources and knowledge by enlisting the help of the Director of the Centre for Family Research at Cambridge University. My analysis of these responses and the conclusions I have drawn are used throughout the book and the nature of the sample and the questions are given in Appendix Two. Several of my findings – on such matters as the impact of poverty, other parent access and domestic violence – conflict with many political and social assumptions made about lone fathers and are at variance in some respects with the conclusions of other studies – usually based on samples of lone mothers – to which I have referred. The problem today is that any challenge to these assumptions provokes immediate accusations of male hysteria or exaggeration. While I do not feel I should entirely abate my passionate feelings on this subject I have tried to avoid these two faults and base my observations and advice on the facts alone. I believe my alternative findings at least deserve a properly funded larger scale professional examination.

My survey seems to demonstrate that men are no less capable of coping on their own with poverty and child rearing, or with work and child rearing than women. Perhaps mothers feel able to depend financially on social security without loss of self respect in a way that men, conditioned by centuries of the puritan work ethic to value themselves by what they are paid to do, still find difficult. But is this men's fault or society's? Is the notion that mothers are endowed with natural superiority as parents a fact or a myth? Is the umbilical link the only one that really counts? Is it sensible that women should annex nearly all the territory of lone parenthood or would a little territorial redistribution benefit many of the children involved?

This book is emphatically not an attack upon women, nor an assault upon their rights. Rather it is part of a necessary attempt to reassert the rights of men at a time when they are under threat. I only pose the question 'Should fathers not be admitted on the basis of equal opportunity, treatment and esteem into the hitherto predominantly female world of child rearing?'

In the 1970s and 80s the more extreme feminists laid all the ills of the world at men's door. It would be equally facile for men to draw attention to the shortcomings of women and then base upon them inferences about the care of children, or indeed anything else, which excluded all women from participation. Neither set of prejudices is particularly helpful in determining who is the better parent to care for a child when parents part. However, women's prejudices about men and conceits about themselves do seem to have become accepted as proven facts and the only sound basis for decisions, in and out of court, in the vast majority of disputes over the care and nurture of the children after divorce and separation. It is this presumption that this book sets out to question, but in the end each individual will have to decide whether or not it is valid in his or her own case.

1

The odds against fathers

There have always been single fathers, but the way men have found themselves in that position has changed completely in the last hundred and fifty years. In 1820 the same proportion of men were left single by death, largely because of the perils of child birth for women, as have their mar riages ended by divorce today. (D1) Virtually all of them would have retained responsibility for the care of their children but, because of extended family networks, rarely alone. Silas Marner, in George Eliot's novel, was the exception. In the 19th century many mothers wrote letters of farewell to their families before giving birth, but 'only fifty per cent kept them afterwards' noted Samuel Butler (QM2) While this may have been an exaggeration for letter-writing middle-class women, disease, dirt and malnutrition would have taken a heavier toll among child-bearing working-class women. Today maternal deaths in childbirth are less than one in ten thousand live births, but divorce in Britain ends one marriage in three. Since nine out of ten people can now expect to marry or cohabit at some time in their lives there are few who are not affected, directly or indirectly, by divorce or separation.

Until 1857 when divorce first, in theory, became generally available,* escape from what Milton graphically called 'the empty husk of an outside matrimony' was available in practice only to rich and determined male members of the upper classes. Between 1857 and the end of the First World War fewer than a thousand divorces were granted by the courts each year, though separation orders were given by magistrates which gave women a degree of financial support and legal protection against molestation by their husbands. Once Legal Aid had been introduced for divorce in 1950 divorce ceased to be the prerogative of the rich and the legally well represented and became an option for the ordinary citizen. In other words divorce ceased to be something almost exclusively determined by the State or the Church and became a matter of choice for

*In this book I refer to the law of England and Wales unless I make specific reference to the different, and usually more enlightened law of Scotland or Northern Ireland.

the individuals concerned. The admission of 'irretrievable breakdown' as a ground for divorce in 1969 so simplified the process of severance that by 1977 this was largely a matter of paper processing by a registrar. The parties did not usually appear before a judge and the annual number of divorces increased sixfold to nearly one hundred and seventy eight thousand between 1960 and 1993. Much more court time was devoted to disposing of the children and the financial arrangements following the break-up of what had ceased, in the eyes of the law at least, to be a sacrament and had become a financial and social contract. About ninety per cent of the time taken by divorce proceedings in court is now concerned with children and finances. (B1)

Today more than ninety-eight per cent of all divorce cases are undefended and virtually no undefended case is ever rejected. Very few defences succeed, in any case, since an over-determined and vigorous defence against a divorce petition can usually be used to demonstrate the breakdown of the marriage. 'Not believing in divorce' is no guarantee against being divorced.

It also needs to be remembered that cohabitation has become an increasingly popular substitute for marriage in recent years. One in four couples live together before marrying and many others never marry at all, so although we do not know the exact number of cohabiting couples there are clearly many and the breakdown of their relationships is not reflected in the official divorce figures. In Scandinavia less than half of the population bothers to marry and in Britain, where a third of all children are born out of wedlock, more than two-thirds of them are jointly registered by the mother and father, although a quarter of the couples named do not give the same address. Almost fifteen per cent of male lone parent families show the father as a single man (OPCS '91) so it seems likely that the great majority of these had been in cohabiting couples. There is still not a great deal of research data about the effects of the breakup of a cohabiting non-marital relationship, but it may be even worse than that of divorce since there is no formal mechanism for ending the relationship and so of tidying up some of the psychological loose ends. (FF1)

However, the fact that divorce has become relatively easy, and theoretically a blameless event, does not alter the fact that the dominant feelings are those of fault-finding, acrimony, and a burning sense of injustice. Such feelings do not help parting parents to reach objective and mutually agreed decisions about children and money. Despite the apparent ease and frequency of divorce and separation today it still comes as a shock to most people even when they initiate proceedings let alone when they are taken by surprise when a partner leaves, as many men still are.

The blow of losing a beloved partner through death is a grievous one for the survivors, adult and children alike. But in many ways loss through separation and the rejection it implies can be more traumatic. We resign ourselves to death and through grief accept its finality and become largely reconciled to its consequences. Children seem able to understand and cope with the death of a parent, to accept that it is final and usually no one's fault. But when a parent leaves home and family in an act which is deliberate and voluntary children often see it as a personal rejection of themselves. The sense of rejection can plunge apparently completely stable characters, particularly adults, into 'profound depression or terrifying mania'. (F14) It is in this confused state that we are expected to make rational decisions about money and children.

Despite the widespread promotion in recent years of the concept of 'no fault' divorce, most of us still look at first for someone to blame for the marital breakdown when we, our relatives, friends or acquaintances divorce or separate. The deserted or sexually betrayed partner feels unjustly treated and the sympathy of friends and family reinforces the sense of righteous indignation. (B1) Only with the passage of time does the support become qualified by criticism, the injury rankle less and the 'injured parties' feel able to look more deeply into themselves for their contribution to the breakdown.

It has been argued that the much more frequent present day break-up of relationships is because we expect more of them. Cynics, however, may prefer to attribute it to the unrelenting promotion by businessmen and politicians alike of the idea that we are entitled to instant gratification of all our personal desires regardless of their impact on others. Adults may see divorce as an avenue of escape from their personal problems and in some cases it may prove to be that, but for the majority of the children involved it remains a turbulent and uncertain path to their future and a devaluation of their past – however short that past may have been. (C3) As one youngster put it 'divorce is like suicide. Instead of trying to solve their problems people just kill their marriage because it's the easy way out'. (P1)

Research suggests that children who are cared for from birth to maturity by the same compatible and harmonious parents have a better chance of doing well at school and college. They are more likely, therefore, to get better jobs, and enjoy better health and emotional stability than those brought up by one parent only of a divorced or separated couple. Children who have known nothing but a lone mother upbringing do better than those whose families break up in childhood and the same appears to be true for lone fathers. The advantages of the traditional nuclear family are not so great or so inevitable as to justify the current political emphasis on it, which has little to do with the way the family in Britain is actually evolving. More significantly, the evidence shows that, in general, the children of single parents actually enjoy a slight advantage over those brought up in seriously disrupted or antagonistic families, or, indeed, in many stepfamilies.

Previous research in these areas has been directed almost exclusively at single mothers. With the reservation that I could not check the fathers' assessments of their children with those of the children's teachers, my own survey suggests an improvement in health, happiness and academic performance of children brought up by single fathers since their mothers left the family home. The fathers of the children with the best overall outcome in our survey have been lone fathers for more than twice as long as those of the children doing least well. (Table One\Table Six)

While divorce or separation may strike the individual involved as a purely personal tragedy, the collective impact of each of these private dramas has been socially highly significant. Nowhere is this more so than in shaping children's attitudes to personal relationships and the implications this has for the family structures of the future.

Consider these sad statistics.

Two-thirds of divorces in England and Wales include children.

The day on which you read this will see some six hundred children confronted with the separation or divorce of their parents and so will tomorrow, and tomorrow and tomorrow ... (P2/OPCS)

In America, precursor of so many European ills, present trends indicate that the figures will be much worse, with something like two-thirds of children born in the 1990s destined to live in a one parent family before they are sixteen. (F7)

Half the children involved are between three and nine years old, the most vulnerable age, (P2) three-quarters are under ten. (OPCS)

Something like fifteen per cent of all children will see their 'resident' parent divorce, remarry and re-divorce before they are eighteen and this takes no account of the changing relationships of their non-resident parent nor of the relationship changes of the unmarried. (F7)

Of the children who remain with their mother, half will, within two years, no longer see their fathers. (St1) This rises to almost two-thirds after ten years and only ten per cent will still see their fathers on a regular weekly basis. Absent mothers see much more of their children, perhaps because of a greater desire to do so, but, from the opinions expressed by the fathers in my survey, it may be equally because of the more constructive attitude to access taken by home parent fathers. I found that of mothers separated for two years or more almost two thirds (64.6%) were still seeing their children regularly, just over half (51.5%) once a week or more. Even after five years a third were still seeing their children.* The children of all the fathers separated for less than two years were still seeing their mothers, but fifty-five per cent of these only twice a month or less.

The number of children in Britain at any one time deprived of balanced, parental guidance from an adult of each sex is approaching three million. Of these more than half will acquire a stepfather by the time they are eighteen (C2). If the 21st century looks like becoming the age of serial monogamy rather than of life-long partnerships, it also seems certain to be an age of serial and extended parenthood instead of one in which a couple take responsibility for bringing up their children from birth to maturity.

In sharp contrast to the explosion in the number of lone mothers, the number of lone father families has only increased fifteen per cent in the past thirty years. Although at any one time (1991) there are only some one hundred and twenty thousand lone fathers in Britain there are, because of the rate of remarriage among men, at least as many again who have been fairly recently. This quarter of a million men and half a

*My survey contained only one lone father of more than ten years' standing, but the frequency of other parent contact after five years is roughly comparable to that for lone mother families. This suggests that the loss of contact may be due as much to other parent weariness and disillusion as anything else.

million children is a small minority of the population, particularly when contrasted with the one point three million lone mothers. But it is an important though neglected minority. Several times this number would like to be the lone parent responsible for their children if they felt they could secure that right. However, only ten per cent of custody arrangements are, in fact, contested. This is more likely to be because men quail at the odds stacked against them than because they do not want to raise their children themselves. All too often it is easier for a man to persuade his ex than a judge that he should bring up a child. Fortunately, if he does persuade her, the judge has little option but to endorse the arrangement except in the most exceptional circumstances. Even in most apparently mutually acceptable residence arrangements one or other of the parents, usually the father, is not happy with what has been nominally agreed. (R1) One consequence of the reforms of the past twenty-five years is that men are now faced with many more obstacles than women in securing the right to bring up their children when this is opposed by the other parent. We shall examine these obstacles later. Whereas for centuries the assumption, in court and cloister, had been that if a couple parted the children remained the property of the husband to be disposed of as he thought fit, the opposite has now become true. Notionally, children are no longer treated as property. In reality, 'property' rights in them have been transferred from fathers to mothers.

My survey suggests that the typical (average) lone father is in his early forties cohabiting or married for a decade* to a woman four years younger who left him a little less than five years ago. One in three of these men still love their exes. For a quarter of them, and a third of their exes, it had been their second or subsequent live-in relationship and was most likely to have foundered on incompatibility (a third), her infidelity (a third) or a variety of other reasons from mental breakdown (17%) to lesbianism (7%). Now the lone father finds himself with two dependant children to bring up aged, on average, very nearly ten. In 1971 one in eight (12.3%) lone parents were men. By 1991 this had fallen to less than one in twelve (7.9%)**. For better or worse the decline of the nuclear family is a woman-inspired phenomenon. Not surprisingly this male\female lone parent ratio of one to eleven and a half has led to lone parenthood being discussed, judged and legislated for almost entirely in terms of lone mothers while lone fathers are virtually ignored.

*Eight years for widowers.
**In the same twenty years in which the proportion of male single parents fell by over a third that of single mothers (ie with no cohabiting male) doubled to 33.8% while widows fell from 21% of the total to 6.3%.

Admittedly it is still usually the father who leaves home, sometimes because he is running away from his responsibilities, but also often so that his children, and indeed his former partner, can continue to have a roof over their heads and the minimum disruption from the break-up of the relationship.

Less than a fifth of the lone fathers in my survey had left home with their children, but three-quarters of the women had left on their own; two had briefly taken the children with them and one couple left at the same time. Before the 1989 Children Act a father would often be given custody, or joint custody* with the mother and thus retain not only a real influence on his children's upbringing, but a lever with which to ensure continued contact with them. The other parent, nearly always the mother, would then be given 'care and control', in other words the daily decisions about the children's lives, but not the major strategic decisions such as education, religion, major health issues nor even in what part of the country they should live, which went with custody. Such split responsibilities became increasingly rare after the 1950s, but had been trying to make the point that the other parent has a right to a say in his child's future. Now, both parents, if married, theoretically retain responsibility for their children, but, as we have seen, residence is almost always awarded to the mother. This contrasts markedly with the situation in Australia, for example, where just over a half the contested cases went in the mother's favour, a fraction under a third in the father's and the remainder were resolved by joint guardianship. All too often society and the courts deem a parent of either sex, but particularly a father, who has left his home and partner to have left his children also, which is very far from being the case.

The Children Act finally abolished the centuries old legal tradition that the father was natural guardian of the child. While it purported to replace rights by responsibilities for both parents, in practice it largely replaced paternal rights, which had in any case been steadily eroded over the previous twenty years, by maternal rights. Ironically, the Act still uses the traditional legal pronoun 'he' to set out provisions which largely empower 'her' at the expense of 'him'. It did, and rightly, reaffirm that the children's interests are the most important consideration when families break up, but it does nothing to dispel the prejudice surrounding the definition of that interest. Nor was the situation improved by the Child Support Act of

*The likelihood of obtaining a joint custody order varied greatly from one part of the United Kingdom to another. In some parts of the north they were virtually unheard of, and joint residence orders will no doubt be determined with equal arbitrariness and unpredictability.

1991 which conspicuously failed to make any mention of children's interests. This is scarcely surprising, I suppose, since the Government drafted it almost entirely in the interests of the Treasury.

The terms 'custody' and 'care and control' have been replaced in the Children Act by definitions that refer to the 'resident parent' and the 'contact parent'. When so many separated parents do not see their children the term 'contact parent' is clearly a misnomer. The extent of absence from the home, usually through economic necessity, of the so-called resident parent who has to leave most of the waking hours care of her children to others, makes this term equally inappropriate. I propose therefore, to use in this book the term 'home parent' for the parent, of whichever sex, who provides the children's main home – the place where the children spend more of their time and keep most of their personal possessions. This is not to discourage further development of the idea of a child having two homes, which we shall look at later, but simply to reflect the reality of the child's eye view of the situation and the child's *practical* priorities, which may sometimes not be the same as his or her emotional priorities. I shall use the term 'other parent' for the parent who does not live in the children's main home, regardless of how much contact he or she may have.

There is also the problem of what to call the members of a couple who live together as husband and wife but are not married. 'Partner', seems to me slightly pompous and makes the couple sound like solicitors or accountants, even if it does underline the contractual element of such modern relationships. 'Lover' seems in many social contexts an unduly aggressive term. To introduce someone for the first time as 'my lover' seems to over emphasise the sexual element of the relationship. 'Cohabitrix,' or 'cohabitor' is pedantic and 'the person who lives with me', is a bit of a mouthful, so I have chosen a much older word, 'mate'. While mate has come to be used of male buddies at pub or work or football terrace it does seem to me to combine the idea of close friendship and mutual support with the older one of sexual partner and co-breeder of offspring. In this book, mate, a word with a respectable and romantic pedigree, will be used to indicate the 'other half' of a cohabiting but unmarried couple or when both married and unmarried couples are referred to jointly.

Reforms in the financial elements of divorce law, the

establishing of the Welfare State – albeit a weakened one in recent years – and much greater if not yet equal economic opportunity in the labour market for women, have given them equal power and opportunity with men to break away from an unsatisfactory marriage or partnership. (M2) Whether this may prove to be a genuine advantage remains to be seen, but for now, at least, women are taking full advantage of their new freedoms. Since shortly after the 1969 Act they have been initiating three out of every four divorces. Although when men divorce it is usually to go to another woman, women often do so solely out of dissatisfaction with the marriage.

Because these changes have taken place within a couple of generations our intellectual acceptance of, and adaptation to, them has often outstripped our ability to encompass them instinctively and emotionally and break free of our childhood conditioning. This is particularly true of those born before World War Two. We may do well to remind ourselves that such major social changes are not new and that the nuclear family is the relatively recent creation of western affluence, privacy and emancipation. Arguably, the childhood on which the effect of parental break-up so concerns us is itself the invention of the Victorians. Until the 17th and early 18th century children were regarded simply as immature adults. In emotional terms at least we seem to be reverting to this pre-Victorian concept. There may today be fewer orphans working in blacking factories or begging for bread on the streets, but there are hundreds of thousands of psychological orphans begging for the love of an 'absent' father and tens of thousands that of an 'absent' mother. Today, both social custom and the law appear to endorse this state of affairs. Why?

2

It's only natural – or is it?

Are women naturally superior, then, to men when it comes to rearing children? If, in primitive societies, there were good biological reasons for women to bring up children do they still apply in the much more sophisticated societies of today? Although conception requires both male and female, gestation, giving birth and breast feeding are exclusively female functions. However, once a baby is born, once it becomes a separate, individual being, how significant are these factors in determining the better person to rear the child? Can fathercare only ever be a poor imitation of mothercare, second best? Or is there a distinctively male style of nurture as valid and effective as the female?

We inherit a complex attitude towards the role of our own and the opposite sex in marriage and child rearing which passes unchallenged or changes only slowly in most generations. Because of the far reaching developments in contraception, child and maternal mortality, the mechanisation of domestic tasks, and new income and earning patterns with their consequent social changes, our preconceptions in the second half of the 20th century of our respective roles have been overturned by what has broadly been termed 'the feminist movement', to which men have also made a significant contribution. The rapid and extensive decline of Christianity in 20th century Western Europe has undermined the philosophic and spiritual justification for a father-based society. God the Father has been usurped from his throne by much more nebulous beliefs; a host of weird cults and religions, including attempts to establish 'God the Mother', or simply by no beliefs at all. The image of the human father has consequently undergone far reaching and, for the male ego, confidence-sapping changes in the past fifty years.

From women's point of view the really dramatic change came with the widespread, if unconscious, acceptance in the 1950s of a new theory on maternal bonding. In 1951, as part of a research project for the UN, a psychoanalyst called Bowlby wrote 'Mother love in infancy and childhood is as important for mental health as are vitamins and proteins for physical health'. This statement has often been taken out of context and had far more built upon it than it would bear – to the lasting harm of many children.

Simplified and perhaps over succinctly summarised the Bowlby argument was that:

1 The mother/child bond is biological in origin, established at birth and therefore an exclusively woman/child phenomenon.
2 The needs of the mother and of the child are reciprocal and complementary.
3 Therefore parental nurture equals maternal nurture and this in turn necessitates the constant presence of the mother.
4 Therefore the father has no directly significant part to play in child rearing, only the indirect function of protecting and providing for mother and child.

While Bowlby did not go quite as far as Bertrand Russell who believed that while 'the ideal father is better than none ... many fathers are so far from ideal that their non-existence may be a positive advantage to children', by the late 1960s and early 70s it had become widely accepted by the mental health professionals who advised judges and politicians in these matters that a child needed a single home only, and a primary caretaking parent – its mother – in that home. This predominant opinion was scarcely surprising in view of the fact that by then the majority of court welfare officers and workers in the field of mental health and social welfare were women. The DSS was unable to provide a detailed breakdown by sex, but of some 30,000 social workers today I estimate from various directories I examined that some two thirds are women. Amongst Court Welfare Officers the proportion of men is even smaller.

This viewpoint coincided with the opening of the divorce floodgates and although eventually the work of Rutter and others showed Bowlby's thesis to be flawed in several respects the damage had been done. Although the strict letter of the law might be said to maintain the equality of parental rights for married fathers, in practice judgements do not seem to reflect that equality. Despite the fact that psychologists such as Rutter had subsequently pointed out that 'it should be appreciated that the chief bond may not need to be with a biological parent, it need not be with the chief caretaker and it need not be with a female', (M1) the courts seem to presume the contrary and favour the claim of the mother in ninety seven out of every hundred cases. It remains exceptional for a man to secure in court the right to rear his children in the face of his ex's opposition. Is this gender discrimination justified by some innate 'parenting' quality in women which is lacking in men?

Every one of us, man or woman, starts life as female and by the same token there is something of a woman in every man – if not of man in every woman. As the pioneering American social anthropologist Margaret Mead put it half a century ago 'all men are born female but some are more female than others!' Because of the greater genetic complexity of the male, both male handicaps and male advantages extend over a wider range than those of the female. More men are conceived (120\100) more spontaneously aborted (106\100) and born alive (110\100) but long before they attain their three score years and ten men find themselves in the minority as a result of the greater natural and social hazards to which they are prey*. Men suffer from more genetically caused disorders, from colour-blindness to haemophilia though the transmitters are almost always female. Measured by IQ tests there are more very stupid and more very brilliant men than women, who tend to bunch around the mean, more criminals and more geniuses. On the other hand more women attempt or threaten suicide than men (though more men actually commit suicide which may say something about the respective importance the sexes attach to verbal and physical action) and many more women finish up in mental hospitals or on tranquillizers.

Above all the male is spared the cyclical hormone release of the female with its effect on concentration, co-ordination and capability. Because these hormonal changes are controlled by the brain it can be inferred that male and female brains differ in some of their functions not just as far as sexual characteristics are concerned, but in other ways. Even today it is necessary to stress that these differences do not imply either superiority or inferiority, simply difference. In the context of this book, however, we must ask whether the differences imply that one sex rather than the other is better fitted to rear children in every case or even the great majority of cases, as happens now.

The most obvious differences between the sexes are

*Perhaps, the involvement of a majority of women in the stresses of paid employment and the, possible corresponding, increase in their smoking, drinking and drug taking while men's diminish, may narrow the widening gap in life span between the sexes. There already seems to be some evidence that morbidity rates are converging.

anatomical. The relative size of the human brain at birth, one seventh of total body weight, is unique in the animal kingdom. The large skull needed to house this brain means that the female has to have a large pelvis – pelvic difference between the sexes is greater in man than in any other species. To reach its full maturity, at nearly four times its size at birth, the human brain requires a slow and prolonged development to which tempo the human body also conforms. Thus the length of time a human child must rely for its sustenance on breast milk (or its equivalent) determined the division of labour between male and female very early in the evolution of man. There is no escaping the fact that most children who are breast fed fare better, physically and emotionally, than bottle fed children and there seems little doubt that abrupt severance of a nursing child from its breast feeding female is detrimental to the child. I deliberately choose the word female rather than mother because, as a long tradition of wet nursing demonstrates, it is the milk and the mothering not who is providing it that are beneficial. While obviously a man cannot lactate enough to produce nourishment, when bottle feeding he can provide the tactile sustenance and the sense of care and protection, the emotional nutrients, that are no less important than the physical ones. Nowadays, formula milk, carefully chosen and made up, can be *nearly* as nutritious as good mother's milk and more nutritious than poor breast milk. What artificial milk does not do is provide the relative immunity from a wide range of infant infections, mostly minor, that breast feeding gives and the Stanays have argued (in Breast is Best) that it can cause other physical problems.

It is true that in the animal kingdom (except among fish!) examples of males regularly and *in the normal course of events,* nurturing the new born and infants of their species are few. However, there are plenty of examples of male animals which, having *lost* their mates, rear their offspring, particularly among wolves, dogs, foxes and higher primates. Laboratory experiments with animals also indicate that men significantly exposed to new born or very young children should become more than usually involved in child care. (F5)

The male usually also has to surmount the stress of transferring his first attachment from a source of good, a role model, of the opposite sex to one of his own sex with the confusion of identity that this can bring about. From this the female is exempt. She not only has a constant same sex beacon by which to navigate through the whole of her development, but spends more time with her. Males do not have the female opportunity in later life to reaffirm gender identity by giving birth to a further generation of the species. Young girls who display male characteristics and interests attract to themselves only the rather approving label 'tomboy'. Boys who display feminine qualities and interests meet with quite strong peer and social disapproval. There is no flattering 'jillgirl' label for them, rather the distinctly pejorative 'nancyboy'.

Anthropological research suggests that in the great majority of cultures husbands had authority over wives and in all but one or two of the remainder it was a joint authority. Although this male authority may have been exercised in Western societies with some of the chivalry inherited from the middle ages it is much more bluntly imposed in the rest of the world. (F5 quoting Stevens 1963) Until very recently there have been very few societies in which any but the most inadequate of men have been encouraged to care for infants. On the other hand, the high esteem in which motherhood is held encourages women's desire to nurture children, particularly when they are very young. It is more than coincidence that both before and after their child bearing years females in many societies are treated but little differently from males.(MF2)

Until relatively recently in the evolution of Man females alone played the nurturing role, men the protective and predatory one. The division of labour between the sexes might be said to have begun with the male both protecting and going out to bring home the bacon – or venison or mastodon or whatever – and the female, usually with a group of other females, concentrating on child care. The male, because he needed to operate with other males in the hunt, naturally became highly mobile and task-orientated while the female depended for the satisfactions of daily life on her interaction with other females and children. It is not surprising that women generally have become superior in verbal skills and dealing with emotional and social relationships while men, with their superior spatio-temporal powers, have coped with the practical and advanced the frontiers of knowledge by their capacity for abstract thinking and conceptual imagination. If society had not evolved beyond this primitive stage it would be hard to argue against the proposition that only females should rear children and only males provide for mother and child. But it has.

Sexual differentiation apart, female development is initially more rapid than male. Although boys are psychologically more inclined to exertion from a very early age than girls, not until the onset of puberty, or just before, do they overtake girls in physical strength, speed and co-ordination, but then the gap becomes large. Recent research suggests that, possibly because of new social pressures, it is not until quite a bit later still, between the ages of seventeen and twenty-one, that boys catch up with girls in other, intellectual and emotional aspects of development, including even some of those in which they were thought naturally to excel. It might be said, with some justice, that girls become women while they are still girls but that boys remain boys even when they are men! Nevertheless, there is ample evidence to show that by adulthood male and female intelligence, on *average*, is comparable but differently constituted. In verbal reasoning, the manipulating of abstract concepts and symbols (as in mathematics), in mechanical comprehension and spatio-temporal skills men, in general, excel. (MF1) In manual dexterity, verbal fluency and social skills women usually excel. It needs constantly to be emphasised that we are talking only about averages, about typical cases. The overlap is enormous and a great deal of human unhappiness has been caused by men and women being forced to conform to sexual stereotypes which stifle their personal inclinations. As that formidable female intellect and leading innovator in her field, Margaret Mead, colourfully put it: 'Males and females respectively forced to reject such parts of their particular biological inheritance as conflicting sharply with the sex stereotype of their culture ... will be doomed throughout life to sit among the other members of their sex feeling less a man, or less a woman, simply because the cultural ideal is based upon a different set of clues, a set of clues no less valid, but different ... We should take instead the primary fact of sex membership as a cross-constitutional classification, just as on a wider scale the fact of sex can be used to classify together male rabbits and male lions and male deer, but would never be permitted to obscure for us their essential rabbit, lion and deer characteristics. Then the little girl who shows a greater need to take things apart than most of the other little girls need only be classified as a female of a certain kind. In such a world, no child would be forced to deny its sex membership ... nor would any child have to pay with a loss of its sense of sex membership for the special gift that made it, though a boy, have a delicate sense of touch, or, though a girl, ride a horse with fierce sureness'. (MF2) Nor, we might add in a contemporary context, for a woman to be an astronaut or a man a home-maker.

Mead also argues, and perhaps with some justice, that 'The mother's nurturing tie to her child is apparently so deeply rooted in the actual biological conditions of conception and gestation, birth and suckling, that only fairly complicated social arrangements can break it down entirely. ... women may be said to be mothers unless they are taught to deny their child-bearing qualities'. (MF2) So, if a mother is breast feeding and committed to it, and if she is willing to rear a child on a full time basis until it is two to three years old then, *all other things being equal,* a presumption of maternal residence being given for an infant when a couple separates is not unreasonable. But, when a mother hands a very young child over to the virtually exclusive care of a nanny or walks out or has a nervous break-down all other things are not equal. Forty-six per cent of the separated fathers in my sample, by way of illustration, were literally left holding the baby and coped with the situation well enough.

The award of residence to mothers, although sometimes unjust to men, need not be totally harmful to the children if the so-called contact parent in fact retains regular, intimate, frequent and prolonged contact with his children. But, as we have seen, this is too often not the case. While men must admit that a substantial number of them walk out on their families with callous irresponsibility, this escape route is not taken by the great majority. On the other hand, there are certainly some men who are deliberately deprived of contact with their children by vicious, vengeful and often obsessive women, determined to exact the full penalty for their own unhappiness and discontent from their exes by depriving them of the love and care of their children, regardless of the psychological damage to the children in being deprived of the visible love and care of their fathers. Fulton found that nearly forty per cent of the wives with custody had refused to permit their ex husbands to see the children at least once – and the children's health, safety or wishes had nothing to do with the refusal. Custodial parents attempting to make a new life for themselves and their children make their decisions and act primarily to keep the other parent at as great a distance as possible. (F9) I am not referring here to women who have suffered brutality and abuse at the hands of their men – they are fully justified for their own sakes, and often for those of their children, in severing all contact.

It is asserted by apologists for divorce on demand that a broken home is better than a quarrelsome one and this is probably true where the quarrelling involves ungovernable rage, soul-destroying verbal abuse, usually by the woman, or physical brutality, usually from the man*. Interestingly research suggests (FF1) that children have a far higher level of tolerance towards the shortcomings, indeed serious defects, of their parents than parents have of each other. For many a 'bad' father is better than no father at all. Since definition of what constitutes a 'bad' father is to some extent determined by women in situations where they feel hostile towards men, or at least their particular man, merely being a father can almost become, by self definition, 'bad'. The feminist literature of the 70s described men as being 'brutal in their muscular strength, aggressive, assertive, success orientated, the cause of international violence, lacking in artistic sensitivity, impatient, competitive, emotionally isolated and incapable of intimacy with women and children'. (F6)

The lopsided view quoted above has since been discarded by most women who have come to recognise 'an uneasiness about an assumption that is often accepted without much examination by feminists and men who support feminism. Characteristics which are commonly associated in our culture with "masculinity" are often just dismissed as bad.' (F10) Fortunately, most women now seek no more than genuine equality and partnership in their personal and working relations with men as well as in the public sphere.

In all cases other than those of the very youngest infants the only criteria for deciding whether a mother or a father should have the rearing of a child should be their respective fitness for the role, commitment to it, and willingness to encourage and facilitate access by the other parent. For social and economic reasons this is still likely to result in the award of residence to the mother in a majority of cases but not, as now, in more than ninety per cent of them. A ratio of sixty:forty or even fifty-five:forty-five would be more likely to benefit the children involved. A massive increase in skilled and free mediation and conciliation services would be needed to ensure sound assessment of the three critical elements in making residence

*One paper (P3) claims that violence may play some part in as many as twenty per cent of marital breakdowns. My own survey bears this out if female violence is included. No research seems to have been done on the role of serious verbal harassment.

orders and to monitor them afterwards. At present these services are less than skeletal, but the Lord Chancellor's April 1995 proposals for divorce law reform, if implemented, could entail a massive and welcome expansion. Such sweeping changes would probably once more shift the balance of domestic and custodial power between the sexes back towards a more equitable and child-orientated equilibrium.

3

Types and stereotypes

Is there, then, a social conspiracy, tacit or overt, to exclude men from child rearing and do men, wittingly or unwittingly, go along with it if there is? Or is it simply that in the war of the sexes the battles are all going currently against an army of men made complacent and insensitive by centuries of more or less unchallenged supremacy because women are now successfully choosing the ground on which the battles are fought?

The process of procreation and child rearing is controlled by women long before it even starts. Men may think that they – the hunters, the penetrators, the initiators – have decided to have a child, or at least that it has been a joint decision with their women. Not so. The evidence (F11) is clear. It is the woman who decides if and when to have a child in nine cases out of ten. Not perhaps, on the face of it, entirely unreasonable, since the burden and the pain will be hers.

Men are often involved today in antenatal activities, they do the exercises, they listen to the child and feel it move in its mother's womb, they look at the scan, they feel that they are partners and parents. What they usually fail to recognise is that they are so only by permission and admission of the mother. Again, not unreasonable, you may say, since the child in the womb is still little more than a physical extension of its mother, totally dependent on her for life.

But even if a father accepts that, what of the next stage when his child has been born and now has an independent existence of its own? Now the women's auxiliary forces take over; the nurses and midwives to whom the self-important male gynaecologists and obstetricians are really no more than technically well-informed satellites. The child is in the orbit of a female planet system with far greater gravitational pull. Father may hold his child – provided nurse or mother gives permission and he hands it back when he is told. Then, in a few days, he will have to go back to work (though it must be said that in Sweden, where extended paternity leave is a legal right, most fathers do not take it). Working and travelling a father will spend some fifty to fifty-five hours a week of his infant child's fifty to eighty waking hours away from home. If his mate later decides to go back to work, probably only part time or at least a great deal nearer home than he, the child will be handed over to the care of another team of females, nursery teachers and child minders. In most cases not until a child is four or five years old and going to school will a father have the chance to play a remotely comparable role, by which time a strong bias towards a female vision of the world has been established through rewards and punishments for children of both sexes. They will have learnt that if you please the woman, or women, in your life then you will be rewarded with cuddles, food, drink, attention; displease her and you are out in the cold, smacks, scolding, worst of all, being ignored. (MF2) Most women, however, seem still to prefer to leave to their mates the serious disciplinary matters, the ones that provoke the conflict and resentment which may be a necessary element of growing to adult independence.

The female child's flying start is built on further by ensuring that this pattern is not broken at school. Increasingly, girls are taught to get and expect jobs and careers as well as learning how to fulfil their more traditional roles as wives and mothers. Excellent! Boys are seldom taught how to be fathers as well as breadwinners. Not so good! In any case, they are so constantly bested by their female class mates in almost every sphere, except sport when they reach adolescence, that as soon as they can do so they take refuge in any form of male exclusivity available to them, particularly in employment and education. In this they are encouraged by social tradition. Anthropologists point out (MF2) that in almost any society in the past whatever men principally occupied themselves with by way of 'work' was regarded as important. If in some other society the same task were carried out by women then it would thereby, for that society, become less important. Male dominance was reinforced by men's exclusive right to pursue certain activities and by status and achievement being gauged in terms of those things women could not or did not do. It is one of the measures of civilised progress in the 20th century that, in Western countries at least, this oppressive definition of success through discrimination is becoming less and less valid. In the Western world today there are virtually no such activities nor are there any places, apart from men's lavatories and sports changing rooms and a corner or two in half a dozen London clubs, to which men can make a ritual therapeutic retreat to be with members of their own sex alone. Women still have many. This rapid upheaval in the definitions of male status and the destruction of refuges for masculinity have made many men uncertain of their place in the world, made them doubt the validity of their maleness – particularly if they are unemployed. Several sociologists have suggested that as a result of these changes 'the potency of the father in the home and his image in society have dwindled, resulting in alienation, irresponsibility, anxiety, aggression, peer group orientation, envy, rivalry and unstable mass movement in the larger society.' (F5) Perhaps it may even account for the considerable increase in overt male homosexuality.

There are many examples of home parent fathers and would-be home parent fathers reporting great prejudice against them shown by the social services. Social workers often seem to assume that if a child of such a home parent has problems they are solely due to the fact that it is being brought up by a man. (F16) Certainly, the courts and social services do little to bolster the self-confidence of lone fathers and if local communities and individuals sometimes discriminate against them perhaps it is because they see the machinery of the state doing the same. Many of the fathers in my survey felt the system was heavily loaded against them – from the hostile attitude of the majority of officials right down to the wording of social service application forms which contain such questions as 'when did your husband leave?' (S31)

These experiences were fairly typical for the lone fathers in my survey:-

'If I have to deal with DHSS, etc ... every time I have a query I have to explain why my ex wife has not got the children or should not have them.' (S31)

'I visited W---- Under 8's Day Care ... to be quite honest I was disgusted at the young man's attitude. I could tell he just could not care at all. He said to me in a roundabout way that I would have to give up working and let the state look after us. I told him I had worked all my life and I would become mentally ill if I had to stay at home all day, whereupon he replied and I quote "We have a lot of parents on anti-depressants" ... I do not need anti-depressants or to become unemployed and I do not need somebody who has just come out of college and has no idea about life and the real world telling me nobody can do anything for me or even wants to. What I need is help.' (S24)

'I had to fight to get Child Benefit paid to me as it was designed to give to mothers. When we temporarily reunited the taxman asked if they should pay it to her rather than to a joint account. When we separated again my ex claimed fifty per cent of the additional allowance for my son and was granted it without reference to me even though she pays no maintenance and sees him one day in seven. I suspect an absent father generally wouldn't have applied for this due to guilt feelings, but would certainly not have been given it automatically.' (S27)

Or, as one of the widowers put it:-

'Officialdom did not want to know at all because I was a man when a woman would have had money thrown at them.' (W18)

The root cause of the problems seems clear whether you are a widower ...

'Trapped!! In a situation which I have no real control over. Government and Social Services totally ignore the plight of the widowed father.' (W11)

or an unmarried father ...

'As an unmarried single father I have felt discriminated against legally, socially and through professionals.' (S22)

or simply as a divorced home parent father ...

'Officialdom does not seem to recognise single fathers, but puts them in a sub group of single mothers.' (S27)

Public failure to recognise that this very substantial minority is not just a footnote to lone motherhood, but has very specific needs and problems of its own makes the life of lone fathers even harder in the majority of cases than that of lone mothers. Nor are many men's experiences of the other state and voluntary agencies supposed to support single parents any less blinkered. One father going to mother and toddler group for the first time is quoted as saying 'I was made to feel that I shouldn't be there. The first time I walked in all the mothers went silent. I stuck at it, but it was difficult'. Another father was even physically assaulted by a woman at his first Gingerbread group meeting because she objected to a man having care of children. Yet another was told by a teacher at school that he should not have care of children and a fourth felt the conciliation service was trying to punish him for applying for custody of his children. (F16)

To what extent are fathers who are deprived of the opportunity to bring up their children the victims of prejudice and to what extent are they themselves to blame for the deprivation? Certainly, many male traditional attitudes do not help their argument. Men must accept much of the responsibility for the gender stereotyping that makes it harder for them to become home parent fathers. Fathers care far more than mothers about the gender characteristics shown by their young children. Most fathers play gently with their small daughters, seek gentleness and affection, praise prettiness or flirtatious behaviour. Naturally, girl children wishing to please their fathers develop and emphasise these characteristics. With even the smallest boy most fathers play roughly, wrestle and box, seek comradeship and help, praise courage, fortitude and aggression. (F5) Small wonder men grow up believing these the prime if not the only virtues.

However, the macho male is slowly changing (F11) and when his children are born his protective and nurturing instincts self evidently come to the fore. This may be because society is becoming less critical of male demonstrations of emotion and affection. A father can be without shame what the Trobriand Islanders called 'a man to take the child into his arms'. (F20) While one researcher has dismissed the increasing tendency of fathers to wish to attend the actual birth of their children as a meaningless gesture (F11), I prefer to think it may express a desire among more men not to be excluded from their children's lives, a rebellion against the medical processing, the clinical detachment, that the predominance of hospital delivery has to some extent made of childbirth. How different from primitive societies where the rituals of couvade might even go so far as to involve the man in the pangs of childbirth by making him literally share the pain. Only as the rituals, and indeed the medical complexities, increased did men find themselves marginalised. Getting off to a poorer start he became inevitably less involved in the subsequent rearing of the children, an involvement which in any case the ever greater demands of an industrial society made less and less practical.

Many women are surprised by the intensity of the desire of

their baby's father to be involved from the outset. Some welcome it. Many are also fearful and resentful of any intrusion into their domain, however tactfully it may be expressed. (F1, F6, F11, R1) There is much emphasis on the need for the man to understand his woman's physiological and psychological needs during pregnancy, to support her during and immediately after the birth, and that is good and as it should be.(F1) We hear very little about the man's needs during this process, or of his sense of being excluded, of being superfluous and that is bad and should be remedied.

The attitudes of the two sexes to the break-up of a longer term relationship which has produced children differs as much as society's expectations of their subsequent respective roles. Male response to marital stress and disharmony is often simply to avoid home, to spend more time at work or in the pub or at some other male dominated leisure pursuit. This option is not open to many mothers. The ultimate expression of this male avoidance behaviour is to leave home, but only when men are allowed to play an equal part with women in the rearing of the children they have begotten is men's growing disillusion with family life likely to be reversed.

Men are generally taken by surprise, regret the break-up and continue to love their ex partners long after the parting of the ways. Nearly twice as many men as women said that they still loved their former mates long after the break (F12), could not understand why it happened and blamed themselves for it. In my survey seventy-five per cent still loved their exes on average nearly five years after separation, but only put their share of the blame for what went wrong at thirty per cent. As Lilian Rubin observed 'Men may make all their emotional investment in one woman where women rarely invest all their emotions exclusively in one man.' (QM4)

Women not only initiate the great majority of separations, but see them coming long before their exes do. Very often in their late twenties and early thirties, having had a couple of children, mothers return to work or study. Their self image brightens considerably, their self esteem and confidence rise. They find they are still attractive to men, as opposed to being taken for granted by one man. These new admirers, predatory chancers though they often are, take, or appear to take, the woman's new identity seriously. This breeds discontent with the woman's home role and leads to escapism. Because of the considerable shift in employment patterns in the past decade or so this experience is no longer confined to women in high executive or professional jobs, but is widespread at all levels. The number of women valuing themselves as wives, mothers and homemakers rather than by the male yardstick of success in their jobs is smaller than it was even a generation ago and those who stick to traditional values are now probably not only in a minority, but are sometimes sneered at by their 'emancipated' sisters for having betrayed 'the cause.'

Women have far fewer regrets about the end of marriage than do men.(MF2) They might argue that this is because they have far less to lose in breaking out of an oppressive, male-dominated relationship than men who are saying goodbye to an unpaid servant. Men, on the other hand, might claim that it is because males are soft-hearted and incurable romantics whereas women are hard-headed materialists. (MF2) This is not a criticism, just an observation based on wide experience and the reasonable inference that the differing roles of Man and Woman in the process of species evolution necessitated different attitudes which we have carried down into modern life. The hunter, thinking himself into the skin of the hunted, missing the constant sexual gratification and comfort of home, anticipating death and danger and devising tools with which to outwit and outkill creatures so greatly his physical superior, cultivates his imagination and inevitably becomes a romantic. Woman's more prosaic life is constantly faced with the practicalities of survival not just for herself, but for the young left in her care and, although she may not consciously have been aware of it, of the very species itself. What we choose to define as selfishness, greed, and materialism, sometimes even putting self, the progenitor, before any single one of her progeny, are the essentials of such survival and millennia of conditioning. Such essentials are not purged by a few hundred years of supposedly more civilised existence. The strength of the nurturing maternal instinct is great, but woman's sense of self perhaps even greater. She is not hampered in her struggle for survival by those absurd masculine concepts of justice, honour and loyalty (a view also expressed by Freud) to an idea or wider group (F5) which may account for the superficially surprising fact that 'divorced mothers generally show less affection to their children, particularly their sons, than married mothers. One described her relationship with her children as like getting bitten to death by ducks.' (F9) At least in the first years after divorce mothers tend to be less nurturant, less sensitive to their children's needs and less supportive of efforts to cope with day to day changes of school, peer relationships, homework and family life. 'Inattention is combined with harsh punitive reactions to misbehaviour'.* (QLP1) Lone fathers, by contrast, usually seem to become even more caring and considerate. This may possibly be because these rare few men have been those most determined to play a good parental role for their children in the first place – hence their persistence in seeking residence. Nevertheless, the myth of the caring mother and the callous father persists.

Another myth with which men have to contend in seeking residence of their children is that men are violent by nature whereas women are gentle. The popular Press revels in stories of men brutally assaulting their women and children, but the weight of statistical evidence also suggests that every year hundreds of children are injured, and sometimes even killed, by desperate or deranged mothers. (C4,D2 & B1) One of the more pernicious anti-male myths is that violence within families is exclusively perpetrated by men upon women and children. In the entire literature of the extensive Home Office campaign in 1994 to combat domestic violence there is not a single recognition that initial acts of violence are also inflicted by women on their mates, nor any attempt to analyse the extent to which male physical assaults were provoked by the psychological, but no less deadly, forms of violence used by women. Only by subtraction of the female victim proportion of the total (80%) can it be inferred that one in five reported acts of domestic violence is inflicted by a woman on the man she lives with. It is no doubt true that much domestic violence in general also goes unreported. How much more so must violence on males be under recorded? A great many men are no doubt ashamed, embarrassed, or too conceited to admit that a macho male is seeking protection from a mere woman by reporting such assaults to the police. When this factor is taken into account it seems not improbable that a quarter to a third of domestic assaults on other adults in the family may be committed by women.

My own survey dramatically endorses this supposition. So frequently did my face-to-face interviewees spontaneously mention violent assaults and threats upon them that I included

*In some cases this may be due to concern not to wrap sons in too much cotton wool rather than to selfishness.

questions on the subject in the follow-up sent to the fifty contactable males of my sample. Forty-three replied, thirty-five of the separated or divorced and all eight widowers. Two of the widowers had been attacked though one only when his wife was driven by the extreme pain of an illness. Of the thirty-six relationships involving the other respondents (one commented on both his marriages) fourteen (39%) said they had been seriously attacked by their exes. Four specifically mentioned attacks with knives, two reported broken bones, one through being hit on the nose with a plate! Four (11%) retaliated and three also volunteered the information that their ex had also attacked a child. One admitted that he, too, was sometimes the first to use physical violence. One other admitted to a single incident of initiated violence (responded to with equal violence), in an otherwise non-violent relationship. This particular case well illustrates the kind of provocation to which many men are subjected. After a long period during which the wife had several sexual affairs and denied him sexual intercourse (which he did not obtain elsewhere) her mood suddenly changed one night and she became amorous. Just as he was about to penetrate she repulsed him and told him to 'bugger off'. He lost his temper, put his hands round her throat and shook her while she flayed his face with her nails. The incident was over in seconds and he says that he was at once deeply ashamed and apologetic for what he had done but she left with her current lover thirty-six hours later leaving him with a five-year-old to bring up. While acts of domestic violence can never be justified, except in self-defence, in many incidents there are mitigating circumstances – no doubt when wives attack husbands as well as the other way around – and actually establishing who starts a fight and the point at which argument spills into blows, fear into pre-emptive self-defence is almost impossible to establish.

When the case of violence towards children is considered women are no less culpable than men. Again in its wisdom (or weakness) the Home Office chooses not to carry out any research into the perpetrators of assault and physical abuse upon children. This is left to the NSPCC. In a comprehensive survey, 2454 cases (0.5% fatal, 11% serious, 88.5% moderate) of physical injury for which information was obtainable during the three years 1988 to 1990 thirty-three point one per cent were caused by the children's natural father *but* thirty-three point nine per cent by their natural mothers. Natural mothers were also two and a half times more likely than natural fathers to abuse their children emotionally and more than eight and a half times more likely to neglect them. Only in cases of sexual abuse were natural fathers (26.8%) more likely to be involved than natural mothers (1.9%) and that may well largely be a matter of male/female sexual mechanics. Taking all forms of injury, abuse and neglect in the NSPCC survey together (4818 cases), give or take fifteen hundredths of one per cent, natural fathers and natural mothers are equally responsible for the harm inflicted on their children. While women may claim that this is hardly surprising in view of their greater involvement with children, men could equally argue that in view of their supposedly greater physical strength it merely indicates a lesser physical capacity for violence in women rather than their more benign intent. This is especially true where older children, who may be presumed better able to defend themselves, are involved. Unfortunately the myth that fathers are violent to their children and mothers are not is still firmly planted in the public mind and no doubt colours some judicial decisions about access and residence.

Perhaps because of their greater verbal and social skills women dwell upon and discuss their anxieties and grievances among themselves far more than men, thus not only making everyone far more aware of them than they are of men's equal agonies, but perhaps even perpetuating and exaggerating them. In so doing women have developed the knack of being able to re-write their personal history so that the relationship, once treasured, is declared, and honestly believed, to have been a disaster from the outset. (B1) Men, by contrast, can get very defensive about attacks on former spouses or mates. Men still take such criticism as criticism of themselves, of their judgement in choosing the woman in the first place, and as the supposed initiator in courtship cannot take refuge so easily in the excuse that they were misled.

As we shall see later, many men still do not play as great a role as they could and should in running their homes and rearing their children. Therein often lies the seed of their downfall should they later wish to become the lone home parent to their children. In this failure to participate they are encouraged by the attitudes of society. Women are still expected to put their children before their jobs, but men to put their jobs before their children. A man who does become involved in child care or who does things it is automatically assumed a woman will do is considered 'highly participant' (F8), a cross between a saint and a freak. Men who, usually with their wife's powerful assistance, break through these barriers are more likely to make good single fathers, but then they are less likely to become single fathers because their adult relationship is based on a greater degree of mutual trust and sharing. (F11)

The consequence of society's low expectation of men's participation in the intact family is that it is generally presumed that they cannot cope on their own if, when a family breaks up, they wish to (or are forced to) look after a home and children. Twenty-five per cent of my fathers commented on the surprise and even admiration with which their taking on the primary care role was greeted by friends and neighbours. Flattering as these responses are to the individual ego, they reinforce the general view that men are neither competent nor willing to play the part. That general view greatly influences the judges who choose between father and mother in contested residence cases. Zika Grujicic's court experience was typical 'I had to fight for three years to get custody of the girls. My wife's barristers stood there asking questions like: Mr. Grujicic how do you bath your children? It made me so angry. A woman would never be asked a question like that'. (QR2) There is no escaping the fact that 'the discrimination against the father is clearly expressed in the divorce court. Just as society treats fatherhood as a second class role so does the law.' (F3)

When men are left as lone home parents they receive more sympathy and, initially at least, more offers of help than a woman in the same situation. But it is often a sympathy tinged with an underlying contempt. The man in the pinny is not a hero but a figure of fun. The man who is left holding the baby is not a tragic victim, as a woman is, but a failure; either a failure as a provider (B1) or, worse still in terms of his self esteem, a failure as a lover whose woman has left for richer or more passionate pastures – or both! His family may even slightly despise him for having 'lost his woman' and he in turn may cut himself off from family and friends through a sense of shame.

The feeling of social isolation came across very sharply from my lone fathers many of whom felt shut out by the single mother syndrome.

'There is an informal support network of single mothers in the area but I am excluded by age and gender.' (M15)

'There are no single fathers locally so there has never been anyone to relate to. All the single mums stick together, even though I am a sole parent, I feel excluded from the sole parent club.' (S17)

'Very few people have offered any practical help.' (S11)

'Slightly less friendly than if I had leprosy.' (K14)

Other fathers were well supported ...

'I have been accepted open-armed, people have gone to great efforts to help me.' (S12)

'I have had several good relationships with single parent women, which has also allowed my son to meet and get on with other children socially and out of school. Parents at school seem cliquey.' (S16)

The school caucus is clearly a problem for many fathers ...

'I have kept away from my children's school unless I have had to attend the concerts etc, primarily because of this Tory castigation of my group. I was very happy when my eldest started school and looked forward to taking him each day but when eventually I realised at the most I was an odd outcast I felt very down. It is mostly women who take their children to school so the situation of a single parent male makes it all even more bizarre.' (M14)

Another problem was out of school socialising for the children of single fathers ...

'I feel discriminated against. At my daughter's birthday party a number of children were invited but only half turned up. I heard the mothers of those that did not come saying that I had only invited girls and that they did not trust me.' (T11)

'Not being allowed to fit in because you are a man and men don't bring up children on their own.' (W17) 'People tend to keep a distance. Society as a whole seems unaware that single dads exist.' (W14)

The majority of fathers react stubbornly to such slights and pressures ...

'My ex wife's friends look on me as a leper when I take them to school as they believed I could never look after them, but I have proved them wrong.' (S23)

But however bravely lone fathers carry on and even though some, myself included, have received a great deal of help, the general impression given by the responses to my open-ended questions is of overwhelming loneliness and isolation. To what extent this is socially imposed and to what extent it is self-imposed out of a sense of failure and destroyed self-confidence is another question.

Perhaps the many contradictions and confusions in both public attitudes and public policy to single parenthood are only symptomatic of the radical changes through which our conceptions of what constitutes family life is going. In the 1989 British Social Attitudes Survey sixty per cent thought an unhappy marriage should end, but only thirty per cent thought a single mother could bring up a child as well as a couple, yet thirty-five per cent approved of a woman having a child without a relationship with a man. Indeed many people still assume that single parents are always unmarried mothers. The attitude of the sexes differed markedly with many more women than men approving of single motherhood. The lower the class of respondents the more convinced they were that a father could perfectly well bring up his children. This may well have been because with more of their wives out at work they had already demonstrated for themselves that they could do this. By contrast four-fifths of upper class respondents thought that a lack of a mother's love would cause problems for the children. Only a quarter of the lower two classes believed this since they have had the good sense to discard the mother bonding theories – if they had ever heard of them – which they had already proved for themselves to be irrelevant. (M2) Nevertheless, a large majority of parents in another survey said that they thought that the parental role should be clearly divided even within an intact family. In their opinion mothers were endowed with the skills of child care, either by nature or as a result of constant practice, while fathers were thought to be less innately capable. (D2)

We thus see public opinion lagging behind reality, as it so often does. In this case it will no doubt continue to do so until a sufficiently large number of fathers have demonstrated their capacity and desire to bring up their children on their own with results no worse, and perhaps better, than those achieved by lone home parent mothers. In the past three-quarters of a century Britain has seen great progress in establishing women's right to equality of opportunity in politics and the professions, commerce and industry, education and legal rights. The 'glass ceiling' that is seen to block the upward progress of a woman of ability is now often only a perceptual one. But there is still certainly one major sphere in which inequality still obtains socially, legally and on a personal level – that of child rearing. As far as the equal right of parents to rear their children is concerned it is men who are the victims of discrimination and prejudice.

The rights and freedoms gained by women entail a need for men not only to change many of their own prejudices, but also to win new rights for themselves. The most important of these is the right to equal claim with women to bring up their children when parental partnerships break up. The rest of this book tries to show how they can obtain and responsibly exercise that right.

4

Catch 22,23,24 ...

There appears to be a move afoot to change the law in the UK so that residence is automatically awarded to the parent already having established primary care. This is, of course, usually the mother. The proposal is based on the American theory that continuity of past primary care is more important than the quality and continuity of care to be provided in future. While it is true that a few fathers have used a trade-off of custody to reduce the financial demands on them this was, and still is, relatively rare and certainly not common enough to justify so great a change in the law. Such a change would not only militate most unfairly against men, who in very few cases will have been the established primary caretaker for more than a brief period, but will raise the whole question of how long primary care has to have lasted to be deemed 'established'. One solicitor, in 1989, told me that there were then many instances where fathers who had reared their children quite adequately for two or three years had been deprived of care and control by a mother suddenly deciding that, after all, she wanted the children she had deserted – and this often despite the protests of relatively mature children. In the case of lone fatherhood, however, the primary caretaker will often have walked out on her responsibilities, so it can scarcely be argued that she is the better fitted to the role of home parent. In other circumstances, too, a father who is willing and capable of taking on the primary care responsibility should at least be assumed to be equally well qualified to do so in the child's interest.(C4)

Many women, confused by conflicting pressures from feminists pressing them to lead independent lives on the one hand and advertisers extolling the virtues of motherhood on the other, do not know what they want. The commercial world, with the enthusiastic co-operation of the media, has engendered the belief that we are all entitled to instant gratification of our every wish from orgasm to a second car, haute couture to holidays abroad. The same applies to marriage. Embarked on with high and unreal hopes of unremitting passion and perfect communication fostered by the image presented through advertising, which is mainly directed at women, the prime consumers, it inevitably disappoints when its nose is rubbed in reality. That resentful sense of disappointment, of having been deliberately deprived of something they are entitled to, seems particularly true of the young women who are the principal target of so much commercial dream mongering and who initiate the great majority of divorces. Over half the decisions to separate are taken by women who keep the children with them, a fifth are taken jointly and a fifth by the absent or other parent. Of these latter the majority are also women. (P3) In other words, it is women, *not* men, who usually decide to break up families.

If past primary care should not be the starting point for judgements about who should have residence what should be? For children of secondary school age – although it is maturity rather than years which is the important yardstick – it should probably be the child's own preferences followed closely by parental character, commitment and willingness to involve the other parent. With younger children, while established primary care must carry some weight, it is the quality of the care past and future, rather than its duration which should be scrutinised. Nor should it be forgotten that one parent rather than the other is usually the primary carer from chance rather than choice.

The courts still do not take sufficient account of good fathers who are willing to change their life patterns in order to provide primary care of a more satisfactory kind than could be, or quite possibly has been, offered or provided by the mother. Judges do not yet seem to appreciate that a substantial body of research demonstrates that deprivation of its father can damage a child just as seriously as deprivation of its mother. The imbalance in favour of women has produced not only many aggrieved and disillusioned fathers, but many damaged children.(D2) Rutter, reassessing Bowlby's thesis in the light of subsequent knowledge, strongly emphasises the *psychological* fallacy of this judicial imbalance. 'A child needs to have the presence of a person to whom he is attached, but it is irrelevant whether or not this person is his mother. He also needs to have adequate maternal care and if this is not provided he suffers. But it appears that this need not be given by the person to whom he is most attached ... The emphasis on attachment behaviour and bonding by Bowlby and others is correct, but its linking with maternal care is misleading. A child who has had the opportunity to form a number of bonding attachments is less likely to be adversely affected by separation than one who has not ... An adult or older child in close interaction with the infant could do so, whether or not he or she was a parent or caretaker ... It may be suggested that for the development of social and emotional relationships in later childhood and adult life it is bond formation which matters and that it is of less consequence to whom the attachment is formed'. (M1)

Other authorities quoted in a major survey of work in the field are equally clear. 'The clear conclusion emerging from the research reviewed ... is that there is no basis for concern over awarding custody to fathers because of gender. The research on gender differences in responsiveness to the young, and studies of fathers in shared care giving and single parent families, all point to the fact that fathers are capable of sensitively and capably caring for children of various ages ... Fathers should be considered seriously as potential care givers in custody disputes, *even if they had not assumed major responsibility for child care in the intact family*'. Research seems to indicate that there is actually little difference either negative or positive in the effect on children of being brought up by a male or a female, a father or a mother. That is to say that men are equally good at parenting. (F12, F14) Emphasising the paramountcy of the child's interests in awarding residence is not in dispute. As Martin Richards points out 'such a criterion has a long history (viz Solomon in 1 Kings 3 v.16 – 28) and should ensure that attention is focused on the welfare of the children rather than supposed moral worth of each parent'. (F12) However, perhaps the 'moral worth' of a parent is itself likely to be a considerable influence on a child's development and an indicator of how responsibly parental duties will be fulfilled. Most of our judges are not endowed with the wisdom of Solomon, inferring erroneously from men's often altruistic reluctance to contest the custody of their children that they do not wish to have it. Judges cannot entirely be blamed for this since even in uncontested custody cases the needs of the children are inevitably interpreted in the light of the (usually female) plaintiff's one-sided testimony. An independent representative in court of the children *as a matter of course* might help to ensure that the unequal bargaining position of one parent has not led to an agreement which is not in their best interests. The more informal this procedure could be the better. (FF1)

Another area in which the courts can lag behind current knowledge is in failing to take the views of the children sufficiently into account although the value of their participation in the decisions which affect them is well established. Recent legislation does now provide for this where they are of 'sufficient understanding'. 'Sufficient understanding' is not defined in the Act because it is indefinable. It can only be a subjective measure of a child's maturity and intelligence not simply a matter of its age, class and education. Ascertaining a child's views through interviews with a judge in chambers no longer need be the ordeal it once was. A court is now entitled to consider video evidence from the child or 'hearsay' evidence from a third party reporting the child's opinion. Fathers need to be alert to the fact that the interviewer, court officer or any other third party legally involved, is likely to be a woman.* Many of these, as the recent Scottish child abuse case tragically demonstrated, are expert at getting children to say what they want them to say. However, if a child is put in the difficult and psychologically damaging position of having to decide between conflicting loves and loyalties he or she may find counselling by a professional 'non-combatant' helpful in analysing its real feelings and expressing them. In my experience many younger children refuse point blank to take sides not only wishing to live with both parents but believing, with some justification, that such decisions should properly be taken by adults.

Once a father, whether married or not, has left the family home and a contact order has been made, he often has less right of contact with his children than a virtual stranger – particularly his ex's latest lover or partner. A father's access may be permitted only on clearly defined terms and these may actually preclude, for example, holidays and overnight stays. He cannot even apply for a passport to take his child on a holiday abroad as only its mother can obtain one. By contrast a 'friend' of the family or one of those sequentially vanishing 'uncles', can be as deeply involved in the children's lives – including sole responsibility for them overnight or during holidays – as the resident parent decrees. A father who feels this may damage, or even physically and morally endanger, his children has to

*No one seems to have an overall figure for the number or sex of court officers but by ringing round a number of the larger courts individually I can make a reasonable estimate of at least two women for every man.

go through a complex, protracted and unsympathetic legal process to prevent it. In other words, 'home' is seen as more important than contact with the father, and a father who exceeds access arrangements can find himself in court, fined or even in jail.

There is the same discrepancy between the treatment of the sexes over maintenance payments. Although women are virtually never sent to prison for refusing fathers access to their children, there are at any one time usually about two thousand men in prison for not paying maintenance. Again in fairness it must be admitted that these are only a small proportion of those who are in arrears or who have paid nothing. This was estimated in one study (D1) to have been as high as 80% of those against whom court orders had been made, although many pay voluntarily without the need for a court order and an increasing number do so through the CSA.

Where denial of paternal access is a necessary protection for mother and children it is perfectly justifiable. Where it stems, as it more often does, from a woman's venom towards her ex it is a cruel injustice. Theoretically, the father can re-apply to the court for access and eventually the court would have the power to commit the mother to prison. However, it never does this as the children would then be deprived of the care of their resident mother and in any case it would probably damage the father's relationship with the children. If he can offer an equally stable and nurturing home to his children, but would in turn allow the mother ample access, logic and justice suggest that he should be given residence. Unfortunately what tends to happen is that the court refuses the father an access order because the conflict could be damaging to the children, or assumes without proof and solely on the mother's say-so that there is some good underlying reason why the mother is behaving in this way. This is totally irresponsible, as in many cases the situation arises from a woman's revenge upon her former partner and she is completely ignoring or suppressing the child's wish to see its father. (D1) If courts were to take proper account of the new criterion in the Children Act that the *child* has right of access to the parent not vice versa more equitable and child-supportive decisions might be arrived at.

'Courts do little to encourage access ... in cases where there is a direct conflict between the interests of the custodial parent and that of the child's relationships with the non-custodial parent, the custodial parent invariably wins'. (N11) Courts, for example, always seem to sanction proposals to take children abroad to live though such permission must be clearly distinguished from abduction – the unsanctioned removal of children without both parents' consent, from the United Kingdom – which we shall look at in greater detail later. Case law on contact is loaded against fathers. For example, although a mother has disproportionately influenced a child to say that it does not wish to see his or her father the higher courts may refuse a contact order on the grounds that to see him now would be to disturb the child emotionally. Not only is this often a specious argument, but no retribution is meted out to the mother for her destructive conduct. There have been a number of cases where the mother's implacable hostility alone has been sufficient to overturn a court order for contact. Fortunately the lower courts, at least, still seem to make the assumption that it is in the child's interest to have contact with the non-resident parent.

The unmarried father is even worse off under the law than the married other parent of either sex; he has no automatic responsibilities at all and therefore no automatic claim to seek the residence of his children. This he can only obtain by mutual agreement with his partner – preferably by obtaining a joint residence or a Parental Rights and Responsibilities (PRR) order before any parting of the ways. A form to apply for a PRR can be obtained from any local court or solicitor's office at the time of a child's birth or later. When signed by both parents and lodged with the High Court this will give the father the same responsibilities as those automatically enjoyed by *all* mothers, married or not, and married fathers. Formally recording a man's paternity in this way is particularly important if a child's home parent mother later dies or leaves. Otherwise the father's right to bring up, or even see, his child cannot be established. Since seventy-five per cent of cohabiting couples who have children register the births in the name of both parents, it would seem a relatively simple reform of the law* to provide that where both parents register a birth both parents automatically enjoy exactly the same status as a married couple as far as their children are concerned. This is not a marginal issue now that almost a third – two hundred and sixteen thousand in 1994 – of live births in Great Britain are outside marriage. Even this might not be sufficient to protect a man's life-long relationship with his

*There is a possibility of legislation to this effect and the Centre for Family Research in Cambridge is currently making a study of what unmarried fathers believe their position to be.]

children without some form of deterrent to women. Perhaps a woman's refusal to register her child's father's paternity at his request should disqualify her from claiming maintenance from him for herself or the child later. Long before matters reach this state, however, the would-be home parent father can do much to shorten the odds in his favour.

5

Improving the odds

Men normally become their children's home parent in three ways: simple acceptance of a situation in which they were left 'holding the baby', either by death or desertion; aggressive pursuit of a residence order by all physical, psychological and legal means; and successful diplomatic negotiation with their ex about the future of their children. These three different approaches often overlap and mix or change with the lapse of time and each may be best in different circumstances.

There are two other minor categories of what might be termed long term temporary home parent in which the children's mother is either in prison or in hospital for a long stay. The responsibility for prisons rests with the Home Office, but it has no idea how many of its female prisoners have dependent children and disclaims any responsibility for them. Since the majority of female prisoners are mothers this is astonishing. If children are neglected as a result that, says a Home Office spokesman, 'is a problem for DSS'. The DSS, according to its figures and a House of Commons written reply on 15 June 1995, looks after about 380 children a year because their parent or parents are in prison. No one seems to have any idea how many lone fathers are bringing up children while their mates are in prison, but an informed guess (by the Director for the Centre for Family Research) is not more than ten or a dozen. In the case of prisoners of both sexes the usual carer is a female relative; for men a partner or ex, for women a mother or other female relative. There are schemes for children to visit parents in prison which seem to work well for mothers, but less well for fathers. Again men are discriminated against. Their children are escorted by their mother or other carer, which deflects attention from the children, while mothers' children can visit unaccompanied. The DSS also looks after about 4000 children a year because their parent or parents are in hospital.(DHSS Figs Oct91\Mar92) Again, the number of fathers who are coping for this reason is not known. (I know of no female equivalent of the man who works abroad returning home to his family on leave only occasionally, though no doubt there are one or two cases and may be more now that the dismissal of pregnant women from the armed forces is considered wrongful). These two categories of men will find themselves in limbo, neither lone parents nor cohabiting, and will have to anticipate whether or not their state is likely to become permanent through death or the stress-related break-up of their relationship. In other words should they sustain the hopes of their children for their mother's return and the resumption of traditional family life, or begin to wean them from these expectations and build a new single-parent-based family life? In the interim, while trying to choose the best course of action, the lone father may be able to get help through the local authority home help service or by his employer giving him compassionate leave, but both local authorities and employers are now under such stern economic constraints that this kind of help is becoming increasingly hard to obtain. This is an area on which I have found no research and which lies outside the compass of my own experience and investigation.

Before looking at each of the three main categories of lone father in turn it is necessary to go back well before the point of separation to see what steps even the most trusting of men ought to take in case what seems at the outset to be the perfect relationship turns sour and breaks up – as it all too often does these days.

There are five golden rules for any man who contemplates the possibility of bringing up his children single handed in the event of his relationship with their mother ending in separation. The first is to recognise that however much in love he is, however loyal, devoted and loving his partner may be, or at least seems to be, the future is unpredictable. She may fall in love with someone else, cease to love her mate and find him so repugnant as to feel compelled to leave him, suddenly become ambitious for a job or career which leaves no place for family, have a mental breakdown, die or end the relationship for a hundred other often astonishingly superficial-seeming reasons.

The second is to prepare the ground when it does not seem necessary to do so, when any steps taken can be seen as a natural part of a couple's mutual love and shared concern for their children. Marriage, for all the financial burden on men if it ends in divorce, is still probably the best means of securing a man's right to apply for the residence of his children in the event of divorce or separation and, of course, automatically secures this if his wife dies. If the marriage breaks up it does not mean that he necessarily or even probably will get the residence of his children, but he is certainly entitled to seek it through the legal system. If the couple cannot or do not wish to marry, then the man should not only jointly register the birth of any children (which currently gives him no rights), but should, as an automatic part of the birth registration process get a Parental Rights and Responsibilities order or, perhaps, better still, get a solicitor to get one for him.

Having secured the right to apply to be the home parent for his children a father can take a number of other steps to strengthen any claim he may one day wish to make. Golden rule number three is one that most fathers wish to follow in any case, but too often allow to be pushed aside by other pressures and priorities – maximum involvement in the care of their children from the day they are born. Fathers do well to remind themselves that in any case this benefits their children.

If a residence dispute comes to court (most do not) the judge will be looking at three things in relation to the management of child care; what has been the pattern in the past, what is it at the time of the hearing, and what is it likely to be in the future. Clearly if a man has shown no interest and played no part in the practicalities of rearing his children, but been content to see himself solely as the begetter and provider, then the judge is likely to cast him in the same role, to his financial and emotional cost. If, on the other hand, he can demonstrate that he has always undertaken a major share of such responsibilities, then he can reasonably claim that he is capable and willing to bear them all if he is made the children's home parent. Ideally, he should have undertaken half or more of feeding, changing, bathing, dressing, and playing with his children, appropriately according to their ages. More usually, from a combination of personal preference and the demands of full time employment, it is only in play that he has achieved his share. Only if his mate is also out at work full time does he really have an equal chance to play an equal role in child caring, but in too many cases he is content to let the mother play two parts while he still only accepts one, or perhaps one and a bit. The traditional division of domestic labour in which the man regards his virtual monopoly of maintenance, repairs, technical and construction tasks, and sometimes gardening, as a valid reason for a minimal share in cooking, laundry, ironing, housework and child minding – jobs for which his education has given him neither training nor inclination – undermines his case for getting residence of his children. The man who can break, indeed insists on breaking, that pattern is more likely to demonstrate a capacity to care for a family of children if it comes to a residence dispute. From the very first day he cohabits with his mate he should bake and sew and dash away with the smoothing iron even if he does not insist that she is as capable of fixing the car and putting up a shelf as he is. It is not so much a matter of skills as of attitudes. Many domestic tasks, although now largely mechanical and therefore more appealing to the male, are more effectively executed by the patient constant application which is a female characteristic than by the sudden bursts of high energy activity which is the usual male approach to a task. Men tend to let the dust, the dishes and the laundry accumulate and then have a blitz, women prefer to keep on top of things piecemeal. As a result women are intolerant of the male approach and criticise their low standards of housework and child care while men think the female approach is fussy and has the wrong priorities. (F12) My own survey shows that the majority of lone fathers have usually played a very significant pre-break-up role in all these domestic spheres and this may account in part for their success in securing and retaining residence of their children although forty-two per cent of my home parent fathers had never kept house on their own before. Three-quarters of the widowers surveyed had done so, presumably during their wives' illnesses.

The fathers in our survey were asked to say what share of household and family tasks they undertook when they were living with their exes. These were rated on a scale 0 to 10 from doing none of a particular job to doing it all. Four claimed to have done all the cooking and four admitted to doing none of it and on average they cooked forty-two point nine per cent of the meals. Two did all the cleaning while six did none and overall they did forty per cent of this job. Laundry revealed men at their least domestic – a situation with which, recollecting my own struggles at the ironing board, I am in full sympathy. Three did it all, eight none of it and their average was only thirty-five per cent. Reflecting the traditional division of domestic tasks thirty-two men did all the maintenance and repairs and none were quite so emancipated as to confess to doing none though one with a housekeeper and another whose family had lived with his mother claimed only ten per cent. On average the fathers carried out eighty-seven point five per cent of this work. Two fathers undertook all child care duties and everyone did something – a far cry from the nursery ghetto of the Victorian middle class family in which mothers did relatively little and fathers nothing at all! Overall child care during cohabiting life was divided almost exactly equally between fathers (49.2%) and mothers (50.8%). If all these duties are taken together it appears that fathers undertook over half (50.9%). Perhaps this is not so surprising since, as I have previously pointed out, undertaking a fair, or better still majority, share of domestic work and child care is a sound precaution for obtaining residence and a good preparation for carrying it out effectively. Even allowing for some exaggeration in the fathers' self assessments they demonstrated that they were 'modern men' before they were obliged to be.

Golden rule number four is don't move out when things get bad. It should be remembered in all circumstances that however virtuous a father has been in playing a full part in family life in all the years leading up to the breakdown of his relationship it will count for little if he is not still playing it at the time of the court hearing. In many cases, when the breakdown of a relationship has been mutually recognised the man leaves his home to relieve the tensions and avoid the risk of conflict, while still providing a roof for his ex and his children. This is almost invariably interpreted by the courts and society as 'desertion', however unjustly. Women leave, but men desert! If a man has genuinely concluded that his children would be better off living with him than with their mother the one thing he must not do is leave the matrimonial home. Staying will be painful, not only because of the constant reminder of a broken dream, but because his mate may employ every ruse and every abuse in the book to get him out, in a surprising number of cases (36% in my survey) not even drawing the line at violent assault. More particularly, she may try to use the children's distress at the rows she provokes and ruthlessly conducts in front of them as a lever on the man's compassion to compel him to go. Nor can he afford to reply in kind. Of course there can be no justification for violence in such circumstances, though there can be sympathy and understanding for how a man may be driven to it. A father does well to remember that, however appallingly his mate has treated him, however promiscuous, profligate, dishonest, or verbally aggressive she may have been, the minute he lifts his hand to her she has won, not only psychologically, but tactically. While a man can get no legal injunction to bar his woman from torturing him with every conceivable device short of violence, a woman can readily obtain one to prevent her man entering their home, or seeing or speaking to her, and even their children, once he has struck her and can be proved to have done so. Nor is the onus of proof always as strict as it should be and there are well substantiated cases* in which the mere allegation of violence or even just of the threat of violence has been sufficient to secure an injunction effectively ejecting the man from his own home. So golden rule number four is that until the court has ruled on residence a father should stay in his home with his children at all costs, continue to provide for all his family, share in the care of his children, and avoid giving his mate any excuse whatever to have him ejected.

The fifth and final rule is the age old one – know yourself. Do nothing in haste. This applies as much to widowers as to the separated. The psychology of uncoupling when a man's partner still lives is intricate and often confusing and it may take him time to sort out what he really feels. If his mate has walked out is he devastated and ready to do anything to get her back, or is he guiltily ashamed to discover deep down a sense of relief that she has taken the initiative in ending a painful situation? If she has taken the children with her, is he angry, desolate and determined to get them back, or secretly relieved that he does not have to look after them, however much he may miss them?

A father should seek the advice of wise friends and relatives and relevant professionals then search his conscience honestly before deciding whether his children will benefit most from having him, rather than their mother, as their home parent. Self-respect and a sense of his own worth can only stem from a clear conscience and the knowledge that what he has decided about the children is right for them. Without that self-respect he will make a poor father. If after such self-examination a father decides he should be the one to care for his children on a daily basis and he secures the right to do so he will have to make many sacrifices – career, friends, lovers, leisure – but he will

*See BBC series in March 1996 A Bad Time to be a Man

also make inestimable gains. If humanly possible fights over children's residence should be avoided, but if it comes to a fight and he is convinced he would be the better home parent the gains for himself as well as for his children are well worth fighting for – in or out of court.

6

Tactics – in and out of court

All this makes the legal system seem biased against fathers, but many solicitors, including women in what is still a predominantly male profession*, *are* sympathetic towards husbands who look like losing home and children, but will still have to pay the bills. All the same, in negotiating with exes, they have to bear in mind the probable outcome of a contested case in a system of matrimonial law whose application at least now seems biased against men. They may well make concessions as part of a damage limitation exercise that infuriate the father. On the other hand there *are* a few solicitors who flourish on conflict and encourage it. A solicitor will also feel he has to fight hard on his client's behalf, so it is important to instruct him firmly and clearly in order to make sure that the battle between ex-partners does not escalate beyond control or, more importantly, beyond hope of the eventual armistice on which the future well-being of the children can largely depend.

The law puts fathers in a difficult position. Theoretically 'There is no presumption in law that one parent is preferred to another for looking after a child at a particular age. However, the courts have said that it is natural for young children to be with their mothers and that this would be particularly difficult to displace where there had been no break in that relationship unless the mother was *unsuitable*'.(WP) A father seeking to be the home parent may thus have little option at present but to prove the total unsuitability of the mother. In doing so he may destroy any prospects, however tenuous, of a co-operative relationship afterwards. For this very reason, many men do not dispute the residence of their children although they would like to have it. They should think seriously, therefore, about mediation before consulting a solicitor. A Citizens Advice Bureau can advise them on how best to embark on this less belligerent course.

Mediation, while sometimes available free in divorce proceedings, is still used by relatively few people. However,

[*Currently by two to one but as each new intake is equally divided between men and women as the older members retire the profession will change further.

mediation or counselling were used by forty-one per cent of my separated fathers. That so high a proportion of the men involved had sought professional advice in this way came as a surprise and seems to belie the generally held belief that men are reluctant to seek professional help with emotional problems. One suspects that it is precisely because the help is *professional* that they find it more acceptable. In any case, mediation is not designed to patch up family breakdowns, only to try to find common ground and compromise between contending partners. Court mediators are usually professional social workers, psychologists, or counsellors, – usually women – or solicitors with the necessary skills who handle approximately twenty thousand conciliation cases a year. The court mediation service usually provides no more than a brief meeting in the presence of a court official to try to resolve difficulties, but at least it is free. Agreements reached are then normally incorporated into a court order. Statements made at these mediation meetings are 'privileged', that is to say they cannot be brought up in a subsequent court hearing. So in a few cases it may not be a bad tactic for a would-be home parent father to get off his chest any weaknesses in his argument that he thinks the 'opposition' may be aware of anyway.

For out-of-court mediation the National Family Mediation organisation, NFM, handles about six and a half thousand cases a year, about a third of which show a complete resolution of differences, a third a partial resolution and a third slight or no progress. It charges a fee based on the couple's means and concentrates on child related matters to the exclusion of any others except in so far as they impinge on a child's welfare. There is also the Family Mediators Association, FMA, which deals, on a fee basis, with about fifteen hundred cases covering a broader range, ie property, maintenance, etc. Independent mediators are not regulated in any way by the Government and charge for the comprehensive mediation on all aspects of post marital dispute which they offer. These mediators usually work as a team of two, one of whom will be a lawyer, and this makes the service relatively expensive. A typical rate is £100 to £120 an hour and a serious dispute is unlikely to be resolved in fewer than seven or eight hours. Financial help may be available for those entitled to Legal Aid, still a minority in divorce cases, if the Lord Chancellor's 1995 proposals become law. Out-of-court agreements tend to last longer than those enforced by court mediation although we don't yet know whether those in turn are better or worse than simple decisions imposed by the court. About three-quarters of these negotiations lead to written agreements, but there are no figures yet as to how many of those written agreements are actually kept. Neither is there any research evidence as to whether children suffer less long term damage if their parents reach agreement through mediation than after other patterns of break-up. At present agreements reached in this way are not binding on the parties unless they are confirmed by a court order, which a solicitor would have to obtain. Mediation tends to favour the articulate and it is sometimes suggested that women are at a disadvantage (although they are supposed to be the more articulate!) because of male pressures upon them during mediation. Some feminists have argued against the use of mediation or conciliation in this context on the grounds that it will favour men because they are more aggressive in negotiation than women. (D1) I doubt that this is any more true than the allegation that women unscrupulously employ subtlety and deceit in this situation. A good mediator will avoid bias towards either sex.

All the evidence in my survey and others points in the other direction. Men are constantly being leaned on both informally and by the official machinery of state to 'be reasonable', to 'act like gentlemen', in other words to yield to the female point of view and accede to any demand, however unreasonable, about money and children. If they wish to play any significant part in their children's lives other than that of unseen banker they must resist the pressure.

The conflicts that damaged a couple's relationship over money – or more usually the lack of it – children's upbringing, where to live and so on are the ones likely to be expressed most virulently during court proceedings if the break-up of the marriage or cohabitation finishes up in court or even with mediators. Negotiation through third parties such as solicitors or mediators can sometimes be both distancing and frustrating and may not provide a sufficient safety valve for the hostile feelings which need to be cleared out. This is particularly true of arguments about with whom the children are to live (residence) and access to them for the other parent (contact). A relatively neutral third party can be helpful in seeking the children's views and guiding the contending parents towards the solution that does least damage to the children rather than the solution that most satisfies the lust for vengeance or soothes the hurt of one or other of them. Such alternatives should be explored conscientiously before solicitors are engaged. The neutral role can be a good one for godparents who have usually been chosen jointly by the parents precisely because they were felt to be the right people to care about the children if anything happened to their father and mother. More than one can be involved if they were separately nominated. Family friends who have taken a close interest in the children can also be involved with advantage.

Such friends, particularly when they know your children well and are fond of them, can be invaluable in finding out the children's thoughts and feelings on the matter. Children often hide their anxieties under seemingly callous practical queries about the fate of pets and toys, holidays, pocket money, bed times and a host of other apparently trivial things which, nevertheless, symbolise for them a small life-raft of certainty in a life that has suddenly been shipwrecked. It is very difficult for a child, who will usually love both its parents, to be asked by one or other of them with whom he or she would prefer to live. They are more than likely to suppress their true feelings to avoid hurting the parent they are talking to at the time. To a trusted older friend a child may very well be prepared to say 'I love my mum very much and want to go on seeing her, but I would rather live with my dad.'

On the whole relatives are less acceptable as mediators because usually they will be thought to be biased. An exception to this may be where one parent has had a particularly close and affectionate relationship with a mother-in-law or father-in-law whose own son or daughter still continues to respect their parent's judgement and opinions. Even if it is sometimes necessary to thrash out the terms of custody through the legal process to have gone through the issues with an objective third party beforehand can clarify, simplify and make the subsequent proceedings less painful.

Although children look at impending separation in terms of its impact on their own lives they are also often touchingly concerned about the welfare of their parents. This may be genuine altruism or equally a reflection of the insecurity which arises from the break-up of the known pattern of life. It is important to deal with their queries in this situation when they arise and not evade, fob off or lie. Children, even more than adults, dread the unknown far more than the truth and the terrors of their imagination are always far worse than the reality. 'One mother told her ten year old daughter that "she was going for a shilling for the gas and she never returned". According to the father, the daughter has never forgotten this'. (C2)

But it is not just as channels of communication with children that friends have a key role to play. Provided they can combine objectivity with their sympathy they can help gradually bring about a less biased interpretation of the situation and, therefore, a more constructive outcome. Women accept this quite naturally and seldom find difficulty in confiding in friends of either sex. Men find such confidences far more embarrassing.

The difficulty men have in building close emotional contacts with other men in this kind of situation (M4) can partly be resolved by substantial disparities in age. To make a close friend of a much younger or much older man can take the competitiveness out of the relationship and make the inevitable confessions of weakness, shameful conduct, grief and fear easier to express.

Men are also supposed to be reluctant to seek professional counselling help and it certainly does not encourage them if they ring an organisation like Relate, as one of my subjects did, only to be told 'you can have an appointment in three months' time'. As he commented to the woman who took his call it was a good job they were not Samaritans! Obviously there are difficulties in playing the role of instant fire-fighter, but if the crisis and departure of a partner has not been foreseen then that is precisely what is needed. Sadly, by this stage the other party to the relationship may already have a closed mind, be determined on their course of action and refuse to discuss the situation with outsiders. Interestingly, it is much more often wives who refuse to go to counselling than husbands and husbands who more often initiate mediation. As one researcher put it 'conciliators try to help parents focus on the present and future without getting caught up in recriminations about the past. Men may find this approach more acceptable and relevant to their needs than other legal welfare services because it is non-stigmatising, impartial and quickly accessible in crisis situations'. (R1)

In 1974 the Finer committee on one-parent families recommended conciliation instead of the adversarial approach in divorce cases, but nothing has yet been done about it and although there are more conciliation schemes now in place they are still not the automatic machinery they should be for separating couples to negotiate about conflicting interests. This may more nearly become the case if the 1995 reform proposals become law. Perhaps most conciliation or mediation services are too concerned with reaching compromise to allow the contending parents the necessary purge of getting ill feeling out of their systems. (F1) They also find it difficult to cope with those situations in which one of the couple is not only completely wrong in their objectives, but wicked and selfish in the pursuit of them and where no compromise is just or appropriate. Nevertheless, mediation, whether successful or not, represents a much more hopeful way forward for a disputing couple than the adversarially-based formal conflict of court proceedings.

There are other less directly obvious professionals to whom a man may turn if he cannot afford or gain access to official mediation services and is reluctant to confide in friends for fear that they may be tempted to gossip – an almost overwhelming temptation in many close-knit communities. Children's teachers will know them well and have a fair idea of the parents' circumstances. Most teachers and head teachers take the need for confidentiality very seriously. The family GP is another good person to talk to though it is a good idea to let him know beforehand what the appointment is for so that he can make it at a time when he will not be rushed. He may recommend a psychiatrist or the practice psychiatric nurse. There is no more shame in this than in his sending a patient to see an ear, nose and throat or a heart specialist. It can be helpful for a few weeks to talk to someone not directly involved, with wide experience of similar situations and who is careful to make no moral judgements of any kind. Once court proceedings are under way, however, caution should be exercised in consulting any child professional as some judges react adversely to this unless they themselves have authorised the consultation. It is as well to seek the court's permission first.

A man may take a very different view from his petitioning wife, and be quite opposed to the idea that she should divorce him because he does not think the marriage has broken down, because he does not believe in divorce, or because he thinks the alleged grounds flimsy and spurious. No matter what the reason, if he does not want to be divorced he must defend the case and there is the first snag he runs into. Although in 1993/4 two hundred and twenty-six million pounds of Legal Aid was provided for matrimonial and family cases it is virtually impossible to get it to oppose a divorce petition. In 1994 precisely £4m, one point eight per cent of the gross Legal Aid for matrimonial cases, was allotted to that purpose. If the man can disprove any allegations on which the divorce petition is based he is little better off, but merely prolonging the agony by at most five years. He may even be accused of unreasonable behaviour for having refused to co-operate. Defending a divorce is unlikely to cost less than three to four thousand pounds, may cost a great deal more, and will almost certainly end in defeat. Under the Lord Chancellor's latest proposals refusing to accept mediation may also mean forfeiting the right to Legal Aid.

In these circumstances residence usually becomes the battleground. Some fathers react so desperately to what they regard as the injustices of the system that they snatch their children, attack their former partner or behave badly, even criminally, in some other way. (R1) Quite apart from the fact that this is morally wrong, it will totally undermine a father's case. He would do better, if his wife has been behaving sufficiently badly in any relevant way (infidelity, however promiscuous, no longer seems to be regarded as relevant) to get his blow in first and petition himself. In that way he stands some chance of winning his costs if nothing more.

If he accepts the inevitable, but wishes to seek residence of the children, contest maintenance or generally dispute any of the proposed divorce terms, it is still likely to prove a costly business and costs will be awarded against him if he does not win outright. Quite apart from the division of the family's accumulated capital and assets that will follow as part of the granting of the decree absolute and the loss of earning capacity that the break-up of a household and family almost invariably entails, unless he is very poor indeed, his legal costs will again be considerable.

It is possible for him to get what is known as Green Form Legal Aid for preliminary work – three hours for divorce, two hours for other matters of this kind, but eligibility is limited to those on Income Support, Family Credit or Disability Working Allowance or who have a disposable income of £70 a week or less. There are also capital limits. If an applicant has savings of £1,000, or £1,535 with two dependents, he cannot get this free help. If there is any doubt about eligibility for legal aid the solicitor's likely fees should be ascertained before any legal action is embarked on. Failure to do this can result in a nasty and even financially crippling shock.

Legal Aid on a sliding scale for contesting cases related to family break-up is again limited to those with a disposable income of less than £7,060 a year and savings of less than £6,750. Even then the litigant may have to pay at least some of the legal cost unless his disposable income is £2,382 and his savings £3,000 or less. Disposable income is calculated on the basis of a personal allowance, allowances for dependents, housing cost, travel and other costs relating to employment. Applications can take up to three months to process. If changes currently being considered are enacted then Legal Aid in matrimonial cases will only be available through certain designated specialist solicitors and may be withheld if mediation is refused.

Fathers fearing with some justice that the courts are biased against them, but wishing to retain residence of their children, will often make exaggerated allegations to the court about the ex's unfitness to be a sole parent, or threaten to do so. Unless this tactic can virtually guarantee success because of clear proof of the mother's serious deficiencies of character or conduct, it can backfire. Judges give short shrift to petitioners and respondents alike who indulge in a legal campaign of petty sniping over relative trivia instead of argument over issues of moment. However, if a father has strong evidence of his superior claim to be the home parent and to be granted a residence order either because of the mother's serious shortcomings or the father's particularly positive qualities as a parent, or better still a combination of both, then he should not hesitate to have it made clear to his ex's solicitors that he will use that evidence to the full if he must. If the evidence *is* strong – a fistful of affidavits from responsible adults who know each parent and the children well can be useful here – then the chances are that the mother will back off at the last minute rather than have a damning portrait of herself painted in court. There is another risk in this approach that must be considered seriously. Such a high level of conflict is unlikely to be conducted without children, or at least older children, becoming aware of the intensity of the hostility between their parents. Awareness of such intense conflict is damaging to children who need two parents psychologically even if they must in future make do with one in practice. (R1) Depending on how the parents conducted their disagreements before the break-up, children may already be well aware of their parents' mutual animosity, in which case a fiercely contested case will make little difference. Clearly such legal conflict is financially and emotionally expensive for all involved so should be avoided unless the woman is using the threat of child damaging conflict as a catch 22 to force the man to give up any claim to his children.

If a robust and aggressive stance is taken by the father the other side may also then employ equally rough tactics. He may find that he is accused of child abuse by a vengeful, disruptive ex or one who wants to get her children out of his care and eventually into hers. Men seem to be at a disadvantage here since the assumption seems to be that they are guilty until proved innocent in such cases. In a sense this is understandable since there has been so much public outrage when social services have failed to protect children against child abuse, but it leads to real injustice.

Sam (S21) had a nightmare series of court cases lasting more than a year after his wife walked out leaving him with a girl of nine and a boy of eleven. When their mother eventually decided she wanted them her tactic, instigated by the court welfare officer, was first to threaten and then, when Sam would not capitulate, bring accusations of mental abuse of the children. The court welfare officer tried to get the children out of Sam's hands by seeking to have them put into local authority care despite the children's insistence that they wanted to live with their dad. This was dramatically illustrated by their running away from the social worker assigned to them and going home to their father. The local social services responded by dragging them out of school and claiming they were 'only carrying out the law'. When she had her daughter to stay Sam's ex used to lock her up in their flat all day and unplug the phone so that she could not communicate with her father while her mother was out. Sam won all three of his court cases and a residence order for the children, but social services still vindictively keep them on the children at risk register. Sam bitterly resents the debt, some £6,000, the series of cases has plunged him into, because he was not eligible for Legal Aid, and the damage the disruption has done his career. He thinks he may even have to give up work altogether. He has channelled his energy and anger into setting up a branch of Families Need Fathers to help other men fight the injustices of the system. With considerable magnanimity he encourages his children to have regular access to their mother observing with a wry smile that his son, who at first refused to see her at all, now goes there for his tea after school 'to save you money, dad'. Sam's ex has contributed not a penny to the children's upkeep since she lost her claim for a hundred per cent of the house, continuance of the mortgage payments and maintenance from Sam and, in order to get all this, the residence of the children based on false accusations of child abuse.

The Children's Legal Aid Centre handbook is a useful source for initial reference in this and other legal issues over children even if it does at times read like a feminist tract. It says that an increasing number of disputes about residence and contact arise from children's allegations that they have been sexually abused. One might suggest that the opposite might equally be true and that such accusations arise out of disputes about residence and contact. Although some foreign research indicates that there is not a high incidence of false accusations by mothers no UK evidence seems to be available. Again the lower courts tend to take a fairly robust and commonsense attitude and do not immediately accept the mother's point of view.

It may be that a child *is* being sexually abused – though it should be emphasised that this is still rare if much less rare than was once thought – by some other member of the family. This is usually a man, though women do abuse, and young people do abuse each other though it is sometimes difficult to distinguish between that and the mutual sexual experimentation and exploration which goes with growing up. For the child's sake, even though it will undoubtedly weaken the father's case for residence unless the abuse is taking place in the mother's household, he should immediately consult his GP about calling in social services to help protect the child. These situations are the rare exceptions and it is in the normal run of cases that a more balanced consideration is needed than is given at present to the conflicting claims of the two parents.

It is not the father alone, but, more importantly his children – and even his ex – who will benefit from the serious and genuine consideration by all concerned, from judges and social workers to family and friends, of his claim to be the home parent. If the members of the family affected all feel that the decision taken is, at the time, fair and sensible and, however painful, the best that can be made in the circumstances, then some good can come of it in the long run. Regular and sustained contact with the other parent, so critical to many children's psychological well-being, can be maximised. Both parents will be more ready to review the arrangements from time to time as the children grow older, to modify contact times, durations and places to meet the children's needs *and* their own. They will usually be able to arrive at common standards of morality and discipline and to inculcate values that are not contradictory. By making it clear that the residence and contact decisions and the patterns and rules of life that are the consequence of those decisions have been agreed and are supported, endorsed and enforced by both parents in their children's interests they will make it much harder for children to play one parent off against another.

If this co-operation can be embodied in a joint residence order the other parent may feel less excluded from her children's lives. By making her loss a little more bearable and by giving her a real say in strategic decisions affecting her children she will be more inclined to adopt a constructive attitude. She will feel less helpless and so be more inclined to recognise that it is in the child's interest to be looked after on a daily basis by its father for the foreseeable future at least. As the years pass the father can also feel more confident about the long term nature of his responsibility for his child's upbringing and that it will not be taken out of his hands by a sudden judicial reversal instigated by his ex. As a result, it gradually becomes the child who decides how much time it will spend with each parent and when. The child feels far less divided loyalty, the mother feels she plays a vital role in her child's life and the home parent father gets a break from the single parent pressure and time to pursue his own interests. This, in turn, will reduce the disruption to the children's lives which separation inevitably causes.

However, a joint residence order is a gamble. Courts, in putting children's interests first, will usually support the decisions of the parent who has day to day legal responsibility for the child – the old 'care and control'. However, the other parent is entitled to have her (or his) view heard and taken into account, in court if it comes to that. This may have no more than nuisance value, though like all court battles for all but the very poor and the very rich it can be financially crippling and thus favour the wealthier of the two contestants. Nevertheless, there are instances when a dispute between joint custodians can completely overturn the life strategy over education, religion or place of domicile, that the home parent has been working towards for his child for many years. The older the child the more likely that his or her opinion will weigh more heavily with the judge than that of either parent in determining who has residence.

Residence orders are not automatically made and this may be a pity as they can help to clarify the situation and avoid disputes. Of course, some parents behave unreasonably even when there is a court order. Even if his children have been left with him voluntarily the home parent father should take care to consolidate his position through a formal court order in case his ex has second thoughts. She may decide at some later date, when yet another upheaval is likely to damage the children still further, that she wants them with her permanently. A father in this situation, whether he was married or not, should seek a residence order to confirm his right to be the home parent while at the same time doing everything he can to ensure that the children, particularly those under ten, keep in touch with their mother a great deal. If he cannot guarantee frequent face to face contact, the best interest of the child *may* mean he should later consider severing contact altogether, specially if his children are very young. We will look at this unconventional proposition in greater detail later. However, the opportunity for access to the mother is usually considered an important factor in awarding residence to a father. The suffering of many hundreds of thousands of other parent fathers who cannot see their children should be a warning to men not to inflict the same anguish on women unless it is genuinely in the best interests of the child.

With or without joint residence, after a lapse of time the ex who has walked out will sometimes try to get back the nurturing of the children she abandoned. This may be from genuine regret at having left them, it may be from revenge and anger at seeing them being happily brought up without her by a man whom, in all probability, she hates – we often hate those we have wronged – or it may be in response to social pressure and the disapproval of neighbours and acquaintances who are much harder on a mother who leaves her children than on a father who does the same.

The expressed desire to have her children back may be no more than a ploy to avoid contributing to their upkeep. 'I certainly won't pay you anything. If you can't manage I'll be happy to have them back'. It may be to undermine the father's confidence. Or it may be to rationalise her dereliction, not only in the eyes of others, but in her own, through making it seem a temporary aberration which she would gladly put right.

If she is really trying to get them back under her full time care then father beware! Although judgements are improving there are still judges who if appealed to by a mother will remove children from the perfectly satisfactory care of their father and return them to the legal care of their mother, even after two or three years during which she has had little or nothing to do with them. Basically, however, the longer a father has had the children the less likely a court is to take them from him provided he can demonstrate that he has done a good job and not obstructed access to their mother.

It may seem petty but keeping a thorough and detailed diary of all parental involvement with the children that shows how competently and conscientiously a lone father is looking after his children and logging every one of the ex's sins of both omission and commission – failure to turn up when promised, neglecting food, health, cleanliness, hobbies, homework supervision and so on – which demonstrate her parental deficiencies – is a prudent precaution against any possible future residence hearing, particularly if joint custody was originally agreed to. Establishing that his ex would not do as good a job as he already does strengthens a father's case. It may also be a good idea to lodge these diaries with a solicitor or other suitably responsible and independent person such as a sympathetic bank manager, head teacher, or magistrate every six months or so. This pre-empts any accusations that they have been made up retrospectively to support a case should they ever have to be produced in evidence.

There is certainly the possibility in a great many broken relationships for reconstructing a new kind of separated family life. While it is not as satisfactory as a conventional two parent family in most cases it has, nevertheless, a considerable potential for good and is infinitely preferable to the isolated, hostile, lone parent syndrome which has been seen as the almost inevitable outcome of broken marriages and cohabitations. With such potential for conflict both parents must always beware of decisions arising from divorce or separation being determined by the needs of the adults rather than of their children. If the hardest sacrifice in the children's interest, to try to make a 'go of it', is obviously impossible or inadvisable, then at least any other decisions must give the children's needs priority. The majority of younger children have not the knowledge or experience to foresee the implications of such decisions nor should they be burdened with having to make them. If they are compelled to make such choices they may feel guilty about them, whichever parent they chose, for the rest of their lives. When the parents were together they thought it part of their parental duty to take major decisions on behalf of their children. Now they are separated they must try to bring themselves to do so still.

7

Child snatchers

The exception to the rule of doing nothing hastily is when a mother, often without warning, has left the family home taking all or some* of her children with her. She may have taken them impulsively to her mother's house, or that of some other relative or friend, or she may, if her 'snatch' was planned, have set up house elsewhere with a lover or on her own. Whichever alternative base she has established the longer she goes unchallenged the harder it will be for the children's father to make a successful bid to be designated their home parent and be awarded residence. Most judges are now reluctant to disrupt children's established patterns of life and more reluctant still to do so where this is under the care of the mother rather than the father.

The difficulty for fathers in this situation is that the law is as anomalous and unjust to men in this as it is in many other aspects of domestic dispute, particularly if they are unmarried. A mother, whether married or not, cannot technically 'kidnap' her own children unless their father has a residence or custody order, but an unmarried father who goes off with his children is, strictly speaking, breaking the law and kidnapping them if he takes them from their home to some other part of the UK and abducting them if he takes them out of the UK.

Immediate application for a residence order should be made by the father if his mate leaves home permanently with their children and an abduction is feared. This normally takes some time, but in certain circumstances the application can be treated as a matter of urgency, as, for example, where their removal from the country is clearly imminent or they may be in some physical or moral danger. He can also probably obtain a prohibited steps order for the same purpose. This is a court order specifically forbidding the other parent to do certain things or take certain actions and if she does not obey the order she risks a fine, or even imprisonment.

There are legal limits to how far a potential absconding mother can go. If the children's father is her husband or has a

*The Courts usually encourage disputing parents to keep siblings together, but home parents will sometimes not have all of their children living with them.

residence order she cannot legally take them out of the country for more than a month at a time without his written consent. If she takes them out of school then the father can seek an attendance order by which a court will order the children to be sent to school, though the mother could perhaps comply by sending them to school elsewhere if that place is her new place of residence.

Abduction, involving as it does what the tabloid press likes to call Tug-of-Love children, who might often more aptly be called Tug-of-Envy children, is not as common as may be supposed. In 1994 the Lord Chancellor's Office dealt with 163 cases (these involved breach of a court order) many of which overlapped with the cases involving 254 abducted children and 176 families in which the help of the charity Reunite was sought by one of the parents. Fear of abduction is more common and Reunite receives an average of one hundred and twenty-five calls on its help line a month. Abduction is usually thought of as an exclusively male crime, but Reunite's figures show that a third of those abducting or threatening to abduct children are their mothers.

Abduction, by its nature, is an international crime and on 25th October 1980 a group of leading nations signed The Hague Convention on the Civil Aspects of International Child Abduction – there are currently fifty-three signatories to the Convention. Under this convention, upon receiving a formal request from the legal authorities in the country from which the children have been abducted, convention members will return them to their normal home so that litigation about their custody or residence can take place there rather than in the country to which they have been taken. This denies the abductor the tactical advantage of taking children to a country where the domestic laws may be more favourable to his or her personal case. This was later reinforced in English law by the Child Abduction Act of 1984 which makes it a criminal act to remove a child without the custodial parent's consent.

When children are abducted the aggrieved parent can apply for their return to the UK by getting in touch with the Child Abduction Unit at the Lord Chancellor's Department, which can be contacted twenty-four hours a day. At the time of writing Reunite was also hoping to extend its helpline service to twenty-four hours a day. The British legal authorities cannot make an application under the Hague Convention unless the parent's rights of custody have been established under Section 8 of the Children Act 1989. Therefore the first thing a father has to be clear about is whether or not he has the right to object to his children being taken permanently out of the country by their mother. He has this right if he is still married to her, or if a court previously awarded him a current custody or residence order, or if he has obtained a prohibited steps order from a British court expressly forbidding her to do so. Even if no residence order may yet have been made when a child is abducted it will still apply as soon as one is obtained. It has been argued that the new Children Act discourages recovery by parents whose children have been snatched and makes it more difficult unless residence orders have been obtained in advance. The Lord Chancellor certainly made it clear in October 1991 that he did not regard the Act as a deterrent to courts from making residence or prohibitive steps orders to prevent abduction, and his department is certainly ready to make applications for the return of abducted children. Most countries co-operate when a request for the return of a child is made and it can be clearly demonstrated that, under the laws of his home country, he (or she) has been wrongfully removed or wrongfully detained. If the child is abducted outside the Hague Convention area the UK legal authorities cannot help, but the Foreign Office consular department can usually put parents in touch with appropriate lawyers and officials in the country to which the child has been taken. Sadly, the chances of getting a child back in these cases is often slight, though in Moslem countries a father may get a better hearing than a mother in similar circumstances.

Realistically, it has to be recognised that a parent who abducts a child is usually so desperate or unbalanced that they are unlikely to give a second thought to the fact that they may be acting illegally, let alone be deterred by such considerations.

A father, whether legally entitled to residence or not, can take certain steps to prevent his child being abducted if he fears that their mother may try to take them out of the country to live. In applying for a residence order or a prohibitive steps order it should be sufficient for his solicitor to make it clear to the court that because of current or future disputes over residence there is a genuine risk that the children will be abducted. This is a particularly strong argument where the other parent is not a permanent resident in Great Britain or has strong foreign family connections. It needs also to be emphasised that even if there is a joint custody or joint residence order it is the laws of the child's normal country of residence that apply.

Obviously, if the taking of a child could have been shown to have the custodial parent's consent it would not be wrongful. However, ignorance of the child being taken out of the country or silence in the sense that no formal objection was made do not imply consent. The custodial parent has positively and provenly to have given consent. Incidentally, the child is ordered not necessarily to be returned to the other parent, but to the jurisdiction which will take the decision. In cases where a child is sufficiently mature its views will be taken into account and the decision will be left to the discretion of the court.

A father who is afraid of abduction needs to tip off his children's school, childminders and anyone else who may be caring for his children in his absence, warning them not to hand them over to anyone not authorised by him. If he is married and there is no residence order then of course his ex cannot easily be prevented from meeting them after school, etc. Once teachers are aware of the situation they are usually quite co-operative about ensuring that a child is returned to its usual home. The children also need to be briefed not to go off with anyone their father has not specifically told them they may go with. Popular grandparents, for example, are sometimes used as an instrument of abduction by vengeful mothers. If a father is forced to act he will have to act quickly so he needs to keep copies of court orders, photographs and descriptions of the children and of anyone who might be involved in the abduction, their addresses, telephone numbers, etc. He will need to keep to hand details of the child's passport, telephone numbers of police and solicitors who would help and of the Lord Chancellor's office and Reunite. He needs to keep passports and birth certificates in a safe place so that a would-be abductor cannot use or obtain a passport, though she cannot be prevented from getting a temporary British visitor's passport and going to countries in which it is valid.

The abduction laws do not apply to children being removed to another part of the UK where only a common law offence of kidnapping would apply. Although an abducting parent can be dealt with under the civil law, orders made in England and Wales may not be enforced in Scotland and Northern Ireland, where the law differs in some respects, without the consent of those courts. An order can be obtained requiring a mother to return children to the father's home because the father has a residence order or the mother is in breach of the terms of a contact order. To obtain the order the home parent will have to prove that the other parent has been keeping or is likely to keep the children for an unreasonable time – several days when no overnight stop, or only a single one, is permitted – or in unreasonable circumstances – ie keeping them away from some important school event, medical appointment, major family occasion or something of that kind. A few hours overdue in bringing the children home or making them miss football practice or a music lesson, while irritating and bad for the children, would not constitute such unreasonable behaviour although repeated and frequent derelictions of this kind might.

Abduction is the extreme and rarest form of dispute over where children shall live. It is important to recognise that such extreme action may be induced by the absent parent's feelings that they are being shut out from their child's life and the home parent should do everything to diminish that fear however paranoid it may seem to him. Men can be very blind and obtuse about women's often different feelings as evidenced by the fact that many do not seem to believe that their women would take the ultimate step of leaving. To some extent children are seen as an insurance policy against this. This attitude is reinforced by the fact that something like half of our women had left the household one or more times before, so the latest departure has often also been seen initially as probably a temporary situation. But if a man continues for too long to hope that his mate will bring the children home he may find that he has left it too late to do anything about it when she does not. Quite apart from anything else legal action to recover the children may jolt the woman into full recognition of the implications of the course she has embarked upon. There is, conversely, the risk that a woman who left only as a ploy, hoping to provoke her husband into begging her to return, may feel herself correspondingly rejected by such action and be pushed into leaving 'for real'. More usually, she leaves and he finds himself soon after served with a divorce petition or, if unmarried, a separation order. This process usually includes proposals for the disposal of the children and a father may only have a few days to decide whether to oppose a divorce petition, or at least its proposed provisions, and this at a time when the intensity of the domestic dispute – the couple may not even be on speaking terms – makes finding out the true position very difficult. Nevertheless, if the father bears in mind the advice of these last few chapters and concentrates all his energy on getting residence of his children he is much more likely to succeed.

8

Getting over it – taking a break

So, by one means or another, father has won the right to be the home parent for his children. Where does he go from there? Once the initial sense of triumph, relief and joy has passed he will be confronted by the fact that, in the majority of cases, he is relatively inexperienced in taking the sole responsibility for home and family. So what must he do?

Selfish as it may sound the most useful priority that he can pursue for his children's sake is to see to his own emotional, mental and physical well-being. If he is uncontrollably distraught, mentally disturbed or sick he will be of little or no use to them.

A useful starting point in the pursuit of self health is to paint two self portraits; the first of himself as he is now, his state of mind, his strengths and weaknesses, his skills and deficiencies, and compare this with a second picture not of an unattainable ideal 'double' parent but of a good one. A good portrait reveals the inner man as well as the outer and that is not always easy to identify in the aftermath of death or separation. Most people feel that their own tragedy is unique and this makes assessment hard. Fathers may find it helpful in placing their own cases in a more reassuring context to be aware of some of the more usual feelings and experiences of widowhood and separation.

'Sensations of psychosomatic distress occurring in waves lasting from twenty minutes to an hour at a time, a feeling of tightness in the throat, choking with shortness of breath, need for sighing, an empty feeling in the abdomen, lack of muscular power and an intense subjective distress described as tension or mental pain'. These feelings of grief, and a preoccupation with an image of the deceased together with a feeling of their presence, a feeling of guilt at the failure of the relationship, hostility and lack of warmth towards others and of aimless search for activity accompanied by an inability to maintain any organised form of activity are the common aftermath of bereavement and separation. (M2)

The process of mourning and recovery seems to follow three general stages; shock, which virtually blocks out all feelings for anything from a few days to a few weeks; then intense grief for perhaps several months, even a year or more, followed by a third long period of recovery in which the sadness fades, the good memories resurface and normal life is resumed. Where death follows a long illness the phases are shorter and many widowers move quickly to and through phase three. But even in these situations, where the father has already largely resolved the problems of reconciling the demands of work and of running a home and family, clinical depression can follow the wife's death. This is more common where that death was unexpected and although some divorced and separated men can also suffer from depression induced in a similar way they form a smaller proportion of that category. How serious and enduring a father's depression may become and whether or not it amounts to a nervous breakdown should be taken as much into account when assessing a father's suitability to have the care of his children as it is in determining whether or not a mother should keep them.

The effect of death on the children also varies according to whether it was anticipated or unexpected. Widowers seem to cope a little better with wives' long illnesses, but these appear to retard children's mental development more than an unexpected death. (M1) It might reasonably be inferred from this that a short intense battle between a mother and father prior to separation, usually the result of one or other being seriously involved with someone else, will be less mentally harmful to their children than the long nagging siege and mutual sniping that stems from basic incompatibility rather than from any single act.

Of all men who lose their mates, for whatever reason, two-thirds suffer depression of some kind, a third frequently and protractedly.(M2) Shock, depression, grief and anger can all have physical effects, so it is important to accept that emotional and physical symptoms need medical treatment (or psychiatric help) unless they diminish of their own accord in a relatively short time and eventually disappear, or almost disappear, altogether. If a man has not wanted his relationship to end, as most home fathers have not, he will find the process of healing will take longer. Before it can begin he has to reconcile himself to the fact that it *is* over. Then those sleepless or nightmare-troubled nights can gradually be turned into a thing of the past as, with his constant reassurance, they can for his children who will probably suffer in the same way. A short term remedy for the father's anxious and sorrowing insomnia may be a stiff alcoholic nightcap or a sleeping pill. But although these, like tranquillisers, may bring immediate relief they do not resolve the problem in the long term and may even do physical harm. Creating a dependency on anything from alcohol to tobacco, cannabis to hard drugs, paracetamol to valium, will eventually entail a cure as painful as the trauma they were supposed to relieve. Far healthier and more effective is to develop techniques of relaxation – be they from yoga, meditation or simply deep controlled breathing to physical exhaustion from work or exercise followed by a hot bath and bed. Supported by regular and sensible eating habits (no over eating of sweet comfort foods, no self-punishing starvation) and regular hours of work, play and sleep these techniques can put a man in control of his emotions again.

If the natural healing process is not taking place within two or three months (for example, if bouts of weeping, suicidal or violent impulses, impotence or other abnormal experiences persist) then the lone father should consult his GP remembering to tell him *all* the circumstances relating to his condition and making it clear that more than just a physical illness is involved. This applies to all lone home fathers however they became such. The best GPs are no great believers in pills and potions as the solution to every problem. They do not automatically give the patient tranquillisers but sympathetic attention and common-sense observations. They may also provide the short term support – usually all that is needed – of the practice psychiatric nurse. There is a much higher incidence of ill health among men than among women when their cohabiting relationships break up which seems to endorse the views of several researchers that men get more out of marriage, or its equivalent, set more store by it and suffer more when it breaks up.(M4) Many men whose marriages end suddenly do not anticipate the severe and debilitating, sometimes almost incapacitating, shock this may have.(B1)

Our natural reaction to bereavement and loss is either to turn in on ourselves and shut off communication with everyone or to develop a kind of Ancient Mariner syndrome in which we talk endlessly on every occasion to almost anyone we can pin down to listen. Friends are often more valuable than professionals in all these confessional and consultation roles except where expert information or advice is required. The majority of professional advisers, such as doctors, solicitors, social workers and so on, are not only less readily and frequently available, but tend to see the problem only from the point of view of their speciality so do not always pick up the nuances or related implications. Because men seem to find it harder to express their intimate feelings, even to a friend, they can find it harder than women to come to terms with death, separation and divorce. Women are the tougher when it comes to jettisoning emotional attachments and a great deal less inhibited than men about telling others what they feel. Men can find it just as helpful and therapeutic to bend a sympathetic ear to which all can be told. By repeating and telling our story uninhibitedly and facing up to the anguish, anger and sense of loss, the events we describe can become ordered and controlled in our minds at least. This may be either by fully understanding them and ourselves or, no less efficaciously (but with some dangers for future relationships) by creating our own myths about them. The role of myth-making in stress management is an important one. Both exes may need to rewrite history for, as one psychologist put it, 'a major element in the adjustment process, for any type of emotional crisis, may be the restructuring of reality into a new form that is more acceptable to the new life patterns the individual is working out'. (QM2) Men, on the whole, are better than women at facing up to and accepting reality and less often need to resort to this device, which can exacerbate the antagonism in a broken relationship. It is extremely provoking to be told that a marriage was a disaster from day one when you know its earlier days to have been happy, fruitful and mutually satisfying.

The experience of loss for the divorced and separated differs from that of widowers in a number of respects. Divorce or separation provoke guilt and shame and undermine personal confidence and sense of worth. The mutual criticism, coldness and negative attitudes that almost inevitably precede the breakdown of a relationship are bound to create feelings not only of guilt but of self-contempt. 'Perhaps what she (or he) is saying about me is actually true.' This feeling persists until an explanation is found or constructed in terms acceptable to the individual's personality that explain so significant a failure in his life. Nor is private satisfaction enough because others, especially children, find their lives shaped by the pattern and conduct of life which grows from the explanation adopted.

Separation is still a great emotional wrench even if the relationship being left was totally intolerable and – in a few 'two-way' cases – is being exchanged for one full of hope and love. Many men are just not prepared for the intensity of their emotional response. Why do they still feel attachment and affection for their partners as well as rejection and even hatred? Why do they still want to have sex with them and indeed sometimes do? Separation as a result of decision is in some ways worse than separation by death. Healing through grieving is not so obviously available. Now grief is made sharper by hope, by a longing, however unrealistic, to put back the clock so encouraging the abandoned person, consciously or subconsciously, to refuse to accept what has happened. With death he cannot do this. Paradoxically the more civilised the parting the harder it can be to come to terms with the strong feelings that parting gives rise to. Rows and arguments may be a necessary process for both understanding what went wrong and reconciling oneself to a different future. There is no blame attached to this response, though those who do not channel their pain into criticism of their ex often turn it to blame of themselves. The deserted half of a couple has every right to feel and express anger, particularly if, though no one is innocent, they have been wronged. Indeed, anger may be a necessary part of the therapy of readjustment for quite a few in this situation. (D1)

There are clear differences in the process for widowers. Among them those cases where the wife's or mate's death was completely unexpected, following a fatal accident, heart attack, stroke or other sudden and swiftly fatal illness (it is surprising how quickly cancer can kill, for example) differ from those where it has followed a long illness, often of a degenerative nature, such as MS. Perhaps the greatest difference between widowers and those whose ex still lives is in the involvement of the children in a common trauma. Following death every member of the family is sharing a common grief and sense of permanent loss. This can make for much mutual support and while a father still needs to control his emotions to some extent for his children's sake he does not have to suppress them entirely nor pretend to feelings he does not have, as so many deserted home fathers must. While both widowers and deserted fathers must resist the temptation to lean on their children for emotional support, the widower does not usually have feelings of resentment or even hatred about his ex to bottle up for fear of harming his children.

Widowers enjoy one other advantage – there is a convention, an accepted pattern of social behaviour developed, if much changed over the centuries, to ease the hearts of the living by formally acknowledging the loss of the dead through funerals, memorial services, periods and symbols of mourning and above all the open expression of grief by those bereaved. Sympathy and sorrow, love and support are shown to the survivor by family and friends. These help him to accept the fact of death and come to terms with his sense of loss. How different for the man whose wife or mate has left him or whom he and his children have had to leave; furtive glances, suppressed sniggers, pointed avoidance of the topic or mention of the departed's name – except to denigrate them sometimes. There is no formal burying of a dead marriage or relationship so perhaps we need to invent one, to help all those involved, all bereaved in different ways, to acknowledge what has passed, to get it out of their systems and to restart their lives.

Usually by the time the first anniversary of significant family occasions, and most importantly of the ex's actual departure, has passed, certainly by the second anniversary, the home parent is likely to have recovered from this destructive experience as much as he or she is likely to. However, sometimes further healing can still come about by involvement in a new relationship, not necessarily a permanent one, or in some absorbing activity at work or home.

It is very important for the stability of the single parent family that the home parent does not crack up under the stresses of separation and the practical difficulties this entails. My advice to new single fathers would be cope at all costs. If children have to go to stay with relatives or, worse, into Local Authority care, because their father cannot cope no amount of comforting or explanation will reassure them or quieten their fears about losing their other parent. This is particularly the case with very young children for whom the terms of reference for adult behaviour are largely meaningless and who expect their parents to be an infallible and unshakeable rock on which they can build their lives. Even temporary surrender of home parent responsibility can provide an opening for a disaffected other parent to raise again through the legal system the issue of residence and reclaim the home parent role. Obviously if a father does have to give up his home parenting duties because of failure to cope he needs to reassess the residence situation himself. Is his incapacity temporary and his long term ability to be a good home parent unimpaired? Or is he just not cut out for the role? It takes courage to come to this latter conclusion, but there is no shame in it (nor in the same situation when a mother cannot cope). Provided the transfer of home parental responsibility is sensitively handled, the children, who will be the first to be aware of the father's shortcomings, will be grateful for his honesty in the long run. The important rider is that the transition should not be abrupt or unplanned and contact should be as frequent and regular as possible with the former home parent even if later it is reduced by mutual consent. Where the mental or physical breakdown of the home parent is serious, sudden and chronic then such a cushioned transition will not be possible and it is up to the new home parent, whatever his or her personal feelings, to make sure that the children understand that they have not been intentionally rejected and to boost the image of the other parent in their eyes as much as possible.

Finding oneself the lone home parent, whether by death or separation, is a traumatic experience. The lone father will find himself isolated, guilt-ridden, exhausted and often poor, but by reassessing himself and his circumstances, perhaps with professional help, he can not only conquer these demons but create a positive and enjoyable life with many unexpected bonuses for both himself and his children. He will slowly gain a new sense of independence and freedom to pursue his own domestic life pattern. He will probably learn what few men do – the art of listening to his children, particularly to what they are really saying to him. He will be forced to discover through the changes and upheavals in his pattern of life who his true friends are and how great is their value. He will find that the bonds and obligations of family are stronger and stretch more widely than he might ever have imagined as he draws strength from them. 'As a result his children's lives will be enriched by contacts with a variety of adults, some of whom will undoubtedly have a lasting and positive influence'. (B1)

He will find that a period of being on his own as an adult is not only a useful and necessary prelude to making any successful new relationship, but of value for its own sake as a mirror to his inner self and a source of confidence and strength. He will learn to reclassify himself out of the old male macho stereotypes and to re-order his values. If at times he feels these egocentric preoccupations are rather selfish he can rest assured that they are an essential first step to becoming a good home parent, to providing that high quality of parenting which can shape his children's future more decisively than the traumas arising from the loss or departure of their mother. In short, his reaction to bereavement or defection will determine his attitude to the task ahead of him and thereby the likelihood of his success in it.

9

Letting go – you're better without her.

The law's delays are usually unnecessary and frustrating, but in the case of divorce and separation they may turn out to be no bad thing, allowing tempers to cool and wounds to heal a little before irrevocable decisions are taken about children and finances. It usually takes time to get residence and maintenance cases heard and where these involve reference to court welfare officers there is often as much as a three month waiting list for the interviews on which reports then have to be made and considered. Hasty divorces nearly always produce residence, contact and maintenance decisions that are regretted by at least some of those involved and later lead to acrimonious disputes that prolong the agony for everyone and prevent them from reconstructing what they can of their lives.

If a man has been abandoned and left with the care of his children, this limbo, although it may inflict all the agonies of uncertainty, gives him time to decide upon and plan his strategy and resolve some of the doubts in his own mind. Has his woman really left him or will she come back? Many women 'run away' and return several times before they finally sever their ties with their homes. Some make several such breaks, but then reconcile themselves to long-term cohabitation. Usually, if the break is a gesture or a cry for help, a woman will return to her children and home within a few days, a few weeks at most. The longer the absence, the less likely she is to return. During his time without her the father has to try to transcend the shock and honestly ask himself if he wants her back. Is her loss really no more than an inconvenience and a break with old habits which can soon be accommodated or is it a rift in the very fabric of his life and, no less importantly, that of his children? If the latter then he must let her know how much she is valued. That may be just the reassurance she is seeking by her actions. He must ask himself honestly and carefully why she has left. Is it just one of those relatively minor mental aberrations or nervous breakdowns to which women are more prone than men, or is it something much more serious? Has he driven her to run away by his infidelity, coldness, indifference, violence, contempt, sexual deviance or demands, or some other wrong? If so, does he wish to amend it and is it in his power to do so either on his own or with help? Or has his mate simply buggered off because she prefers another man or is just a selfish bitch – both common enough occurrences? If there is another woman in the man's life he needs to ask himself whether his relationship with her is really so important as to risk wrecking his children's lives and possibly breaking their mother's heart, specially in view of the fact that a second relationship has even less chance of survival than the first.

The hardest conclusion of all for a man in these circumstances is that the relationship is irrevocably dead, however much he may have wished it to live, and its continuance likely only to warp and twist the lives of all concerned, children included. Then he must decide whether it is in his children's best interests to remain with him or to make arrangements for them to join their mother either by moving out of the family home and letting her come back or by sending them to her. This is certainly not a decision to be rushed. A few months of managing his children's lives and a job – or lack of it – will not only give him an idea of how well, or badly he can cope in practical terms, but a better idea of how essential a part of his own being his children are and his role to them. The majority of residence orders given to men are awarded because a father has found himself bringing up his children willy-nilly and has demonstrated, for some substantial time, that he is perfectly capable of doing so. A father must always bear in mind that once he passes his children to their mother the chances are no better than even that, within two years, he will *ever* see them again. If, even so, he concludes that they need the daily care of their mother even more than they need his he must prepare the ground so as to secure his future contact with them as carefully as possible – again a transition which should not be rushed and is probably best negotiated through solicitors or mediators if that can be afforded. At least written conditions of access should be secured before he agrees, formally or informally, to anything. That by itself is no guarantee of contact, but it is a starting point and negotiating it may give him a truer idea of where his ex really stands on his future relationship with his children. If he suspects an agreement on contact may be broken as soon as the divorce or separation is secured, then he should fight for a residence order himself.

In many ways the man who finds both himself and his children abandoned from the outset by a woman who is adamant that she wants no part in family life, or has simply vanished altogether, is better off. Despite the heartbreak he must usually endure he can at least buckle down at once to the task of rebuilding family life around himself as home parent, unconfused by having to take account of a host of other options and possibilities.

Letting go of a mate who remains precious can be made very hard by the repeated assertions of exes and social workers that the deserted party should immediately relinquish all ties and make no demands upon her. His ex is probably seeking to absolve herself from the guilt of what she knows to have been a selfish action in leaving home and family. If her partner can be seen to be tacitly rejecting her by rapid and total willingness to 'let go', then she can justify her action and sooth her conscience. Most men's instinct when deserted is the opposite. They wish to put pressure on the ex to return by refusing to let go and their behaviour can sometimes become obsessive. John, (J11) one of the fathers in my survey, stole the key of his wife's new flat from her handbag, had it copied and returned it without her knowing so that he could read her letters to try and find out the real nature of her relationship with her lover and whether or not there was any chance of the reconciliation and return for which he so desperately longed. Only when the duplicate key did not fit was it suddenly brought home to him how stupid and obsessive his behaviour had been. Although he recognised this intellectually and took steps to remedy his obsessive conduct, it was two or three years before he fully came to terms with the fact that his ex was not coming back and had no wish to do so. Even after that the notion would briefly and painfully resurface whenever she was having difficulty with a current relationship. The love and longing never entirely dies even when a new life has been successfully rebuilt. There is nothing unusual, or indeed within limits harmful, about such fantasies and obsessive behaviour. It is not easy to confess to conduct of which one is ashamed, but this is the kind of situation in which calling on the help of the community psychiatric nurse or other professional counselling can be helpful in channelling and sublimating these regressive feelings to constructive ends.

Demented behaviour is usually manifested in different ways by men and women. Men often seek relief in violence, not always against the offending ex, though that is all too common, but also frequently against the ex's new man, 'her' children, or some innocent bystander in the pub who makes, even inadvertently, a wounding or offensive remark. This gets no-one anywhere except into court or even prison and certainly does nothing to improve a father's chances of gaining or retaining the residence of his children. But it is absurd to ignore the fact that male nature is intrinsically and by conditioning prone to express the emotional extremes, hate, fear or anger, in physical and often violent action. The sensible course for the angry or frustrated man is to recognise and accept his feelings and find a harmless means of giving vent to them. The competitive games and strenuous physical pastimes enjoyed by most men and mocked by so many women actually serve a valuable purpose as acceptable and constructive vehicles for these otherwise dangerous and destructive impulses. John used to run up and down the mountain behind his house every day and swam two or three times a week. Eventually he lost too much weight, falling below that at which he had left school thirty-six years earlier, but by then with the pounds he had burned off he had also burned off all his feelings of aggression, if not his sense of loss, and was able to slow down to a more normal existence. While I can strongly commend physical exertion to men in this predicament it does need to be tempered by caution so that it is exercised within the bounds of each individual's capacity and state of health. I suspect that for those not so inclined a competitive game of golf (or even snooker!) or a brisk walk could have the same therapeutic effect. If companionship can be blended with the competition it will be even more healing.

If a man feels or acts violently towards his ex or his children then he needs to try to work out what triggers these reactions and avoid exposing himself to that trigger. He also needs to find out what relaxes him (alcohol is usually a bad idea as it disinhibits) and if necessary get help with dealing with his anger. It makes sense for a lone father who is worried about his feelings of anger and aggression towards his children to contact social services for assistance. The problem is that he may well fear that they will then take his children away, since the presumption tends to be against fathers in such matters.

Similar anxieties may inhibit the father who feels strong sexual attraction to one of his children. In this case he may not only need help to prevent his feelings being translated into actions fearfully destructive to his child, but also to confront the fact that the child may be better off for the time being in the care of its mother or some other close relative. Going through a good GP rather than direct to social services can give the father some insurance against the over-reaction of a social worker whose professional instinct may be to take the child into care immediately. Notifying a solicitor of any proposed pre-emptive appeal for help may be another wise precaution. The encouraging fact for fathers who find themselves tempted to violence or sexual abuse is that therapy, counselling or medical treatment or a combination of them can usually bring these aberrant feelings under control provided they are recognised and faced up to before they have ruined a child's life.

Women's resentment tends to be expressed verbally, though unbalanced practical expression of it, from cutting off the sleeves of all an unfaithful husband's suits to cutting off his penis is not unknown and should not be entirely unexpected by the cautious male half of a broken relationship! Jokingly expressed hostility may be the sublimated expression of real anger. However, this book is not the place to analyse the nature of women's negative feelings on the break-up of a relationship, but simply to advise men to recognise and sympathise with them. Any bizarre behaviour they may observe in their ex may be a mirror image of their own turmoil.

The finality of death has a depressive effect but the usually indeterminate nature of separation leaves the father in a limbo of uncertainty and many men are so shattered by the experience that they contemplate, and even occasionally commit, suicide and display many other psychological symptoms. For those who pushed their wives out, for whatever reason, these considerations might seem not to apply, but even they frequently express a sense of loss. The very absence of companionship, however bad, can be disturbing and generate much resentment at wives who go off without any consideration for the children's welfare nor for the burden the man has to bear as a result.

Two-thirds of the men in one survey (M2) felt anger or bitterness at the time of the wife leaving and half these still did a couple of years later. The other half had become indifferent or reconciled. The early anger may be a healthy response, creating bitter energy and a refusal to give in. This is precisely what is needed at first, but while a scapegoat may be a necessary mechanism in the short term it is not helpful in the long run because it holds the victim in a backward looking posture instead of looking forward. In the first year eighty-six per cent of the men in the survey referred to, missed their women. In the next two years it was down to seventy-four per cent and by four years down to sixty per cent. The more remarkable thing is that even after all this time more than half the men still missed their exes, particularly their companionship or when confronted with things that a partner specifically used to do like sewing or buying a daughter's new clothes. One man in my own survey found himself bursting into tears almost twelve months after his wife left when he took down from the shelf the last jar of the home made marmalade she used to make every year. The resurgence of grief that the most trivial incidents can bring is quite natural provided it does not persist for too long.

In a way those whose mate leaves them for another man can more easily handle the crisis because it is part of the classic pattern of male rivalry and can be attributed to a failure of the woman's judgement. If she just leaves, then there is no escaping the fact that she has rejected him, full stop. Even though the departure of many wives is obviously because of their desire for independence rather than of any animosity towards their particular mate of the time (something they appear to have failed to think about before they paired off) it still leaves the man with a strong sense of personal failure. Social workers are reporting this trend of women leaving their mates simply because they think an independent life would be preferable, or even just more fun, as increasingly common among those in their early thirties. Eighty per cent of the women in my survey had left home in this way, though that includes the irrational flight of those suffering from mental breakdown or alcoholism. The irony for the deserted lone father is that his children's happiness and his chances of doing a good job as their home parent depend to some extent on how good a relationship he can now form with the woman who left him.

10

Ex marks the spot

The aim of responsible parents in the ordinary intact family is to raise their children to be able to live happy and fruitful lives as independent adults. There is an expected (if not always very precisely planned) programme of cutting the parental ties one by one until the child becomes an adult and can stand alone needing nothing more than the knowledge of the parents' love and sympathy. The goal is never in question, only occasionally the method and timing. (M1) If the job of detaching a child is done well, its demands for independence progressively and sensibly met at the appropriate moment, then its ties to its parents as an adult will be stronger and more mutually supportive than if a sharp and sudden rebellion is the only way to break free. The intensity of feeling created by the child/lone parent relationship can blind a home parent father (or mother) to the fact that their aim is no different, although balance and emphasis may be. When a child has two parents to turn to at any time there is a built-in safety mechanism that usually prevents its needs or feelings being misunderstood or neglected for long. If dad will not help mum may, if mum will not listen dad will. For the lone parent the absence of the second point of view means that he must listen more generously and more carefully than he might otherwise sometimes have done. Nowhere is this more important than in a child's relationship with the other parent. The home parent must try not to lose sight of this because he is too absorbed in his own concerns and anxieties. As one child put it 'If a child wants to stay with its father or mother, there's a reason for it and parents should *listen* instead of doing all the talking'. (P1)

A mother who has left home and become the other parent is still a vitally important person in her children's lives, perhaps in some cases still the most important person, even though they are not living with her. For their sake the home parent must foster as close a relationship as he can – and as she will permit – between mother and children. In the case of death, or total loss of contact, then the memory of her, however idealised, plays an important part in a child's emotional life and needs to be kept bright. The overwhelming indications of the research in this field, biased heavily though it is to analysing the role of absent fathers, indicate that the closer to pre-separation normality the children's relationship can be kept with both parents, the better the outcome of the break-up for them may be in terms of health, happiness and educational achievement. (D2) There is no reason to suppose the part played by children's relationships with an other parent mother will be any less significant in most cases. My emphasis is on 'as close to normal' for, as can be seen in my own survey, spasmodic and infrequent contact is of little and probably even negative value. The Children Act 1989, by its redefinition of parental responsibility, recognises post-separation involvement with both parents not only as a parental duty but as a psychological necessity for the children and treats it as a central issue in family law.

According to one study, (M2) forty per cent of fathers said the children's mother had not seen them since she left, twelve and a half per cent saw them once a week or more with the rest in between. These figures may be partially explained by the fact that a mother will experience much greater social disapproval for leaving her children than would a man. She may feel so guilty that she finds it easier to cut herself off from her children completely. However, my own research points to a much higher level of contact between the children of home parent fathers and their other parent mothers; between sixty-five and seventy-five per cent between two and five years and still thirty-three per cent after five years. Whether this is because mothers were more conscientious or fathers more encouraging of contact would be hard to prove. I think it must be largely up to the home parent father to encourage mothers to keep in contact with their children. He may hesitate because he fears that if she becomes deeply involved in the children's lives again she might want to take over his responsibilities for looking after them and that as a mother her claim for residence would be the stronger. Although it is true that the process of persuading judges to award custody to fathers is a slow one it is also true that judges are increasingly reluctant to disturb well-established arrangements for child care. The longer a man has been looking after his children the more relaxed he can feel about keeping their mother in their lives.

We shall look later at the advisability of replacing the female element when death or total severance make that the only option, but widowers can console themselves that children brought up for a few years by widows on their own who subsequently remarry seem to perform in all respects as well as those of 'normal' couples. (LP1) The same will presumably apply to widowers.

How can home parent fathers, whose feelings may range from the small minority who hate and reject their exes to the great majority who still love them and often long to be reunited, involve non-resident mothers in the lives of their children? The most effective way of sustaining an other parent's involvement in a child's life is to see that they spend as much time together as is compatible with properly running the home parent family itself. The principle is easy enough to state, defining an 'optimum amount' is a different matter and the definition is likely to be continually changing as the age and circumstances of each child change.

As soon as a couple has parted the home parent should make provisional arrangements with his ex about such things as contact and then try them out on his children for size if they are mature enough to understand what is involved. Early visiting patterns should be extremely predictable in both time and place so as to reassure children that they will return home when the visit is complete. The fact that they cry or express reluctance to see the other parent before they leave home may not mean that they do not wish to go only that they are anxious about failing to return. Their certainties of parental care have already been seriously undermined by the departure of one parent and it will take time for them to accept that the new pattern of life is a reliable one. For several months John's (J11) five-year-old would burst into hysterical tears if he went so far as the garden gate without telling her first what he was doing and for a while he could go nowhere without taking his child with him. Regular times and durations of absences from home can be helpful in easing such fears.

Making contact arrangements is easier if the couple try to find a neutral place and a time when neither parent is rushed or harassed, perhaps in the presence of a mutually acceptable third party. It is not a bad idea to have a clear agenda for such meetings and sometimes even to send a note in advance if there is something particularly complicated or a potential source of emotional conflict which needs to be discussed, but care must be taken to see the note does not sound like an ultimatum or an unchangeable statement of fact! A proposal is best put in the form of a number of questions to which the writer offers possible answers and asks for suggestions rather than merely seeking endorsement of decisions already taken. It is also tactful to use the plural personal pronoun, rather than the singular, what should *we* do? rather than what should *I* do? Not, 'Jane wants to give up the violin, but I do not propose to let her for at least another three to four months – I am sure you will agree'. But 'Jane wants to give up the violin – do you think we should let her or insist she keeps it up for another three or four months? Any other ideas?' And so on. To realise the wisdom of genuine consultation a father needs only to consider how frustrated, depressed and enraged he would be if he were the other parent and never consulted, only presented with decisions already reached. Real compromise rather than superficial acquiescence to the ex's point of view is the way to develop genuine co-operation to the children's benefit. Because both parents usually love their children the other parent's suggestions, or emphasis on one element of a plan rather than another, frequently improve a course of action or guide the home parent towards a better one.

In four out of five cases the mother is escaping from her mate or her domestic circumstances *not* her children – though 'circumstances' are often tied up with the boredom and frustration that being at home with small children can entail. The chief responsibility for ensuring a close relationship with the other parent lies with the home parent and the best means of achieving it depends on the children spending adequate time with the other parent. This in turn requires a couple to keep good lines of communication open between them, but one pessimistic researcher considers that 'Most divorced couples simply are not capable of the kind of continuous, courteous communication that is required if both of them are to play major roles in bringing up their children'. (F7) Another believes 'that parents who could not reconcile conflicts while living together are even less likely to be accommodating to one another while living apart'. (D2) It is true that in some cases, however friendly a man's overtures, his ex will remain bitter, resentful and unfriendly, but more usually hostility will diminish with time – though women tend to harbour resentment for longer than men.

Even allowing for its basis on fathers' opinions the section of my survey dealing with relations between lone fathers and their exes throws doubt on some popular assumptions about their impact on the children. The first surprise is the very high incidence of violent attacks on lone fathers by their exes during the relationship when the assumption is that men are the perpetrators not the victims of domestic violence.

That a history and recollection of violence presents a serious obstacle to improving post-separation relationships is confirmed by the fact that in eighty per cent of my violent examples the relationship continued to deteriorate after the break-up. Only in seven per cent of the cases did things improve and they remained the same in thirteen per cent. By contrast, among those who reported no violence from their exes only forty-seven per cent of the relationships continued to get worse. Thirty-two per cent stayed the same and twenty-one per cent improved. How much this matters except for the peace of mind of the father is a different question.

The circumstances leading to violence by a female mate vary as widely as the causes for the break-up. When adultery, preferring another man or financial disagreement ended the relationship there was no marked increase in female violence, but where incompatibility or mental disturbance was cited as the cause there was quite a significant increase. It is possible that being physically assaulted itself led some men to define their exes as mentally ill.

Not surprisingly lone fathers felt themselves less at fault than their exes for the break-up of the relationships. On average they accepted thirty per cent of the blame.

Paradoxically, those who were attacked were only half as hostile to their exes as those who were not, suggesting, perhaps, that the removal of a cause for anxiety, even actual fear in some cases, had enabled the men to look more kindly on their erstwhile mates. Moreover, the fact that the victims are four times worse at communicating with their exes than the non-victims seems to endorse the view that in the case of marital separation distance does make the heart grow fonder even if, as I suspect, this change of heart is prompted by unrealistic nostalgia for what might have been and memories of good times surfacing again. It also suggests that frustration at lack of verbal communication may be a common trigger of physical violence.

But what of the impact on the children of these two factors, violence and self-blame? In my survey I asked the fathers to rate their children at the time for health, happiness, behaviour and academic achievement on a scale of minus ten for total disaster to plus ten for complete success. Taking the overall average of these scores there is no significant relationship between the children's scores and their fathers' experience of violence, which the children must usually have been aware of or even witnessed, nor with the extent to which fathers blamed themselves for the break-up. Moreover, the means by which men became lone fathers also seems equally irrelevant in this context with three-quarters of the amicable agreements being between the parents whose children fall into the lower two groups. Although one might also expect the hostility implicit in a court case to be reflected in a poor outcome for the children none of the court case families appears in the lowest group.

As the table below shows, there were only two surprises, one minor and one more significant perhaps, when the extent of the lone father's agreement with his ex over the issues most directly affecting their children was examined.

	NR	NC	0	0-5	6-9	10	Avg
Separated							
Access	–	05	10	06	07	16	6.10
Education	2	06	07	04	11	14	6.38
Upbringing	–	06	07	09	10	12	5.95
Religion	7	06	07	06	04	13	5.61
Finances	3	05	14	08	06	08	4.08
Widowers (before bereavement)							
Education	1	na	00	00	03	04	9.0
Upbringing	1	na	00	01	04	02	8.1
Religion	1	na	00	00	03	04	9.14
Finances	1	na	00	02	04	01	7.29

NR = No Response; NC = No Contact; Avg = Average score excluding no reply and no contact. Scale 0 = absolute disagreement to 10 = absolute agreement.

The minor surprise is that over access, supposedly the most contentious issue, a considerable degree of consensus (only marginally exceeded by education) was found. Access had the highest proportion of absolute agreement (41%), including one that there should be no contact, and the second highest (25.6%) of absolute disagreement, suggesting that this is not a subject on which compromise is easily reached between exes.

There is less surprise in the fact that finance was easily the most contentious issue by some way and that even the usually charitable widowers were less inclined to think well of the departed about this than about anything else. The widowers, in rose-tinted retrospect, recorded not one single absolute disagreement with their exes. Thirty-nine per cent of the responses were of absolute agreement and another fifty per cent of between six and nine on the zero to ten scale. When this is compared with their gloomy self-assessment of their happiness and health (Table Five) it is hard to escape the conclusion that perhaps a more realistic view of their former spouses might help them to cope with life more positively themselves.

The major surprise is that the outcome for children, as assessed by their fathers, (Table Fourteen) is *not* better for those whose parents achieved the greatest overall agreement on our five chosen issues. On the contrary, the reverse is true. Of the thirteen fathers whose average agreement was eighty per cent or more only two (15%) had children in the best outcome group, while six (46%) had children in the worst outcome group. Of the twelve fathers whose average agreement was fifty per cent or less only two (17%) had a child in the worst outcome group but they also had two children in the best. Here is another instance where a more objective assessment of the outcome for children than I have been able to undertake might cast some interesting light on these tentative conclusions.

It remains true that both parents have a responsibility to their children to communicate constructively. As one child put it 'If parents are going to get divorced in the first place, they should expect to pay the consequences, which include talking directly to each other – even if they hate each other. The kids shouldn't be dragged into their problems'. (P1) The majority of couples recognise this, but do not always practise it. It has to be confessed, however, that in terms of maintaining good communications it is usually men who are less effective. Nearly a third of my fathers had no communication at all with their exes and only nine per cent complete communication on everything necessary to the well-being of their children. With an average of only just over three out of ten, men are not doing too well though this survey has not tried to measure the extent to which lack of communication is due to the obduracy of their exes.

Sometimes it may seem (and sometimes actually even be) better for couples not to see or speak to each other because of the way angry or painful feelings get in the way of constructive communication. If it is difficult to communicate with exes vocally, because conversations rapidly degenerate into shouting matches, a careful, polite and friendly letter can often be better than entrusting an unfortunate child with the daunting task of go-between. Tempting as it can be as a means of avoiding the abrasive consequences of direct communication, using children as spies or messengers attenuates the communication and puts them in an impossible position. It was customary in ancient times to cut off the head of a messenger bearing bad news! That only reflected a natural, if somewhat extreme, response – psychologically a couple's children are equally vulnerable!

If there had not been profound disagreement, mutual antagonism and dislike between the couple, in most cases, they would not have parted, so it is clearly absurd to expect instant amity when they first separate, but things often improve with time. How often though do you hear the remark 'I get on much better with him/her than when we were married'. This is no more than a recognition that removing the sources of friction to a safe distance is more than likely to diminish the friction itself. More than a third of single fathers in an earlier survey reported that their relationship with their ex was better than during the marriage.(M3) In my survey this was only eighteen point six per cent, but a further twenty-three point two per cent reported that at least the relationship was no worse. Moderate contact can be good for the exes too and in observing this the children will be learning the necessary virtues of forgiveness and understanding – in that order! The children may have been one cause of friction themselves, but differences involving them may also have meant that they had become a vehicle for conveying disaffection with the other parent. One thing physical separation will imply is that a conscious effort will have to be made to resolve conflict over the children, but this may prove easier than anticipated.

When a couple communicate about their children it is wise in the immediate aftermath of any but the most friendly parting to confine the discussion to practical matters – the when and where of access, what clothes a child needs and so on – and to steer clear of emotional land mines. Written notes between parents can (and should) be carefully considered and drafted and telephone conversations broken off if they become too heated with a firm but courteous 'I'll call you later', though these severances tend more usually at first to be an abrupt slamming down of the instrument rather than a gentle return to its cradle. It may well be that an ex has fled to a bedsit or parent's or lover's home where there is no telephone, but only sixteen point seven per cent of the mothers in my sample were reported as having no telephone. Of the home parent fathers eighty nine per cent had phones. This compares with figures from a much earlier survey of one in six for employed fathers and only one in eighty for unemployed. Where the other parent is phoneless a home parent who can afford it can usefully offer to help meet the cost of putting a phone in and renting the line so as to keep the communications open. BT and Mercury unfortunately seem to have no concessionary rates for lone parents. I know of no one who offers this kind of subsidy at present. Perhaps this would be a suitable object for support for one of the children's charities interested in sustaining child-parent links. If telephoning is out of the question then children who are able, however hesitantly, should be encouraged to write and it is a good idea to supply them with pre-addressed and stamped postcards or envelopes so that they can do this privately as and when they wish. Nor should either parent pry into communications with the other. As one little boy rightly objected 'When I talk to her on the phone my father and stepmother always want to know what we talked about, and that upsets me'. (P1) Some children want to be totally absorbed in the life of the parent they are with without uncomfortable reminders in the shape of telephone calls about the solitary existence of the other parent. The majority like the reassurance of regular contact when they are away.

It is up to the home parent to try to maintain a constructive and courteous tone to the dialogue with his ex, remembering that those other parents who want to be with their children feel anguish and frustration at being out of touch with them on the daily basis they previously enjoyed.*

*Mothers experiencing difficulties about being apart from their children should contact MATCH Mothers Apart From Their Children. Fathers in the same situation can try Families Need Fathers.

It helps to reduce the frustration, and the antagonism that goes with it, if the home parent talks about positive things, particularly children's achievements, as well as problems. If the parents meet or telephone each other regularly this will help to get a balance in the substance of their exchanges. A mother will greatly miss those tiny day-to-day evolutions towards adulthood which the home parent is privileged to share so she needs to be kept well posted on all of them for her sake as well as the children's. This will enable her to pick up the threads more easily when she sees her children. If a father cannot bear to talk to her face to face or on the telephone at least he should drop her postcards, though conversation calmly conducted tells the story so much more vividly. Children themselves will convey most of their own news, but there are some things they cannot, or should not, be asked to tell her involving themselves or personal aspects of their parents' lives. This is particularly true where the information might provoke an outburst directed at the child who may then feel at fault. Generally it is better not to involve them in exchanges on any subject that does not directly, practically and uncontroversially concern them.

Even when a mother does not communicate directly with her children the father should continue to feed her with information about them if he can. Despite the fact that one study (M2) shows increasing numbers of children year by year *saying* that they were no longer concerned about seeing their mothers, I suspect that this is often the bravado with which they contain and control their sense of rejection and that if the option to communicate can be kept open, more mothers and children would eventually avail themselves of it.

Misunderstandings are all too easy and likely in the emotionally strained atmosphere that follows the break-up, when judgement is clouded by strong feelings, so it can help to put in writing such things as 'who does what' agreements and visiting or holiday arrangements. I know of one case where two non-communicating parents each gave their seven-year-old son a bicycle for a 'surprise' birthday present. He was, to say the least, a little puzzled as to what he was supposed to do with two identical bicycles! Division of special days, such as birthdays, can be a source of parental conflict. If the parents live near enough to each other then it is best, if possible, to split the day between them otherwise the least provocative plan is to alternate them and swop them round – this year father has Christmas day, next year Boxing day, mother the reverse.

There are other more mundane events which also need to be fairly and generously shared. It is sensible to ask the children's school or playgroup, if they attend one, to send second copies of all communications to their mother direct at her new address and under whatever name she now wishes to be known. To make sure the other parent knows about these things and as a gesture of his willingness to share them the home parent can make photocopies of events diaries and invitations and similar information from school, drama and sports clubs, music teachers and so on and get the child to pass them on. School also needs to know with whom to get in touch, where they are usually to be found and who is the back up contact in case of an emergency. It is sensible for children to have in or on their school bags an airline luggage type card with each parent's telephone numbers or even a bracelet or medallion of some kind upon which they are engraved.

If the home parent father has a new wife or mate or the other parent mother has a new man, then extra tickets will be needed for various school functions – even if on different occasions. Usually a child will want both its parents to see its starring role in the school play, its winning run – or even its losing run – in the sports competition and for some of these events there is no alternative to both parents being present on the same occasion. There is nothing, of course, to prevent them sitting apart. For other events which are repeated more than once it can be an advantage for one parent to attend each different session, thus giving their child support throughout. If everyone has to be present at the same time at any particular event, from the school play to a family wedding or funeral, children will be on tenterhooks with anxiety lest the parents quarrel publicly. Polite and courteous mutual behaviour is important so as not to spoil the occasion for the children and because it can gradually induce more positive feelings in the adults. As one researcher put it 'we heal ourselves by offering goodwill.' (M3) Sharing pleasure in watching a child's cultural and sporting achievements (and occasional embarrassment) can remind both parents of happier times and common delight in their child and so slowly help to reconstruct friendship between them.

Small children usually want their estranged parents to do things with them together as part of their innocent strategy for bringing mum and dad together again. This is not easy at first and the poignancy of walking along with a child holding a hand of each now parted parent can be almost unbearable. (The objections of new mates can make this even more painful). The awkwardness can be covered with jokes, games and shared pastimes, and perhaps within a couple of years joint expeditions will become a source of pleasure rather than of emotional stress. Paradoxically a child's quite common initial reaction to any growing friendship between its parents can be jealousy and it will do its best to make sure they get no opportunity for private conversation. Children, having once been wounded by the independent decision of their parents to part, hate the thought of being left out of any subsequent discussions and decisions which affect them.

Geographical moves can present another serious problem. Many studies show that distance does weaken the bonds between parents and children. (F7) A working rule of thumb suggested by my survey seems to be that a journey time of more than forty minutes between the two households, by whatever means, does result in a marked reduction of contact time with the other parent, though it is hard to disentangle this diminution from that brought about by the naturally increasing complexity and egocentricity of children's lives as they grow older. With remarriage or re-cohabiting with a new mate after the break-up of a parental relationship being the rule rather than the exception the likelihood of one or other parent moving away to be with their new spouse increases. Where this happens sustaining the contact relationship by phone, letter and frequent holiday visits becomes more important. However, like many of the other theoretical post-break ideals and fancy solutions (many of American origin) it also becomes increasingly expensive and therefore beyond the reach of the majority of divided parents who usually find themselves poorer than they were before. It also rarely works. The research on which I have based this book indicates that for a successful outcome for the child it must be face to face contact or nothing. If the other parent is more than forty minutes away it is increasingly likely to be nothing.

Whether a child's absence be long or short, the home parent will naturally be anxious about what goes on in the other household. Not only *can* he do very little about it, but he *should* do very little about it. There is not much doubt that it is not the other parent's ultimate responsibility to decide about a child's education, religion, long-term medical treatment or other strategic matters of that kind, though it is sensible to consult her on such matters. Only where financial liability and responsibility is concerned does the law impose the same joint responsibility that was exercised naturally across a wide range of issues when the parents lived together. That does not mean, of course, that there were then no disagreements or that children were not fully aware of differences of opinion between their cohabiting parents about how they should be brought up, only that they had to be resolved within each particular family pattern. Once a couple has parted the division of responsibility about such things as discipline, bed time, television watching, diet and so on is not so clear. Each parent can act independently of the other while their child is in their charge and they do not have to consult each other or the child about day to day matters even though if one parent has a residence order he or she is legally responsible for them. In other words, the home parent cannot compel the other parent to behave reasonably or to communicate effectively. There may, therefore, be a degree of what he regards as excessive interference in the day-to-day care of his children, but he can be oversensitive to this.

It is important that the parents should not undermine each other's authority otherwise their children will become hopelessly confused. They will sometimes complain to one parent about things, particularly disciplinary things, in the other parent's household. The home parent should support his ex if he possibly can and be careful to discuss any differences without a value judgement unless the issue is one in which her attitude is so deeply repugnant to him that he feels compelled to explain to the children why his attitude is right and hers is wrong. Drug taking, dishonesty, promiscuity or racial prejudice might be typical areas in which a home parent has diametrically opposed views to the other parent which he feels have to be upheld at all costs. There is nothing wrong in firmly asserting strongly held moral convictions, it helps a child gain a sense of security from knowing where it stands, but where matters of belief or opinion alone are at stake, for example in religion or politics, it may be as well to qualify that strongly expressed view with the rider that other good and intelligent people think differently. Having spelt out his attitude and the rules based upon it the home parent must insist that, at least while he is present and in charge, his word is law. If he does not his children will become so full of doubts and uncertainties that they do not know what is expected of them.

Any difference in gender roles, philosophy, politics, moral standards or anything else between the home parent father's household and that of his ex needs to be described and discussed dispassionately. Generally speaking, even where there are quite strong differences, it is as well simply to lay it down that in the home parent's house his rules are obeyed but that in the other parent's house it is reasonable for her to expect her rules to be obeyed. Ideally there should be not only common rules but common standards in the two households, but between parents who could not bear to live together this is highly unlikely in practice. If there is a really serious issue then it is necessary for the two parents to take it up openly. Although this may cause aggravation at the time some mutually acceptable balance can often be struck. Only if a home parent thinks that what is happening in the other household is seriously and consistently damaging to the child should he consider restricting or denying access as the solution to the problem. He could also ask a solicitor to seek a prohibited steps order or a specific issues order which should give the desired protection without depriving the child of contact with its mother. This fairly draconian approach is likely to be resented and to destroy co-operation with the other parent so should never be lightly pursued. It may be better to put up with two different codes of behaviour. Many parents are surprised how quickly and readily children adapt to this, but they have to do it the whole time as between school and home and even as between one teacher and another within school. We tend, quite reasonably, to have different rules for children of different ages, for different times and places – term time and holiday, concert hall and football stadium – so why not for children in different households?

Difficulties can also arise from different values rather than different rules or moral standards in different households. One parent may like classical music, good literature, restrained make-up and modest clothes, his ex may listen continuously to pop music, read only the Sun, make-up heavily and enjoy flamboyant dressing. The home parent just has to let the parallel world go on without interference and with his own dislikes politely expressed if at all. His children will eventually choose those elements from each set of values which suit them best and they may not always be the ones he likes. Nevertheless, if he presents his ethos confidently and with evident enjoyment the chances are his children will like and pick up a large part of it eventually.

Another pitfall for the home parent father is jealousy of his ex's new male partner or fear that he will alienate the children's affections. The fact that the other parent in these circumstances can now offer a 'complete' family will not of itself persuade a court to transfer residence to her, so there is no real need to be defensive about the relationship. Similarly he should recognise that his ex may find it more awkward to visit him when he has a new mate and help her overcome that barrier to maintaining contact with her children.

Hard as it is to swallow at first, it is better to look on the new man in the other parent's life as an additional adult who may enrich the children's lives or at least extend the range of people who are kind to them. Often the man with whom an ex sets up house is kind and generous to her children as well as to any of his own. That is not to say that a home parent father is not fully justified in satisfying himself that the man is kind and a suitable one for his children to be with and he should monitor the relationship closely but tactfully. The fact is that although child abuse is much more rare than the tabloid Press implies, its perpetrators are often stepfathers.

Just as the home parent's personality will be continually evolving in his new circumstances, so will that of his ex. It may be, therefore, – after all it was perhaps divergence of personalities that parted them in the first place – that they will find each other's ways even more alien as the years go by. The parent with residence will then have to be careful to distinguish between those issues which are really significant for the welfare of his children and over which he may feel justified in insisting on his own way and the far more numerous ones where they are not significant, or indeed even relevant, and differences, however wide, should be generously accepted. The home parent must not deny the other parent the right to influence her children too, particularly in view of the fact that she spends less time with them.

Alternatively the couple may become quite close again in time and regain the ability to see each other's good qualities and different talents in the way they presumably once did. In those circumstances a child's oscillation between the two households can have compensating benefits to offset the undoubted disadvantages. The two homes can be very different in many ways and if both can be made welcoming to a child that is a great bonus, as is tapping into the differing gifts of each parent. If a balance is struck in this constructive way a child is unlikely to echo American eleven-year-old Heather's complaint 'switching is definitely the biggest drag in my life – like it's just so hard having two of everything. My rooms are so ugly because I never take the time to decorate them – I can't afford enough posters and I don't bother to set up my hair stuff in a special way because I know I'll have to take it right back down and bring it to the next house'. (P1)

The success or failure of the damage limitation exercise for children depends more than anything on the good will the home parent father is able to show his ex in her relationship with them whatever his private feelings may be. The extensive research (F5,C3, etc) into the role of the 'absent' father and the custodial mother's attitude towards him has led to conclusions which should be equally valid when the roles are reversed.

The first simple rule is one that applies to all cohabiting couples, but was probably not in operation in the months before they parted – no rows in front of the children. Once the couple no longer live under the same roof mother and father have greater opportunity to back off, to walk away from confrontation – leave the house, put down the phone, shut the door – than they may have had in the often cramped conditions of family life where angry voices through thin bedroom walls have turned many a child's sweet dreams into nightmares. In the period immediately following most separations the motivation for restraint is at its weakest. Anger, jealousy, resentment, a million practical problems arising from the ex's absence, are all bursting to be expressed in harsh words, raised voices and even blows. The wounds these uncontrolled outbursts cause cut deeper into the children than they do into the ego of any ex.

The second simple rule is similar; no fighting through the children, either by making them the bearers of waspish exchanges or by abusing and denigrating the other parent to them or in front of them. Children themselves provide the most revealing evidence of the effect of such conduct. 'One of the reasons I may have bad feelings now toward my mother is that I feel she tried to turn me against my father' says one. (P1)

Another, Tracy, aged 16, when she does something that her dad does not like, objects to him saying 'you're just like your mother.' Just as a mother's derogatory comments about the absent father can contribute to a boy losing self confidence and to a girl developing a distrust of all males (F5), so a father's expression of negative views of the other parent simply makes it harder for his child to cope with the separation. Inevitably in the early days in most separations tongues cannot be guarded against every bitter or resentful remark. The important thing is to let any child who hears one know that it stems from the parent's own upset and anger at the time. Even if he meant every word, the speaker whose tongue has slipped should try to convey as soon as possible that this is not what he really thinks of the child's mother and certainly not what he expects the child to think of her. If a home parent does make cracks about his ex, or more likely her new partner, then it is necessary to confess his prejudices to his children, apologise to them and try to explain the jealousies and uncertainties that have given rise to the remarks. In purely selfish terms the home parent father should know that in children's eyes it is often the critic rather than the criticised who is diminished. He can safely leave it to his children's own experience of the relationship between him and his ex and of their own relationship with both parents to draw their own conclusions.(C3)

This does not mean that confrontation or criticism should always be avoided in the hope that this will create a better atmosphere among all those involved. While being placatory may defuse the immediate situation, if there is a fundamental issue at stake retreat will not resolve the differences in the long run. Tolerance and understanding and even affection for an ex should not be confused with false acquiescence in standards that are believed to be morally wrong or practically damaging. The home parent cannot inculcate a sense of right and wrong in his children without emphasising his own views. At the same time he should, in general, acknowledge that he may be wrong and give his ex the benefit of any doubt. It is praiseworthy frequently to swallow one's pride, but never one's principles.

All too often the attitude of the parent with the children to the parent without them has tended to be at best dismissive at worst downright hostile. Once they have parted mothers with residence seem to see the involvement of their children's fathers as 'bothersome, empty rituals' (F7) and argue, quite fallaciously, that if a father did not love his children enough to stay at home then he cannot love them enough to be allowed to see them. One American survey showed over half of the single mothers rarely or never talking to their exes about the children. (F7) Another survey showed mothers with whom the children did not reside developing a higher opinion of their exes than those with whom they did. (F12) Mothers with residence reckoned their relationship with their exes had grown worse while fathers with residence thought their relationship with their wives had improved. (M3)

A child's transition to life divided between a home parent and an other parent will be much easier where both parents have been fully involved in decisions affecting it when they were together. Nevertheless, however co-operative they were then and however amicable the parting and the current relationship, it would be surprising if there were not differences about children's upbringing now – they are, after all, common among intact families. What a father can be certain of is that his children will usually want to be with their mother more often and for longer than he, at first, may think appropriate. (B1) Home parent fathers do not come well out of some research into their perceived value of other parent contact. One survey (F1) found only a very small proportion who thought the contact beneficial for the children, their negative attitudes to their exes making them blind to their children's needs. Home parent mothers seem no more enlightened with the added irony that the less frequent the father's contact was the more excessive the home parent mother thought it to be! (P3)

If a mother has deliberately severed all contact with her children and persists in keeping aloof*, the home parent father will find himself faced with the difficulty of sustaining a myth which he knows to be untrue – namely that his ex loves her children even though she neither speaks to them nor sees them any more. There is much talk about the necessity to make children feel that both their parents, particularly the absent one, still continue to love them, but sometimes one has to face up to the fact that the inability to love her children is one of the things which has driven a parent to leave and no amount of bluffing can disguise that from the child. As it is, many children will experience sharp feelings of guilt that their mother (or father) has left home and continually search their consciences for some fault of theirs which might have driven her away. A typical

*23.3% three per cent of the children in my sample had no contact of any kind with their mothers.

five-year-old may repeatedly ask if her mummy would come back if she promised to be tidy, quiet, well behaved or whatever the principal cause of the child's conflict with the mother may have been. It is no easy thing to reassure a child that he or she is still loved by the absent parent and is in no way to blame for that absence. This is particularly true where contact is minimal or non-existent because the absent mother is still coming to terms with her own feelings and attitudes towards her children. The slightest evidence of interest and affection should be seized on and emphasised for the children's sake. What the home parent can truthfully say in all but the severest cases of mental breakdown or selfishness by the ex is that she has left to get away from the home parent because she does not love him any more. Unless the permanence of that departure is categoric the possibility of return should only be gradually excluded as time goes by. However, there comes a point, usually long before the deserted parent's own hopes are extinguished, when children must be helped to face up to the fact that they live with only one parent and must, as surely as their home parent and in partnership with him, build a new life on a new basis. That, after all, must be the prime purpose of any man bidding against the odds to be his children's home parent.

The best outcome for the children is secured when the terms of their residence with the home parent and contact with the other parent are not only agreed between mother and father, but are actively promoted by them both. Fathers who find themselves the home parent as a result of desertion or after a successful legal battle over residence should, nevertheless, work all the time towards the diplomatic, mutually agreed solution to the rearing of their children. This will, sadly, not always be possible, but in many cases it becomes so as time passes. False hopes, anger, despair, grief, poverty and lack of domestic confidence can make co-operation over their children's upbringing, education, residence, conduct, contact and much else almost impossible at first. As the weeks go by love for the children and mutual desire for their future good come to predominate over adult goals which loomed so much larger in the early days. The parents will probably agree on most things eventually and when they do not are able calmly and constructively to discuss their differences without the discussion degenerating within a few sentences into acrimonious argument, as it does at first. It may even become possible for them not only to work together for their children's future, but again to become, largely as a result of that common bond, affectionate friends.

11

Contact – communication and access

Good communication between the two parents and between the other parent and the children is usually important in reconstructing acceptable lives for all of them and nowhere more so than in the tricky matter of contact meetings and visits. When a couple first part, a mother and younger children will usually want to see each other often, the mother to reassure the children that she still loves them, the children with the mixture of hope that she will return and anxiety lest she has rejected them. Though short frequent contacts of this kind may partly provide that reassurance they will generate their own tensions by their unnatural brevity and by re-enacting the original parting each time they end.

Much has been written about the importance of other parent contact for children if they are to emerge relatively unscathed from a lone parent upbringing. Of the dependent children of separated parents in our survey a quarter had no contact of any kind with their mothers (Table Seven). The average length of time since the parental relationship ended in these families was twenty per cent longer than for those still in touch. In three of these cases some of the children had regular contact, but the sibling(s), by their own choice, had none.

Of the children with contact a quarter saw their mothers less than once every six weeks, just under a third from once a week to once in six weeks and forty-four per cent twice a week or more. When regularity of contact is related to the length of separation it suggests either that a more constructive approach to contact with other parents is taken by home parent fathers or that home parent mothers are more conscientious about keeping in touch, or a combination of both. Whereas other studies quoted earlier show that after two years' separation when mothers have residence over half the children have been cut off from contact with their fathers, two-thirds of my lone fathers separated for more than two years ensure that their children *maintain* contact with the other parent. The common wisdom is that these children should, therefore, thrive more than lone mothers' children, but the relationship between the extent of contact and thriving children is more tenuous than is generally supposed – or at least more complex.

The main reasons why contact between other parent mothers and their children varies so widely in home parent father families is the obvious one – distance. Of the twelve families without any face to face contact for which data was secured six had no car and of those that had cars half faced journeys of three hours or more. Only half of all the no contact families could travel to their mothers in under forty minutes by any means, so it is reasonable to infer that a contributory element at least, and perhaps even the determinant one in most cases, was the difficulty of getting children to their mothers. I have not been able to establish how easily or otherwise mothers could have travelled to their children (as so many fathers are expected to do). Only one of these separated families had no phone and in two only one parent had a phone so the absence of phone calls or letters among all of them suggests that contact was either neglected by the mother (some fathers volunteered this explanation) or was denied by the father. In three of the families, where some of the children did see their mothers but others did not, these explanations are not valid. Of the families in which there was some contact, but less than once a week, only half had cars and over half faced journey times of three to thirteen hours.

At the other end of the scale, of the six families making contact four to seven times a week none had journeys of more than twelve minutes and only one had no car. In the next most frequent contact group only one of the nine families had no car. Six families in this group had journeys of forty minutes or less. Of the eight families in the once a week to twice a week contact group six had cars and five journeys of under forty minutes. Two out of three fathers in my survey had a car.

Contact divides into three clear groups. The first is of those twenty families with an average shortest journey time of just over two hours who make less than one contact a week on average; a second group with one to four contacts a week consists of seventeen families with just under one hour's journey time on average; the third group is of six families with four or more contacts a week who were only five minutes apart on average.

What else then determines whether or not contact is maintained between children and their other parent mothers?

There is a correlation between frequency of contact and the children's relationship with their mother, but this should probably be ignored for two reasons. Firstly there is no telling which is cause and which is effect. A sense of having been deserted, particularly if reinforced by the father's attitude, would naturally generate hostility. The second reason for doubt is that the child's relationship with the mother has been assessed by the father who is likely to have been influenced by his own attitude to the mother. This is borne out by the fact that the greater the affection and the less the hostility of the father towards the mother the more contact a child has with its mother.

The route by which the non-widower fathers in our survey became such also seems to have some bearing on the frequency of face to face contact between child and mother. Happenstance, being left with children to care for willy-nilly, is the most common (46%) reason if the eight widowers are included. However, among the separated and divorced alone, voluntary arrangements predominate (46%). Thirty-nine per cent of the families were also eventually subject to various court orders, but nearly half of these as part of the tidying-up of a voluntary agreement – very necessary for the avoidance of misunderstanding and taking advantage of tax benefits from maintenance payments. In general the more the happenstance in the way men become lone fathers the less the contact the children have with their mothers, and the more voluntary agreement the more the contact. These two factors presumably reflect the mutual attitude of the parents. Court proceedings do not necessarily reflect attitudes. Indeed, there are slightly more court orders in force for the families with most contact. This may suggest that certainty and clarity about contact can be beneficial.

Nor is there any correlation between contact frequency and either employment or unemployment, occupation, or income (Tables Nine and Two) which are the same in the lowest and the highest frequency contact groups. Neither available free time nor money are, of themselves and unrelated to the distance to be travelled, significant in determining how much contact there is between children and their other parent mothers. This pattern of similarity between the effect of the experiences of the groups with the least and with the most contact mirrors the pattern we shall see later in studying the groups of children with the apparent best and worst outcomes from lone father upbringing.

If in the early days after separation children cannot see their mother frequently, then, for her sake at least, until a decision about long term contact can be taken, they should be kept in touch daily by telephone or letter. Even a little child's drawing can convey so much love and mindfulness and a mother's postcard can be a reassurance against rejection. If there is a telephone with a programmable memory in the home parent's house it is a good idea, for smaller children particularly, for the father to programme one button with the mother's telephone number. He must also make sure the children do not feel inhibited about calling her nor constrained when they do. A father should not hover near the phone without very good reason when children and mother are speaking. They need to be able to say 'I love you billions mummy' without fear that they will sound disloyal to the home parent. Nor is it just the children whose emotional turmoil needs to be calmed by contact. Most women who leave their homes are racked with guilt and anxiety about their children. Being able to communicate with them regularly will allay some of their worst fears and make them more amenable to suggestions about the children's future, but constructive contact cannot be maintained for long by these remote means alone.

So just how useful a part do alternative forms of contact with the other parent, such as telephone calls and letters, play in the children's lives? Compared to the findings of earlier surveys our single fathers seem to have more of the amenities of life for communicating. (Table seven) Only one in seven had no phone (one in five no car). In only one household where the father had no phone did the children make phone calls to their mother. In the other six there was no contact of any kind. One in ten exes definitely had no phone and for seven there was no data. Of these latter six had no contact of any kind with their children, and of those with phones three had no contact and two only minimal. In only two households where both parents had phones was there no contact of any kind and possibly in two more where it was not known if the mother had a phone.

In a tenth of the families the absence of phone calls may have been due to the closeness of the parents' homes. Outside the no contact group lack of phone calls does not seem to have been a major negative factor. In a third of our families phone contact was made one way or the other once a week or more, in two daily. (In two other families which reported calls the frequency was not known.) In every case but one the incidence of phone calls closely reflected the level of face to face contact rather than being a substitute for it.

If corroboration is required that the art of letter writing is dying then this survey can provide it. Two families exchanged letters each way twice a year and one once. One mother wrote weekly and got six replies a year, in one family the three children wrote weekly and got four replies a year and in one family the children wrote once a month but got no reply. In one family only were letters evenly exchanged fortnightly; the rest was silence.

It seems reasonable to conclude that, even if they provide useful reassurance immediately after separation, in the long run neither phone calls nor letters play any significant part in maintaining contact in the majority of families. While common sense suggests that remote contact is better than none most other parents in this situation cannot cope with the anguish it gives them and sever contact of every kind. It is face to face contacts, or lack of them, that will count – or not.

Animosity between the parents can remain so intense that hand-overs for that face to face contact are acrimonious or have to be conducted through a kind of no man's land where the other parent leaves the child at the yard or garden gate and moves off before the home parent collects it. When parents indulge themselves in this kind of perpetual enmity or are psychologically incapable of breaking out of the cycle of hate and self-pity, children are likely to be exposed to more conflict rather than less and will suffer accordingly. There *are* better solutions. If relations between the adults really are so bad, then the best format of handover is through some intermediate place and person, such as school or the venue of some leisure pursuit, in which the child can become absorbed on leaving one parent before rejoining the other. Involvement in school activities dissipates the tension otherwise often evident in a child during the last few hours in one household and the first few in the next. If parents are on better, but still distant, terms school can be a neutral place for them to meet and discuss their common concern about a child's education and welfare in the presence of a third party. Such a formal atmosphere can impose restraint and reduce tension. The fact that they are doing so will in itself help the child to get over the separation, and may, indeed, help the parents themselves to become more reconciled to each other. Children who show serious and prolonged signs of stress after their parents have parted (some is almost inevitable in the immediate aftermath) may benefit from the child counselling provided by many child mediation agencies and often paid for by Children in Need. The promising work of the Cambridge Centre for Family Research on this provision indicates that it can be valuable provided what passes between child and counsellor remains confidential unless the child asks for a specific message to be passed to one of its parents. It is up to the parents not to press the child about what was said.

Except where the parental parting has been mutually and amicably agreed it may be best at first for mother and child to meet on neutral territory, such as a friend's or relative's house, rather than in the family home where their mother will feel uncomfortable or in her new home where the children may feel uncomfortable, specially if she is with a new partner. The place of these meetings may also need to be one where the father is confident they will not be submitted to undue pressure to live with their mother or otherwise be distressed by her conduct. This is particularly important if the children's contact is likely to be protracted long past the agreed time or there is a risk that they may not be returned to the home parent father at all. If no relative or friend's home is available or mutually acceptable then, through the remarkable initiative of Mrs Mary Lower, a network of professionally supervised centres has been set up in most parts of England, Scotland and Wales. There are now well over a hundred and thirty of these. Telephone numbers can be found under the name of National Association of Child Contact Centres, NACCC, in the local directory. Although they are usually used by so-called 'absent' fathers to see their children in private, but on neutral ground, they are equally open to 'absent' mothers. The father may remain in another part of the building if he wishes to allay his fears about the return of the children at the end of the contact period.

At first children may become anxious about not getting to see the other parent or about returning to the home parent. Regularity and punctuality are, therefore, important in early visiting patterns. When children return from the other parent they may be difficult and temperamental for a short while until they settle down into the new routine. Visits to absent parents, however eagerly anticipated and actually enjoyed, can also be occasions of great tension for children – so much so that on their return they may even show physical signs of distress such as being sick. This does not mean that they want those visits to stop and should not be taken as an excuse for ending them. The bad behaviour and displays of temperament on return from a visit to the other parent are usually a mixture of reawakened distress at breaking contact with their mother and confusion over different surroundings and codes of conduct in the two households. As they get used to the switches this disturbed reaction should become shorter. These difficulties are made greater if the other parent has nowhere suitable in which to make the children feel at home. This may not seem to be the home parent's problem, but it is because it concerns the happiness of his children. He should agree to meetings at the homes of his ex's parents or relatives, with whom the children will usually want to maintain contact anyway (unless they are deliberately encouraging the children to reject or leave him). Later on he may even find that in some cases with little children the best thing he can do is to go out of their home for a while and let their mother visit them in familiar surroundings – no easy thing for her either. Alternatively, he may find himself having to take or escort his children to see their mother or arrange transport for them. This he should ungrudgingly do. One father (J11) in our survey does a round trip of eighty miles every Friday and every Sunday to deliver and collect his child to her mother's home though he can ill afford the time or the expense.

All these arrangements become complicated, emotionally at least, if either or both exes have live-in mates, so the home parent should not encourage children to tell catty stories about his ex and any new partners she may have. Pleasurable as indulging in such malice may be, a child's adverse comments must be recognised as part of a classic ploy for retaining the parent's attention for itself. (M3) This does not necessarily mean that a child should be prevented from expressing negative feelings or making critical comments about the other parent, but they should be listened to neutrally and without comment rather than deliberately elicited. If comment is made it should be open ended, encouraging the child to explore the mother's motives for itself – 'I'm sure she had a reason'; 'I wonder why she did that?' and so on. The child's criticism of one parent to the other – and it *will* be a two-way traffic – is not only a device for declaring loyalty, which also yields useful information about his or her feelings, but a very necessary safety valve in a stressful situation. Before 'bad-mouthing' the other parent the home parent father must seriously ask himself if he wants his child, particularly a boy, to grow up despising women or subconsciously so distrustful of them that when he becomes a man he will be incapable of a sustained adult relationship with any woman. Unless the child is encouraged to understand and even sympathise with the female viewpoint in the marital dispute the bare fact that the most important woman in his or her life has inexplicably deserted may have just that effect. The difficulty is to balance this positive and uncritical approach with a keen ear for any genuine cry of unhappiness and distress caused by the other parent.

Another temptation for home parents in any ongoing battle between them is to be late or miss out altogether in making children ready and available for contact visits. Similarly, the other parent may be deliberately late in returning them. This not only induces anxiety in the children, but the kind of anger or despair in the parents which leads to the erosion and often eventual ending of all contact to the probable detriment of the children and no advantage to the adults. Contact may be broken just by creating a situation in which the children feel it is emotionally risky or disloyal to the parent with whom they live to visit the other parent.(C4) Children may be equally confused by having enjoyed themselves when away because they feel they have been disloyal to the home parent. The lucky ones are the ones that can benefit from two sets of parents, two sets of friends and two sets of people to love them.

The practical difficulties of frequent transition from one household to another cause children additional stress. Things such as school books, sports kit, and musical instruments, can provide all sorts of problems by being in the wrong place at the wrong time. It is largely up to the children, with a little parental guidance, but not too much nagging, to manage these transactions for themselves as they get older and in so doing learn to take responsibility for their own lives. At first things frequently seem to be in the wrong household, but gradually both children and parents learn to plan ahead a little more carefully to avoid this on most occasions. Few families can afford two complete sets of everything, and in any case children also form strong attachments to familiar objects as reassurance during the process of readjustment. A teddy bear taken to and fro from one household to another can be a talisman, a magic sign that the child will return.

The sooner both parents can bring themselves to accept a pattern of longer visits involving at first overnight stays, then whole weekends, and eventually holidays and other visits of several days' duration, the better it will be for the children unless they obviously do not want to be away from home for so long. Children will often *say* that they do not want to go away, but unless they persist or are seriously disturbed by the prospect this is usually a sign of the sensitivity and innate compassion of most children who fear that the home parent may feel lonely and unhappy without them, rather than real aversion to the contact. 'Research has confirmed that it is the duration of each visit not the frequency that is most important'. (B1) This gives both children and parents the opportunity to express natural feelings, such as anger and irritation, uninhibitedly and also to go through the process of reconciliation which usually follows. Regular and sustained contact with their other parent mothers enables children to learn to make realistic relationships rather than create myths and fantasies about other people.

Visits to the other parent need to be long enough for the children to become part of her normal life rather than be seen as a sequence of special occasions. Many home parents complain about the 'unfairness' of one parent having to deal with all the discipline and dull routines of life while the other parent seems to provide nothing but treats. If so, this is probably the home parent's fault for keeping access visits too short. The normal ups and downs of family life need to be experienced in the other household as well as in his own. A parent who sees her children only for brief and too infrequent encounters cannot be blamed for wanting to express her love by filling them with pleasure. Children will happily accept such spoiling, and even be enticed by it for a while, but they are not so gullible as not to see what may be behind it nor so naive as not to recognise where their long-term interests really lie. Most children will give neither more nor less love to the parent who spoils them in this way than they would were they treated in a more balanced manner. In due course a lavish other parent comes to see that children's love is not conditional. Once she can accept that she will not be deprived of her children's company she will revert to a more balanced approach. Sheer economics will also play their part, particularly when visits become more frequent and of substantial duration and the high level of expenditure can no longer be sustained.

The conventional contact arrangement made by courts and solicitors of one weekend a fortnight is neither frequent enough nor long enough to create the kind of mother-child relationship that is necessary for the emotional health of both. Indeed, my research suggests that such apparently constructive compromise can even be damaging in some cases. Fortunately, what is laid down by judges and solicitors seldom has much connection with the reality after a while and the home parent father can feel fully justified if he increases the contact time with the other parent to a level which makes it truly effective. His ex is hardly likely to complain! The reverse process is harder to justify though my survey suggests that if frequent and lengthy contact cannot be sustained some children *may* be better off with none. What is quite unjustifiable is to deprive the other parent of substantial contact where this is practicable, there is no serious threat of moral or physical danger to the child and the child wants it. It is a *child's* right, in law as well as in terms of its well-being, to see its other parent.

In my view, if access is constantly refused then the courts should exercise their power to reverse residence and give it to the other parent – something they rarely do. This should certainly be the case if the other parent undertakes to allow his ex good access to the child and fulfils that undertaking. This just redress has to be set against the possible adverse impact on the child of changing homes, but it is strongly arguable that the parent who is so bent on revenge and so full of hostility to the former mate (except in cases of proven serious physical or emotional danger,) as deliberately to keep them apart cannot really be said to be a good and effective parent. Were the courts to exercise their discretion to reverse residence orders in a number of well-publicised cases then no doubt many more fathers and a few mothers would gain much greater contact with their children to the benefit of everyone involved. The home parent should know that a grudgingly permitted occasional visit is probably worse than no visit at all.

It is generally argued that a high level of contact with both parents is essential for the well-being of a child of a separated family. Whether or not this may be true where single mothers are concerned the situation is considerably more complicated in the case of single fathers. When the four child characteristics which I analysed in my survey – happiness, health, behaviour, and school performance – and the combination of all four are compared to the frequency of contact an interesting W pattern emerges. (See Figure One)

In all five categories the highest ratings, all of a closely comparable level, are achieved, at the opposite end of the spectrum, by those children with no contact with their other parent and those with almost daily contact. In terms of school performance the no contact group is significantly superior to the maximum contact group and fractionally so in terms of happiness and behaviour. In health and overall performance the high contact group is fractionally better. In health and behaviour (but *not* happiness, academic performance or overall) the groups seeing the mother between once and twice a week are roughly comparable to these two. (The lowest of these three groups in terms of behaviour is the high frequency contact group which perhaps suggests a little spoiling!) The two plunges in the graph are for those children seeing their mother between once and eighteen times a year and those seeing her between once and twice a week.

This comparison suggests that the proposition by some researchers that contact is a critical element in the prognosis for children of single parent families is not always a valid one in the case of single fathers. In the great majority of lone father families either no contact at all with the mother or almost daily contact were more beneficial than the intermediate stages. This would seem to confirm the subjective impression that children thrive on certainty and predictability, almost regardless of whether that certainty and predictability is of a positive or negative future, other than in circumstances of extreme mental or physical cruelty.

Contact arrangements can and usually do become increasingly flexible as both exes feel more at ease with the new situation and more confident with their own roles vis-a-vis their children. The children themselves will start to express very strong views about these arrangements as they get older. They will wish to make contact as and when they wish and not necessarily during the prescribed access periods. In practice, they will start to make their own arrangements from their early teens on and, wherever possible, the home parent should not stand in their way. If he does have to refuse an impromptu proposal because it is genuinely inconvenient for the rest of the family he must explain the reasons carefully and such prohibitions should be exceptional. Year by year it becomes increasingly important that children should be able to call on their other parent ad hoc, when they want to rather than when either parent or a court has decided. Paradoxically children, specially teenagers, do not like similar unexpected visits from the other parent and often resent having to break into what they had planned to do when she turns up. As children grow older they must be expected to try to rearrange their contact arrangements themselves as they become increasingly interested in their own peer group activities and so want to spend less time with either parent. It is quite possible that they will even wish to change residence altogether in adolescence. It is important to be prepared to be flexible, even very occasionally to the extent of recognising that such a change could be to a child's benefit.(B1) For example, if a home parent plans to live abroad the children may want to live with the other parent who is remaining in their native country. They may run away to the other parent to make their point. Unlike children in two parent families, who will often fantasise about running away from home, in separated families they actually have somewhere to run to.

Sometimes when they are angry with the home parent children will threaten to go and live with the other parent. It is a mistake to respond to this either by telling them to 'damn well go' or trying to argue that this would be a bad idea. If the child is behaving badly and this is part of a tantrum then it should be checked and reprimanded in just the same way as it would for making any other threat of anti-social behaviour. Very often in these circumstances contact with the other parent and with the realities of the alternative home will be sufficient to restore a better perspective on life with the home parent. If the child's mother is inciting such threats then the home parent must make it clear that this is not an acceptable post-marital weapon and that because its continued use will damage the child will result in less contact not more. There may be some circumstances in which the home parent would be perfectly justified in terminating or at least supervising visits, for example if there were serious behavioural problems or risks of physical or verbal abuse or deeply disturbing scenes with third parties. However, it is as well to remember that children can cope with a great deal of such conflict in exchange for love. If the child's threat to leave is not made in the course of a parent\child contretemps, but in a more general way, it is probably a form of testing. The response to such insecurity should be as much affection as the child will happily accept at the time and a tactful enquiry at the first opportune moment about what the underlying cause of discontent might be. Temporary changes in contact arrangements may also need to be made to allay any anxieties the child may have about its relationship with either parent.

A joint residence order (what used to be joint custody) is sometimes thought to be a solution to the problem of divided lives and loyalties inflicted on children by the physical separation of their parents. Depending on how it is interpreted it may or may not be. One of my respondents called joint residence 'about the best way to rescue children from the mess of a broken family and marriage ... it became obvious that ... the next best thing to the children having their parents with them together, was to have their parents with them but separately.'

Joint residence as a means of giving the other parent a reassuring, theoretically equal say in the major decisions about their children is valuable in its limited way, though the parent with day to day care will carry inevitably much the greater weight in such decisions. Where joint residence is literally interpreted as exactly equal division of very young children's time between one parent and another its value is less certain. In fact such arrangements may put children in an impossible position. Time too equally divided may not reflect the true division of their needs and loyalties. I certainly know of cases where such a child has become seriously disturbed by not knowing clearly which place to call home or which parent to turn to in a particular crisis. For many children this is no doubt a temporary phase, if more protracted than the disorientation experienced by all children of separated parents, but with more likelihood of longer term consequences. I should admit here to generalising from a few particular cases as I know of no comprehensive formal European study of the outcome for children under joint residence compared to those with a clear 'lead' parent and primary home. Joint residence is sometimes referred to as co-parenting, but in the majority of cases so-called co-parenting is no more than very well organised, documented and previously agreed contact, with one parent still having by far the greater number of critical nights at his or her home although the division of waking hours may be more nearly equal.

In America the term co-parenting is more widely interpreted and indicates a more broadly balanced division of time and responsibility between the two parents. The consequences for the children seem, in the more affluent American context, to be better than those of lone parent families. Children's attitudes to such arrangements varied, as might be expected, from one extreme to the other. We have already seen Heather's opinion (Cf page 96) and another child in the same study (P1) endorsed her view. 'I always feel awkward and stiff when the family is together. I prefer for just one of my parents to come – like last year, when I was in a play. My dad came one time and my mom came another, and it was no big deal'. Zach, aged thirteen, expressed an opposite opinion. 'Even though I live with my dad and my sister lives with my mom, my parents have joint custody, which means we can switch around if we feel like it. I think that's the best possible arrangement because if they fought over us, I would have felt like a bill in a restaurant.' Most children can cope with the situation described by another child in this study. 'My parents have very different rules and philosophies about life. For example, my dad's attitude is that he lets us learn by our mistakes, and my mother does exactly the opposite.' (P1) From the children's point of view it is clearly a case of horses for courses and some American evidence seems to be contradictory. A few recent studies suggest that joint physical custody is not necessarily better for children's adjustment than the alternatives. (F7) The benefits of joint residence arrangements may also have been exaggerated in these studies by the way the samples interviewed have been selected from conscientious and highly motivated families. (F12/D2)

To work the equal co-parenting version of joint residence must be willingly embraced by both parents (F7) rather than imposed by judicial decree and there must be trust between the parents that each will put the well-being and peace of mind of the child above any desire to undermine or strike at the other parent. Co-parenting is also impractical in nearly every instance where parents live further apart than the forty minutes' journey above which contact diminishes with time.

Sometimes the solution put forward is to split the children between the parents, though British courts sensibly prefer not to divide siblings if it can be avoided. When they do this it is usually on the basis of age – infants to mothers being the usually justifiable rule – or of sex, for which there is little scientifically based justification. Indeed, common observation suggests that while children may model themselves on their same sex parent, their emotional bonds are often stronger with the parent of the opposite sex whom they do not regard as a rival.

A much more serious rival in the child's eyes is the potential stepmother and we shall look next at the implications of introducing her into the equation.

12

The next step?

Within five years half the divorced and separated people in Britain will have found a new partner and, in general, a slightly higher proportion of men than women will remarry. At least three out of four will either remarry or find a new mate within ten years and so become once again part of a couple. (D1) In America seven out of eight single fathers will eventually remarry. (F11) One third of divorced women re-marry within three months, nearly half within four and a half years. (M4) Sadly, this triumph of hope over experience proves short lived. More second marriages (50%) end in divorce than first marriages (35%), they last on average only seven years as opposed to an average of ten for first marriages and women remarrying are twice as likely to divorce as their contemporaries marrying for the first time. Men are one and a half times as likely to re-divorce. Perhaps the lesson is gradually being absorbed that remarriage solves no problems of itself if the declining rate of remarriage – less than a quarter of the 1971 rate for men, forty per cent for women – is any indication. However, this may only reflect a growing general disenchantment with marriage rather than reluctance to re-partner.

More than six million people in the UK live in stepfamilies (F15) – that is families where one of the adults is not the biological parent of one or more of the children. On current trends sometime early in the next millennium the stepfamily will be the most common form of social grouping in Britain. Sadly for the future social stability of the country and the happiness of its families few politicians either see or are willing to recognise this fact and the legislative consequences it should have. The education system has not even begun to consider preparing children of both sexes for life in step families. How difficult this mental readjustment to 'the complex family' will be for adults and children alike was illustrated by a piece of research (F7) which tried to establish what members of stepfamilies considered to be 'our' family as opposed to 'my' family. When members of such families were asked to list who they regarded as their family only one per cent of parents neglected to mention the biological child who lived with them, but fifteen per cent omitted a stepchild. With the children ten per cent did not list a biological parent in their home, but a third left out a step-parent. (F7)

Children experience similar difficulties in defining their relationship to stepbrothers and stepsisters let alone to the children of an unmarried new parental mate. My daughter resolved the problem of terminology with a useful new (to me at least) term. She described the two daughters, a little older than herself, of her mother's first new mate as her URSs - UnRelated Sisters – at first, but later came just to call them sisters. When a new half-brother was born of this relationship she always referred to him as her brother from the outset. When her mother changed mates again and remarried the network became so complex she simply referred to everyone by name rather than relationship.

There are plenty of social and psychological maps for negotiating the difficult territory of step-parenting, so I shall only point out a few landmarks relevant to home parent fathers. Any single father who has not become a complete misogynist as a result of his experiences needs to think very carefully about his relationships with unrelated women, whether or not he will eventually live with them.

Many people contemplating remarriage are determined not to put their children through the agonies of a separation again and feel very committed to making a second relationship work, but the sad statistical fact is that it is just as likely to fail as not. Moreover recent research from the University of Exeter (R3) shows that children who are the victims of a second break-up perform less well in terms of school and general health even than the children of single parents let alone of stable relationships. A slight consolation is that (no doubt through practice) the participants in second and subsequent marriages and cohabitings recognise their breakdown more quickly – or give up more easily – and end them early. The second cohabitation that survives its first five years has as good a chance of life-long survival as the first. If the second pairing does hold fast and is a good one then the evidence indicates that in both emotional and academic terms the children may benefit from it and do well. However, in the majority of cases they probably will not. As Elliot and Richards pointed out in 1991 (QLP1) children with lone parents are just as likely to perform well educationally and get higher qualifications by the age of twenty-three as those living in a stepfamily. The difference in achievement between children of the divorced and intact families is of the order of thirty per cent at GCSE level, twenty-seven per cent at A Level and forty-one per cent at University level (where the mother has died, children perform better than those of intact families at GSCE, but worse at A Level). (M5)

A less objective criterion for measuring the impact on children of different family structures is their general happiness as reflected in their social behaviour. One verdict (F7) is that 'It seems likely that growing up in a stepfamily increases the risk of encountering problems relative to growing up with two biological parents but that, on average, the added risk is rather small ... Researchers have not identified which children or which family situations are the major source of the problems'. The National Child Development Study of seventeen thousand children born in the first week of March 1958 reports only slightly more conflict and problem behaviour among stepchildren than among those living with natural parents.

Any difficulties encountered are not surprising in view of the fact that the complexity of the sub-cultures to be blended, or at least mutually tolerated, might be said to be squared when one partner has children and cubed when both have. It is hard enough for two adults who have *chosen* to live together to modify their personal habits and predilections for the sake of harmony and the older they are – as step-parents will tend to be – the harder it is. How much more difficult it is for their children who have not only not chosen the new relationship, but in many cases are actively hostile towards it. No wonder so many stepchildren leave home earlier on average than their intact family peers.

Of many bad reasons for a lone father to consider remarriage two are probably the most common – to find a substitute mother for his children and convenient copulation.

Although the home parent father will have had to take over most of the mother's nurturing functions he may cause confusion in the children's minds if he tries to usurp her iconic role. Children, particularly when young, need their female model and however flawed she may be in her ex's eyes this will almost certainly be their mother. Children themselves may come to replace her by a stepmother or father's new partner, older female sibling or friend, but only in their own good time. If the children's relationship with their mother has already totally broken down because it was marred by fear, violence, cruelty or abuse or because their mother has deliberately lost all contact with them the situation is different. However, it is still important to remember that the children may mix their negative feelings with love for their mother, or at least for a mythical, idealised mother. In these circumstances it may be a good idea to provide them with opportunities to form a voluntary attachment, or attachments, to a woman or women, who will show them affection both physical and emotional. Grandmothers and aunts from both their parental families and godmothers or other women whom they see regularly are ideal because of their probable permanence and continuity. The problem with the women who may now come into their father's life and be important to him is that experience suggests that most of them may go out again! For children to have to relive, in however minor a way, the heartbreak they have already experienced damages them by reinforcing their sense of rejection and failure. Most men, exploring potential new partnerships, are very mindful of the inter-play between the woman concerned and their children. This is a considerable burden for these women to bear, but one the terms of which need to be fully understood by everyone involved before any commitments are made.

Children, small children especially, often seem to like the idea of getting a new mummy or daddy in theory, usually when the absence of a second parent is seen as causing inconvenience or hardship to them. If the theory becomes a real prospect the attitude can be very different. For this reason it is as well not to make too much of new relationships with female acquaintances, friends or even lovers, but be fairly discreet about it all and also encourage the women to be discreet as well. Children will quickly pick up any air of anxiety on their father's part about how they may react to his women friends and pounce upon it for the fun of giving him a hard time and of protecting their territory. On the other hand the way a new female in a father's life may respond to his children and they to her is a pretty good indicator of what sort of person she is. Exploring the potential of a relationship within these constraints is difficult because while a father will not want to get his children involved in relationships which may prove to be only transient keeping things from them can inhibit the development of those very relationships.

A substantial degree of openness, tailored to the maturity and understanding of the child, is probably the better course, but one to be followed cautiously. From the knowledge or observation of their father's intimate relationships children may infer either more or less than is intended by them.

If a child is not to be confused by conflicting signals the same pattern should obtain in the mother's house as is adopted in the father's – particularly if the next generation of children is to escape from the still widely made assumption, whatever may be said on the subject, that different standards of conduct, personal responsibility and mutual care, particularly with regard to AIDS and pregnancy, apply to men and women, boys and girls. Sadly, common practice in the two households is not very likely since differences of sexual drive and ethics are one of the most common causes of cohabiting relationships breaking up. But if common practice is not the reality at least each ex should not condemn in the other, conduct he or she is seen to follow themselves. Unless the ex's sexual behaviour is causing serious problems for the children it is probably better not to comment on it at all.

The home parent father's problem is more likely to be lack of opportunity to meet potential mates than temptation to pursue them too rashly. The very isolation of domestic life for those who decide to be full-time housefathers, rather than to go out to work, prevents them meeting many women in circumstances where they can develop closer relationships. There are too many eyes and ears at the school gate or in the high street (though it can be managed!). Nor has the housebound man the opportunity for casual or chance encounters enjoyed by housewives visited by all those seaside postcard milkmen, postmen, gasmen and so forth. His far fewer female callers are more likely to be debarred by their occupational ethics as social worker, health visitor or community psychiatric nurse from seeing him in anything but a professional light!

The lone father will probably not have the time, energy or even money to go out much to meet new people. Agencies and advertisements are a chancy and expensive way of making new contacts and are often regarded as slightly sleazy although in many cases this is unfair. I know of several men who, even if they did not find new mates, did make good new friends who substantially enriched their lives and those of their children. Being too obviously on the lookout for a new partner can have the opposite effect to the one desired. It can also deter women who have nothing more in mind than friendship and giving a helping hand from offering it for fear of misinterpretation – not only by the lone father, but by their own men.

There is no need for the home parent father to be in a rush to repeat his mistakes. The more he learns to cope with those aspects of life with which his former partner used to deal, the less likely he will be to enter unwisely into a new relationship simply to get those practical problems solved. A period of being on his own can be both strengthening and instructive and in most cases is a necessary preliminary to any new relationship. It also gives children the time to adjust to *their* loss without the confusion of having to come to terms with a new relationship at the same time. It is sometimes thought that a single father who remarries is looking for a replacement mother for his children so that he can wash his hands of his responsibilities. However, in practice, it is much more likely that a new partner will find it difficult to persuade him to let go of many of the things he had been doing for his children on his own. As one writer puts it 'Men who have struggled to rebuild a satisfactory family life for themselves and their children out of the ruins of a broken marriage do not necessarily believe that their family is incomplete without a woman'. (B1)

If sticking together for the sake of the children can be a mistake (if not as often as is generally supposed) remarrying in order to provide them with a substitute mother is even more likely to be. The only valid reason for cohabiting again is a desire to live with another person both so strong and so carefully considered as to make the risks to father and children worth taking. A man who has taken the serious decision to assume day to day responsibility for his children's upbringing in place of their mother is not entitled to bring another woman into their lives, however passionately he may feel about her himself, unless there is a very strong likelihood that this will be greatly to their benefit. Nor is there any need for him to do so, least of all because his judgement is based not on logic but on his loins.

Sexual confidence is not usually at its greatest at the end of a cohabiting relationship and it is not uncommon for people to have a series of short relatively uncommitted affairs with sexual pleasure and exploration as their main aim. Children exposed to these superficial sexual relationships can find them very confusing. It is probably better to keep such things well away from them, at least until such time as any relationship looks as though it might have a serious potential for either long-term partnership or even long-term friendship. However, if a lone parent father is going to adopt this course he has to adopt it successfully. Partially hidden casual sexual relationships are probably even more damaging for the children than open ones, giving them the impression that sex is something illicit and shameful to be indulged in only furtively. If children then imitate such an attitude in adolescence, particularly where child and lone parent are of the opposite sex, it will make very difficult the building of the mutual trust and exchange of confidences necessary to support them in a healthy development of their own sexuality.

Lone parents' sexual activity can present a special problem for teenagers experiencing the excitements and disturbances of their own burgeoning sexuality. When the myth of a parent being too old for sex is obviously exploded, it can be hard for children to adjust, even in an intact family. Most of us find it impossible to imagine our parents copulating however vivid our sexual imaginations in other directions. Parental sex is seen as 'disgusting', even unnatural, and a father having sex with another woman can be seen by children as a betrayal of their mother even when she is long since dead or departed. (C3) Where children are over exposed to their lone parent's sexuality there is a tendency for girls to become promiscuous themselves, boys less so, though dual standards seem to apply in reverse to the usual pattern. This is one of the subjects where it seems quite legitimate to say 'don't do as I do but do as I say', but it will take a great deal of tact and skill to convince the teenager of the justice and benefit of this approach.

Very young children may be oblivious to the implications of a woman not their mother sharing their father's bed, but awareness comes early these days. So does the kind of balanced and sensible view expressed by twelve-year-old Sarah, 'Neither of them should worry about my getting upset, because I am old enough to understand that grown ups are allowed to have private lives, which includes other people. But if someone is going to spend the night, I think it's better and less awkward if I know about it beforehand, so I'm not taken by surprise'. (P1)

Perhaps because most societies set such store by a male's sexual potency as the confirmation of his masculinity, being deserted by his woman (more so if she has gone to another man) can render a man virtually impotent. Being sexually desired by a new woman is usually the only cure for this state. Fortunately for the men in this situation there seem to be equally large numbers of bored or sexually frustrated married women, impatient with what might be termed their husbands' or lovers' shortcomings, eager to restore his self confidence. As one man put it 'I had six girlfriends at a time, all of 'em wanting to jump into bed with me ... I thought I was past it ... of course I was completely wrong'. (B11)

The logical outcome of this search for potency is often the begetting of a child with a new woman. As one writer bluntly but accurately put it 'this is the absolute guarantee that the penis works'. (F1) Sadly quite young men have had vasectomies for the sake of their former wives or lovers (who may have been aware long before the men were that things were not going well and that more children would be inappropriate) only to find that they have deprived themselves of the opportunity to have children with a new mate.

Attitudes to post-widowhood or post-separation sex vary as they do for extra-marital sex generally. This is now usually accepted, or even approved of, when based on mutual respect, pleasure and consent. In the case of the lately uncoupled there is the added feeling that they are entitled to try to replace what they have just been deprived of. There is still a substantial minority whose view is that there should be total celibacy until remarriage and at the other end of the spectrum another minority who think it does not matter how many different girlfriends children see in their father's bed (or boyfriends in their mother's). Apart from any moral considerations the essential criterion should be whether or not the conduct of a home parent father's sex life is likely to upset or even psychologically damage his children's own sexual development and general mental health, or whether it will help them to happy, healthy and socially responsible sexual relations of their own. As good a guide as any to whether or not a home parent father should let his children be aware of a sexual relationship and to what extent, is whether or not he feels uneasy about it. If he does he is almost certainly doing the wrong thing.

The poverty which so often burdens lone parents of both

sexes after a break-up often compels them to seek escape from it through remarriage. Remarriage can certainly improve a lone parent's standard of living. It may restore gross income to pre-divorce levels by creating the option for two wages or salaries or by freeing one partner to work more lucratively while the other runs the home and family and perhaps works part time. It also reintroduces the 'two can live as cheaply as one' situation. There are, however, a number of financial snags to be considered. Firstly any payments to a stepmother from a former husband (or, much less likely, to a stepfather from a former wife) may quite legitimately be ended by the payer when the ex remarries, though, in another hypocritical absurdity, not if she only cohabits. Payments for children are unaffected by subsequent marital status. Secondly, since the Child Support Act, the dependent children of previous relationships who are not living with the new couple are given higher priority than they were previously and any second family will find it much harder as a consequence to attain a satisfactory standard of living. Thirdly, if a step-child had been treated as a child of the family by the step-parent, child maintenance can be sought through the courts from the step-parent in the event of the marriage ending. The Child Support Act does not apply to step-parents. Eligibility for state financial support may also be affected. As George (S12) found, if both have small children and were living on benefits they may be financially worse off married than their combined incomes when living apart and single. George and his two children recently moved in with his girlfriend and her two – all under six. 'From being two single parents on Income Support to a family has come as quite a shock to the pocket. Between the two of us we have lost nearly £50 a week in Benefits. Yet we have the same amount of children, eat the same amount of food, wear out the same clothes at the same rate as before, etc, etc. It seems the state not only hates single parenthood but does not wish to encourage single parents to re-enter the family classification.*'

Lone fathers need to do a careful cost benefit analysis before speculating on whether such financial gain as there *may* be in remarriage is not more than offset by the upheaval, complexity and conflicting loyalties created by any new family structure.

These complexities and their financial implications make the drawing up and regular revision of a will even more important than for the conventional couple. This can either be done

*I do not intend here to deal with the problems raised by homosexual relationships since the number of known practising homosexuals who obtain or retain residence of their children is still so very small.

through a solicitor or with one of the do-it-yourself will packs available from such organisations as the Consumer's Association. Unless the financial affairs of the new couple and their exes are particularly complex the DIY approach will probably suffice. The important thing is to be quite clear about the intentions, to express them clearly in writing, and to get the signing of them independently witnessed.

Equal clarity is essential in any financial agreements between the new mates, particularly if they intend to cohabit rather than marry. If there is any ambiguity in how a dead mate's assets are to be distributed bitter quarrels can be generated between survivor, children, stepchildren and even exes. This is particularly true where the new couple have bought a home together or when the incomer has bought a share or loaned money to reduce a mortgage in the lone father's existing home. If the dead person's wishes have not been made known, then the survivor and children could even lose their home as a result of a forced sale following a claim on the dead person's estate by his or her heirs.

I would advise a couple planning to cohabit where one or both of them have children and/or exes, to draw up an agreement (or better still get the solicitor of one of them to do so) and get it checked and witnessed by two outsiders (better still the other person's solicitor). It should stipulate that in the event of the death or departure of either of them neither will make any claims upon the other or his estate apart from those set out in the agreement. Most parents want their natural children to benefit financially on their death, but this has to be balanced against the need to secure a home for the mate and any dependent children, be they stepchildren or bred by the couple. Marriage largely solves these problems, but even then, where there is a marked discrepancy in age, when the older person dies his heirs can feel aggrieved at having to wait as long as forty or fifty years, until the step-parent dies, to inherit. As well as pre-cohabitation agreements, trusts can be set up for children, stepchildren and widows (or even widowers!) in various ways, but they can be complex and since each case is different, except in those where neither owns or ever expects to own anything, professional advice can be a good investment not only financially, but in happiness and peace of mind for all.

Severe and dislocating as the financial impact of losing a

mate can be it is as nothing compared to the emotional consequences for survivor and dependent children if decisions about post mortem residence have not been anticipated and planned for. Whether the dead person was married to the survivor or simply lived with them, unless specific provision has been made to the contrary his children will have to go to live with their natural parent even if they are on bad terms with her, may even not have seen her for years, do not wish to go and would be going to someone unfit to have the care of them in psychological and material terms. A parent who has the parental responsibility (but not a step-parent) may appoint another person, including his new partner, as the child's guardian on his death by making a formal appointment in writing, signed and dated by two witnesses or in his will. The guardian will in this way acquire parental responsibility. This appointment will not take effect (although it may by court order) if the child's other birth parent is alive, unless a residence order has been obtained by the deceased parent to the exclusion of the other natural parent. In this case the appointment of a guardian by the will or other witnessed document takes effect.

The only other legal recourse for a stepmother (or stepfather) who wants to claims rights and responsibilities for her stepchildren is to adopt them while their father is still alive. This is quite likely to be opposed by the children's biological parent, if she or he still has regular contact with them. It may not be welcomed either by children who do not see all the implications. Nor can the children's name be changed by deed poll without the consent of both their biological parents. Step-parent adoptions can cause distress to children upon the death of their natural home parent if their links with the other parent and family are strong. Where they are old enough to understand what is involved and to make sound judgements their wishes should be carefully ascertained and regularly reviewed before any formal steps are taken.

For younger children their father, his mate and if feasible his ex should try to arrive at the best answer for the children, which may differ from child to child. What must be avoided, however bitter the feelings a home parent father may still harbour, is any revenge on his ex in the event of his death by depriving her of the right to have her children and to bring them up if she wishes to. Recognition of the justice of this is hard for the stepmother who having lost a loved mate is also faced with the loss of stepchildren whom she has probably grown to love. Her position in retaining contact with them is even more ambiguous than that of the children's grandparents which, because of belated recognition of the claim of blood ties, has improved in recent years. It would be possible, but not easy, for a step-mother to seek a contact order if she felt that the children's natural mother might try to prevent them from seeing her. If she was not married to their father her chances would be even slimmer.

We have looked at a number of very good reasons for *not* remarrying or re-pairing, but are there any for doing so and how should the lone home parent father go about choosing? The answer in a word is – carefully! If he falls in love again, fine. He may already have done so and thereby caused the break-up of his previous relationship. He may just have found or eventually find someone he loves – a less intoxicating but more equilibrious state than 'being in love' – and likes and whose physical, mental and emotional company he enjoys – someone he would like to live with.

We have already considered the notion that a period without emotional attachment is a valuable part of greater self-knowledge. If the home parent father is already deeply involved with a woman then he should ask her to be patient about setting up house together. If he is not he can use a period of being unattached to learn more about himself. Since we are nearly all susceptible at heart the best way to do this is, for a little while, to avoid putting himself in situations where romantic attachments might develop rather too rapidly!

The first use to be made of a home parent father's singular state is to examine in cold blood not *what* went wrong last time but what *he did* wrong last time. Were there conflicts and character flaws unresolved and uncompensated for because the relationship broke up before they could be worked out? Is he, by any objective measure, divorce prone? A great many lone parents find they only enter into a committed new relationship after advancing and retreating like the lobster quadrille ('will you, won't you, will you, won't you?' etc.) for several years and with much trepidation and caution. Nor can a man embark with any hope of success on a new relationship until he is quite sure he has completely broken free of the pull of the old one – at least in all significant ways. 'Unfinished business' (F7) can hopelessly clog up the new agenda. Before entering into a second cohabiting partnership it is necessary to make sure that all the baggage from the first, if not jettisoned, has been carefully identified, labelled and stored. (F1) The arrival of an OHMS buff envelope and a scrap of paper from the county court recording the fact that a marriage has been 'dissolved', as if it were a lump of sugar in hot tea, hardly seems a sufficient rite of passage to mark the end of something so important as a marriage nor, for that matter, of a long cohabitation.*

It takes no great mathematician to deduce that men, whose first marriages last on average ten years, are still pathetically seeking the elixir of youth in their second unions. Their second wives are only four years older than were the first at the time of marriage. (St1) Pure guesswork (the lack of statistics on what is *really* happening in family life in Britain today is a scandal) suggests that of an estimated** 50,000 re-marrying lone fathers each year perhaps a third will be taking new wives who themselves have been married before. The courting lone father does well to remember that personal freedom comes high on the list of reasons why women divorce or leave cohabiting relationships before he tries to re-impose a conventional domestic pattern. To work, second marriages probably have to be more egalitarian and enlightened than first so the home parent father must take care not to put his by now well-developed domestic and parenting skills back in the broom cupboard when he carries his new woman over the threshold – if he can manage both these physical tasks at once!

Overall the best advice about remarriage or its unofficial equivalent would seem to be 'don't', but overall the advice is pretty certain to be ignored. The great majority of home parent fathers re-pair within ten years of going solo. So what can they do to give themselves the best chance of success?

It can take a long time to rebuild a good relationship with an ex and the entry of a new person to fill the vacuum she has left can cause a surprising amount of resentment. Exes can sometimes have very strong feelings about potential new partners particularly where they feel they may have played some role in the break-up of the marriage. If the first priority is to help the children come to terms with the arrival of a step-parent in their daily lives, the second can be to help an ex come to terms with the same event. If their mother is hostile towards their father's new mate and continually criticises her the children may feel like doing the same. The new partner will feel equally

*At one time Birmingham probation service recognised this in devising an end of marriage ceremony in which the couple formally relinquished their claims upon each other. (F19)

vulnerable, unsure until many years of the new relationship have passed, that the ex's hold over her man is entirely broken. She may have good cause for these doubts for ten per cent of divorced men have been sexually unfaithful to their second wives by making love to their first (M3). Perhaps the hostility that develops between some ex partners is a form of protection, a kind of incest taboo that makes forbidden that which might otherwise be too tempting.

While guilt about the rupture of the first relationship can inhibit the development of the second, overcompensating for it also carries its risks, unless the first wife is also safely re-partnered. It augurs badly for the new pairing (and for its likely impact on the children) if the only way to preserve it is to weaken the ties of affection and friendship and common concern for children between home parent and other parent. That will inevitably make it harder for the other parent to sustain her necessary relationship with her children. If, however, the ex wife can acknowledge the new – and even allow some kind of friendship to develop between them – it will be greatly to the advantage of the father and children. Some exes are positively delighted to lighten their consciences by seeing their former mates safely paired again – One American thirteen-year-old girl living with her father and stepmother declared it 'much better for everybody, and I'm a lot happier. It's especially improved my relationship with mommy – I spend every weekend with her – because now she's more relaxed. Maybe it's because she does not feel so responsible for my actions – like if I don't do well on a test, she doesn't feel it's her fault. We are much closer than we have ever been because we don't fight any more'. (P1) Where the partings have been predominantly amicable this is not uncommon and I know several second relationships where the ex wife has not only retained the friendship of her former husband but gained that of her successor. Though not infrequent, these cases are the exception and it is more likely that remarriage will produce rivalries between biological parents and step-parents that sometimes aggravate dormant hostilities between formerly married partners. There is a risk that a father's new partner will try to diminish children's contacts with their mother which is not good for anyone. This will be particularly true if a pattern has developed whereby the children's mother feels free to drop by and see them without notice, treating the father's home more

** By Erica De'Ath, Chief Executive of Step Family and a determined campaigner for better statistics. The charity, Step Family is a valuable source of both printed and oral advice.

or less as if it were still her own. If the stepmother feels neglected because of the priority that sometimes has to be given to the needs of the children and their mother then it is up to the home parent father to make her feel correspondingly singled out for attention and cosseting at other times. (B1) She is the most vulnerable of the three adults in this context.

Fairy tales are full of wicked stepmothers with little mention of wicked stepfathers. Feminists say this is sexist and arises because the tales were written by men – odd for an oral tradition largely in the mouths of women child carers – but a more charitable interpretation might be that wicked stepmothers are highlighted only because cruel behaviour towards children is considered quite unnatural in women, but perhaps to be expected in men. Whatever the explanation, it is true that society's notion of the proper role for the 'woman of the house' places a far greater burden on stepmothers than on stepfathers and many women make that burden unnecessarily heavy for themselves. Their instinctive belief that they can change (some would say control) their man and his life for the better makes many women feel that they must take on full-time, full-scale domestic and child care duties from the outset, believing that a man can be wooed through his children – a not unreasonable belief in many cases, as we have seen. (B1) While treating this approach with a certain amount of scepticism, the home parent father should be careful how he attempts to interfere in or dictate the pace of development of a step-parent's relationship with his children once she has moved in. A step-parent has to achieve acceptance by each individual child and no third party can grant it to her. The chances are that the home parent father's natural children will treat his new mate like dirt at first and if so he should interfere only to impose the normal limits of good manners and civil behaviour that he would in their conduct towards any adult and preferably only if she actually asks him to do so. It is better if she can fight and win her own battles for their respect and perhaps for their tolerance and co-operation. Only then can she move on to win their affection and even love, a much more common outcome than is often supposed. While most relationships between natural parents and children are resilient and can be affectionately resumed even after many quarrels and differences, the step-parent relationship has to be continuously worked at. What is more, the step-parent will frequently get little or no thanks from the stepchildren for a long time, and sometimes never, for the effort that she puts into it and may often suffer a great deal of rudeness and hostility. The children's father will be doing them no favours and seriously damaging the chances of making a new family relationship work if he does not establish a common set of rules with his mate. Both adults must then enforce them in their own ways but with equal rigour and impartiality. This does not mean instant draconian response to every misdemeanour or testing provocation. On the contrary, the relationship network will develop most smoothly if both adults are patient and do not feel they have to solve every problem of child discipline instantly, here and now. It can help if both father and step-mother, or potential stepmother, can develop the knack of seeing the situation from the children's point of view – without necessarily endorsing it.

Most home parent fathers became such because they either actively obtained or willingly accepted their role, but they are also entitled to consider their personal happiness and re-pairing can certainly contribute to that. This need not necessarily be to the children's disadvantage. The evidence suggests (M1) that children do not suffer if their natural parent's new pairing is long lasting and harmonious and the additional or substitute mother cares for them well and with affection. Ferri's study of 1984 (PF1/LP1) also concluded that 'The development of children with stepmothers did not differ very markedly from that of their peers in unbroken families or of those living with lone fathers ... results relating to children with stepfathers, however, were rather less reassuring. These children, and particularly the boys, frequently compared unfavourably with those in unbroken families and differed little from children living with lone mothers ...'.

But that is about as far as the good news goes. The bad news is that stepfathers can expect 'A modest but significant increase in disruptive behaviour for stepfamily children compared to lone parent children. In adolescence the transition to stepfamily life can be difficult for children of both sexes.' (PF1/LP1). If the second relationship is also unhappy and breaks down, the outcome for children is worse than if they had remained with a lone parent. (M1) They have already experienced considerable upheaval and if separation from their other parent is relatively recent they will not be keen on still further change. This is particularly true where they can see a very close relationship with the home lone parent being threatened. It is important to talk through all the implications with them and help them appreciate that they cannot be displaced in their father's affections.

Their own views are often unequivocal, as one eight-year-old girl made clear when her mother was considering re-marriage. 'I hope they don't get married because I like it just the way it is and because I only want to have one father. I also don't want my father to get married to his girlfriend, because if they had a child, then I would feel he would not really be my father any more'. (P1)

Conversely, if the father's anxiety not to make a mistake in his second pairing results in a series of short relationships broken off at the first sign of difficulty then that will undermine the children's ability to form relationships with adults because every time they make friends with someone that person disappears. Such childhood experiences could even make it harder for them to form stable adult relationships themselves when they grow up. Preliminary courtship is best kept entirely private, but anything becoming serious should involve the children before long-term commitments are made. There is a very difficult balance between making children feel they are party to decisions about personal relationships on the one hand and allowing their attitude towards a potential new partner to weigh so heavily in their father's decision making as to give them a tyrannical veto over all future personal development.

From the child's point of view, by remarrying the home parent seems tacitly to be accepting that a new adult relationship will be more important than his relationship with his children. The parent seems to be putting his own needs first – which he is. Children will often accept this providing the new partner is an addition not a replacement. For this reason it is vital in step-families for parents to have ample time alone with their own biological children. While telling children frequently that they stand first in their father's love and care is good, demonstrating it is better. Doing so in a balanced way that makes sure children do not become selfish nor new mates get hurt by an obviously secondary status is hard. The re-paired home parent has to play two distinct parts, child-orientated in the ensembles and mate-focused when the new couple is in private dialogue. Most children come to like the idea of each of their parents having a new partner and being made happy by that – unless they are blaming the new partner for the break-up.*

Perhaps the conclusion of one writer (D1) that the 'discovery that your second partner is not so very different from your first, that your own responses are depressingly familiar or even that, constituted of the daily trivia of domestic life, one marriage is very like another, brings its own bitter disenchantment' is unduly cynical, but it is a fair warning. Yet despite the obvious hazards and poor prognosis for step-parenting all the social pressures are calculated to drive the home parent father into re-pairing even more than they do the lone mother. Family, friends and professional advisers all combine to propose a solution to the psychological and practical problems of single parenthood in remarriage.

The entire legislative and social structure in Britain is based on the assumption either that families consist of couples and their own biological children or of single mothers qualified by their gender alone to bring up children. What is not assumed is that it might be a good idea to give boys the necessary skills and attitudes to cope successfully as men with the role of single parent rather than relying on their ability to recruit another woman to do it for them. No wonder so many of them eventually remarry.

A child's balance sheet of "Step Family" (home parent fathers) Limited might read as follows:

Assets:

New income and capital or the opportunity for dad to earn more.

Two adults to share the demands of housework, child care, etc. so more time for play.

Sexual and emotional companionship making for a happier dad.

Liabilities:

Destruction of established routines and habits.

Possible renewed hostility between biological parents.

*It would be interesting to know whether second marriages without children endure longer than those with, but broad national statistics are an unreliable guide since the majority of childless people remarrying are fairly old and their relationships are therefore likely to end in death rather than in separation.

Further withdrawal of mother from family life.

Dad too involved with new mate to have time for children.

Child no longer number one.

I am not sure that this is a company any sensible child would invest in!

13

My worldly goods? – dividing the family assets

Not surprisingly the division of the family assets becomes a vital and contentious issue, usually complicated by the fact that for the vast majority of families their only significant asset is the family home. In many earlier societies, when a married couple divorced, the wife's property was returned to her or her family, but in the later Christian Church the mutual endowment of worldly goods at marriage became, in effect, the transfer of all a woman's rights in her property to her husband with only the most modest protection for her and her children. Divorce or desertion were deliberately made unattractive prospects for women. Any capital, or indeed earnings, which came to a wife after marriage automatically became her husband's to dispose of as he wished. Not until 1967 was a wife protected against third party claims on her home by those to whom her husband might have mortgaged, pledged or sold it without her consent and then only if her 'ownership' was registered under the Land Charges Act – not a precaution likely to occur to many wives! However, with the 1969 Matrimonial Causes Act the position changed decisively in favour of women.

The courts now had absolute power to dispose of the joint and separate capitals of both spouses and to allot whatever proportion of one partner's earnings it thought fit to the other – the old rule of thumb had tended to be one third of a husband's earnings. Previous property rights became irrelevant and the matrimonial home, in particular, came to be regarded as equally the property of both partners regardless of who had paid for it. Mates or common law wives, while still less favourably treated, also began to acquire similar rights. The catch for the man was that occupation of the family home, and indeed sole ownership of it, tended to be awarded to whoever had the children and, as we have seen, this was usually the mother. Since she seldom had any other cashable assets and was very unlikely to be able to get an increased mortgage there were no means by which the man could be bought out or compensated for his lost share of their joint asset. Moreover, he would often find himself not only deprived of his capital but obliged to go on paying the mortgage.

There was until relatively recent times a general, if ill-defined belief that the division of a couple's assets should to some degree reflect their conduct during and at the break-up of their relationship. This conduct included, of course, willingness to care and provide for any children. The implication was that the parent who did not have day-to-day care of the children, particularly in the case of the 'innocent' father, was still entitled to maintain contact with them, provided this was not obviously harmful, as a quid pro quo for his financial support; no cash, no access. Not so today. Since the Children Act the almost unconscious sense of what was right has been replaced by the concept that the only right involved is that of the child to maintain contact with its absent parent. Since in eleven cases out of twelve this is the child's father it is becoming established that lone mothers, full of bitterness and hatred towards their exes as they may be, are the sole arbiters of what contact other parent men may have with their children, regardless or not of whether the fathers are making a financial contribution to their upkeep. This is in marked contrast to the situation in which the mother is the other parent when, as my survey shows, despite the fact that the vast majority of them make no contribution to their children's upkeep, few are denied access to their children.

However, a fair division of a couple's assets on break-up is not as simple as it might at first appear. The home may not be easy to dispose of and why should both have to leave it? While pensions and insurance contributions may be equally spread over the contributory period the growth in their terminal value may be greatest as they near maturity, quite possibly after the break-up of the partnership, and in any case they may not be realisable until maturity in which case a wife may lose out. Proposed amendments to family legislation may remedy that. On the other hand a man marrying later in life may have been paying to redeem a mortgage and build up a pension for many years before marriage. Is it right in these circumstances that a wife leaving her husband after perhaps only a couple of years of marriage should be entitled to half his life-long accumulation? And how is an appropriate share for children to be decided? Whatever legislation is introduced this will remain a minefield.

Chattels may never have been valued or may be costly to value. Which are to be deemed joint possessions and which personal ones? Then add the complication of children and the problem looks even more messy and the solution far from simple. The legislators have tried, and are still trying, to enact provisions to cover these complex and almost infinitely variable situations. A wife, for example, may enjoy the use of the marital home while children are growing up, but the husband may maintain his capital interest until it is finally sold – but then who has been paying the mortgage in the meanwhile and with wildly fluctuating rises (and now falls) in property values at what moment are the respective shares to be determined? The fact is that with any divorce legislation conceivable, fairness will always be an elusive concept, particularly at a time when anger and pain are likely to give the parties very different ideas of what is fair. It might be argued that this could be anticipated by a pre-marital contract at a time of mutual harmony of the kind currently popular in America, but these are unenforceable in Britain because it is deemed contrary to public policy to make legally binding an arrangement which anticipates the failure of the marriage. Ironically, such agreements can be made and enforced between couples who live together without marrying.

For a while after the 1969 Act there was the occasional unsavoury spectacle of a vindictive 'alimony wife' sitting back in idleness living off the life-long payments of a former husband. These cases were far fewer than is commonly supposed and nowadays it is rare for maintenance to be awarded, in addition to her share of the family assets, to a young woman free to earn her own living. Maintenance is, of course, still awarded for dependent children, although strictly speaking these are still designated payments to the wife and benefit her as much as the children – an added cause of resentment in men. (D1) Sometimes a wife takes over her former husband's share of their home or accepts a larger share of the family capital in lieu of maintenance payments for children. There seems to be no redress if the children are later brought up by their father as Neil's case on page 152 illustrates.

The Child Support Act 1992 rubbed large quantities of salt into this often raw wound by ignoring such clean break settlements when imposing maintenance or increased maintenance payments on non-resident fathers. This book is not the place to scrutinise the general and all-too-obvious defects of the well-intentioned Child Support Act and its administration, currently under review, but the Child Support Agency for three years declined to tell me how many lone fathers it has helped as opposed to lone mothers. In February 1997 it gave me a figure for August 1996 of 405,900 assessments completed for resident mothers, about a third of the total, and 20,462 for resident fathers, a sixth of the total. The disparity speaks for itself. The only man in my survey who reported CSA payments had received derisory awards – £3.84 a week reduced from £24.30 – for two children whose mother and new partner had a weekly income of £600. I should add that I also know of similar derisory awards against fathers living the life of Riley.

The other major shock for better off men will be the probability that they will lose their homes. Much of the family's collective striving for status and the man's most patent evidence of his success as a provider is embodied in the home. Having the children will not necessarily save it for him since as many homes are sold belonging to separating couples with children as to those without. I know of no man who has benefited from the Matrimonial Homes Act of 1983 and been able to use it, as so many women do, to retain occupation of the family home until all the couple's children are grown up. In law there is no reason why he should not. In practice it does not happen that way. In any case, the increase in expenditure and the drop in income the home parent father is almost certain to experience often mean he can no longer afford the family home and must buy something more modest, or even rent. If he can hang on at least for a year or so it will be one less disturbing disruption in his children's lives, but in trying to do so he may land himself badly in debt. Renting will become an increasingly popular option as mortgage tax relief is phased out and is probably the wisest interim move while longer term plans are being made. It can be a relief to be a tenant for a few years with a landlord shouldering many of the responsibilities of the ordinary home owner. Provided the landlord is reasonable and the tenancy agreement secure, the home parent can be left free to attend to the many other things he now has to do. In financial terms the comparison to make is between the rent paid and just the interest element of a mortgage on a comparable property. With house prices unlikely to rise significantly for several years and even still liable to fall, there are many better ways today of investing capital than buying a home. It is a healthy trend that has made people look on their houses as homes again rather than investments.

As with houses, so with most capital assets; other parent fathers, who often escape with lighter maintenance payments than they should, are hit hard when it comes to the division of property and assets. If they are home parent fathers they get the worst of both elements for, as we have seen, they very rarely get any maintenance from their exes. Many an ex wife or mate has no sooner taken her suitcase down the garden path than she is demanding not only the sale of the house and half the proceeds but the disposal or division of all the other family assets down to the last stick of furniture. The courts will usually back her if it comes to a fight. Not only do they not make any calculation of an element of capital transfer on behalf of the children for whom the home parent father has to provide a home, but they take no account of any discrepancy in the equity value each partner (here the term partner *is* appropriate) brought into the partnership in the first place.

Usually on marriage or cohabitation the man still brings in far more in terms of property, investment, savings and accumulated pension and life insurance, but the discrepancy in value between their respective initial contributions is tacitly ignored. Even here forward calculations of the value of pensions and insurances are now being made in assessing the wife's share of the family assets. If of each £100 a family starts out with the man brings in £80 and the woman £20 and the family increases the value of those assets by twenty per cent while the couple are together, the division on divorce or separation will still be fifty-fifty (sixty pounds each) rather than the initial four to one (ninety six pounds to twenty four) which, perhaps, in fairness it should be. The return of their original share plus half the increment would still be more fair than the present division. Women also tend to be more persistent in the pursuit of their 'share'. Where most men will say 'take what you want and just bugger off and leave me in peace', many women will fight their corner down to the last teaspoon.

With the encouragement of the courts, in the majority of cases where there are some assets, a clean break is made in order to remove a potentially contentious issue. No more arrears of maintenance grievance on the one part, no more resentment of having lost mate, home and family yet still having to pay on the other. (M3) The CSA, however, in its short existence, has managed to regenerate a great deal of the conflict by ignoring clean breaks in making assessments. It remains to be seen whether the recently proposed new guidelines will end this grave injustice to men. Let us hope that we do not yet again follow the American example. One American woman reported, without apparently any sense of irony, 'I made a deal with him. I said I'd keep everything we had at the time, and that would be it'. (M3) Some deal, but a fairly common one!

There are two things the home parent father should bear in mind when dividing the family capital. The first is that, provided enough remains to provide a reasonable home for the children, the rest is just not worth the stress and acrimony of a battle. The second is that he has a legal duty to make full and frank disclosure of his financial position before the hearing by the registrar to settle these matters. He may be cross-examined, as may his ex if she has to make a similar statement.

Although Legal Aid is available in divorce proceedings, once property division has been made it nearly always has to be repaid, or partly repaid, depending on the sum involved, out of any assets acquired through the settlement and will be deducted by the solicitor before he passes on the balance. Protracted battles only enrich solicitors at the expense of the couple. The important consideration for the home parent father in both division of capital and maintenance is the question of sufficiency rather than of fairness. On a scale of values adjusted to the priorities of his new life has he sufficient to provide a reasonable home for his children and income enough to give them a happy and secure upbringing measured by sensible and probably much more modest standards? If the answer is yes, he should abandon the pursuit of 'fairness', remembering that what is one man's fairness is another woman's injustice. If he behaves generously and openly towards his ex, even at the cost of thinking himself not a little ripped off, he stands a much better chance of creating the kind of post-separation relationship with her that his children need.

When a mother keeps children the father's burdens remain, although his privileges and pleasures in his children are drastically curtailed and often totally removed. It is no wonder that so many fathers are tempted not to pay maintenance, but that misses the point. However 'blameless' they might be they cannot shake off responsibility for the economic well-being of their children. While it is frequently exasperating for men to think that the money they are paying for their children's upkeep is being spent to make life easier for their ex, they must recognise that this has to be a matter for the mother's conscience and at least their own can be relatively clear.

The would-be home parent father might, therefore, reasonably assume that he could expect child maintenance payments from his ex. He would be mistaken. Despite having taken the freedom to lead their own lives, the majority of women who leave their families even when they take up paid employment, which they usually do, (more divorced women go out to work than married women) are far from generous in making payments to their exes for their children. A recent national survey (P3) showed only three per cent of other parent mothers paying cash maintenance of any kind for their children. This contrasts with the thirty per cent of men doing so. A 1984 survey showed seventy-five per cent of lone mothers getting or not wanting maintenance or having had some other acceptable formal settlement, such as a lump sum 'clean break' payment. Lone mothers were also three times as likely to receive occasional cash payments as men and the level of maintenance paid by men was three times as high as that paid by women. Even allowing for the lower proportion of women employed generally and their lower levels of pay this is another area of blatant sexual discrimination – against men. In my survey only seven point seven per cent of the exes were paying maintenance, three by court order, one through the CSA.

The whole area of maintenance is a highly contentious one and a principal reason why ill feeling persists for so long between so many divorced and separated parents. Often both partners in a divorce feel that they have had the worst of the financial deal for the simple reason that if 'two can live as cheaply as one', one will suddenly find himself living a great deal more than half as expensively as two! Things have not been quite so antagonistic since the 1984 Act set limits on how long exes should receive payments in order to encourage them to go out to work themselves. Orders for children normally continue until they are eighteen. Nor have we yet quite reached the absurd situation in America where a husband's 'career potential' – how and by whom defined? – may be regarded as part of the matrimonial property of which the divorcing wife is entitled to a share. (M3) Research by the Cranfield Institute of Technology found that 'the unending nature of maintenance payments to ex spouses was the cause of bitter resentment, especially when the ex spouses were thought to be capable of supporting themselves and were living in the former matrimonial home with another man. Appeals under the new Matrimonial Act brought relief in some cases. It was noticeable that the men did not object to paying maintenance for their children'. Men who were particularly unwilling to pay maintenance for exes nevertheless expressed themselves quite willing to pay for their children. As one absent father put it 'I don't believe a man should have to pay for his wife, in circumstances like mine, where she could work. Nor do I think I should be the only one of us who has to pay for the children. I know now why some men disappear. If it weren't for my vast love for my children I would do a bunk myself'. Another complained 'She got five-eighths of my salary and then went out and got a job herself'. (M4) I suspect that even more feel this since the Child Support Act, fearing that the impositions of the CSA, if they remain in contact with their children and thus easily traceable, may completely ruin them.

Those in the Cranfield study who actually paid tended to be those whose assessments had been low and by court order. The principal excuse for non payment was that the money was not spent on the children and that the father was being deprived of access to his children. No one thought maintenance should be unconditional. There is about a five to two correlation between male maintenance payments and non-payments and male child contact and non-contact. The subsample of women paying maintenance in my own survey is too small to be significant, but it so happens that all of them were still seeing their children. The Finer Committee proposed that a guaranteed maintenance allowance should be paid to all lone parent families irrespective of how the loss of a parent occurred rather like a widow's pension. New Zealand has had for many years a general domestic purposes benefit which operates in this way.

Theoretically, a father could apply to the CSA for a contribution from his ex. But what about the CSA? Is it worth his making an application? When the Government created the Child Support Agency it was with the declared intention of 'making fathers pay' (no mention of mothers, as usual) and of releasing many single parents from the poverty trap. It was also hoped that it might take much of the hostility out of post-separation financial disputes. If the lone fathers in this survey are anything to go by it has lamentably failed on at least the last two counts. I will quote from only two of the many adverse responses as they best illustrate the two principal dilemmas facing a lone parent of *both* sexes in dealing with the CSA:-

'I was in full-time employment as a single parent when they finally forced me out of work through stress and anxiety. I now no longer pay maintenance for the child my first wife kept. However they are attempting to force me to make a claim against my ex wife. I am expecting a personal visit from them any day now. I understand that any maintenance I receive will be deducted pound for pound from my benefit so the children gain nothing anyway. The resulting grief it may cause my youngest son really would not be worth the risk as he is just now coming to terms with his mother deserting him. I certainly don't wish to start all that up again.' (S13)

This extremely important consideration is not considered an excuse by the CSA for not pursuing a claim! For the agency violence constitutes the only let out. The second father had a different problem and one not experienced by any significant number of lone mothers.

'Three months after my wife left for her boss the CSA doubled my maintenance payments for a second child from my first marriage (I have custody of the eldest, but have never received a penny). The CSA were simply not interested in my situation and demanded and threatened election from my employer with extra costs if I did not comply.' (S25)

This home parent father constructed his own solution to the problem of the CSA's making.

'I was not living within my means anyway. This proved to be the final straw and I ended up on the verge of a nervous breakdown and on tranquillisers/anti-depressants and was off work for several months. I was forced to finish work and claim income support. I sold my car to rid me of that debt, cancelled all the standing orders, claimed for my mortgage interest payment and became a different person. I had time for my children, my depression faded as did my aggression, short temper and bitterness. My health improved, I came off the tranquillisers etc, and eventually no longer needed to visit the community psychiatric nurse – though I still have my moments.' (S25)

Probably the best thing most home parent fathers can do is steer well clear of the CSA, not just because of its apparent anti-male bias, but because it has helped astonishingly few men and once its wheels have been set in motion they cannot be stopped. The intervention of the CSA is as likely to cost the poor applicant money as it is to secure him any additional income. It is probably only worth applying if he is earning over £9,000 to £14,000 himself (depending on the age and number of dependant children he has) his ex is paying nothing, contributing nothing, sees the children for less than two nights a week on average and is earning over £10,000 a year with no new children or step-children of her own to support. Moreover, if the home parent father is not himself below income support level he will have to pay the CSA a fee of £40 for making the assessment. If he also wants them to collect the money because he does not trust his ex to pay him or wishes to have no further contact with her, then it will cost him a further £28 a year. If he is living on benefits he will be no better off unless the amount she is obliged to pay is more than he receives from the state, otherwise the Treasury gets the money and the home parent gets none of it. The net result is that while in 1992/3 the CSA collected only forty-four million pounds from other parents – it refused to say how much of this was from other parent mothers – it saved the Treasury £165 million in benefit payments. Its predecessor department in the DHSS collected four times as much with a quarter of the staff in its last year of existence.

An application to the CSA is regarded by most other parents as a hostile act* and would be likely to alienate the applicant's ex. Pursued by the CSA the other parent's co-operation over the children could diminish or cease altogether and the net amount, if anything, that the home parent father might receive would be far from enough to offset all the benefits in kind that his children, and even he himself, might previously have been receiving.

If a lone parent has applied for Family Credit or Income Support this information is passed on to the CSA and it can then demand that he make a claim for maintenance from his ex. If he refuses to name her, locate her whereabouts or make a claim against her without formal exemption from the CSA (a long drawn out and often complicated process) he could have his benefits reduced by almost £10 a week for six months and

*Some absent fathers are denying paternity to defeat the operation of the Agency (so there is a provision for DNA tests but they cannot be compulsory). This, at least, absent mothers will find rather difficult to do! (WP)

half as much for a further year. Once the CSA process has been started a home parent can only refuse to give information about his ex if he can show that it will damage the child, but, at least in theory, the parent with care should be believed initially unless what he says is inherently contradictory or implausible.

If the home parent father is earning above Income Support level then he will wait for ever and a day for an assessment. To complete the thirty-two page form you need a PhD in semantics and gobbledygook. Already many women lone parents have found themselves worse off after CSA assessments than they were before, losing benefits and consequently also the right to such things as free school meals, clothing grants, free dental treatment, prescriptions, home improvement grants and social fund loans. CSA payment is both taxable and counts towards income for purposes of assessing Income Support. If the new level of income is higher than Income Support level the lone parent will lose assistance from Housing Benefit, and with Council Tax and water rates rebates and any mortgage interest payments that may have been paid. Since there is a ceiling on how much the Agency can make someone pay the lone parent may be better off without maintenance secured through its intervention. A CSA payment will also be reduced if the children spend more than one hundred and two nights a year with their mother thus discouraging home parents from giving that extensive degree of contact to other parents which their children need.

On the other hand an ex can make the home parent money 'gifts' – ie with no legal, CSA or other contractual obligation to do so – of up to £3,000 a year without the recipient being taxed on them though the donor cannot claim tax relief on payments unless they are made by an order of a court or the CSA. If the couple are still married, ie separated, but not divorced, there is no limit to the untaxed gifts she can make to her 'husband'. The children's mother can also make untaxed payments to the children themselves of up to £3,000 each year.

Probably the most effective way for an ex to support her (or his) children without giving to the Treasury money intended for their benefit, is for her to take on certain financial responsibilities directly. She can buy their clothes, (but not the weekly household shopping) pay for their holidays, hobbies, school trips, school fees if they are at private schools and anything else the couple can think of. Being able to take advantage of many of these untaxable subsidies assumes that the ex lives nearby – or is at least in regular touch with her children and the home parent – and that she wants to co-operate in minimising the material impact of her departure on them. The greater the opportunity the other parent has to maintain her parenting role with her children the more likely she is to ease the home parent's financial burdens in this way. However, an ex cannot be compelled to do any of these things and precedent suggests that very few women will give a home parent father direct or indirect financial assistance however reasonable he has been about other matters.

Prospects are a little brighter for the home parent father getting another major source of help an other parent mother can give – help in kind. This will be particularly useful if he is still going out to work. It can embrace activities from household support – still doing the children's laundry, ironing, mending and even preparing meals and cleaning house – to an unemployed ex fitting her contact time with her children into the home parent's timetable so as to provide the out of school hours back-up that he will need. It will have been an amicable parting and a generous hearted woman indeed if she still does any domestic chores for a man she has left, but she will probably be inclined to do things for her children, particularly if they can be done in her own new home. I know of one parted couple where the children call on their other parent, who works from home, on the way back from school each day until their home parent gets back from work – an arrangement that suits everybody. If the other parent is working full time in conventional employment this will not be practicable, but can be for part time workers. There are also a few enlightened employers who not only provide creche facilities, but minders for children after school.

The serious poverty of many home parents of both sexes is a national disgrace breeding a legion of problems for the future as the children of these families reach adulthood. However, even if all the home parent's financial difficulties can be resolved, the big question remains – to work or to stay at home?

14

Home or away?

The so-called work ethic makes the false assumption that work, simply being occupied regardless of how, is necessarily desirable in itself. In fact work for many is often boring, badly paid and stressful. A home keeper has much more control over life's timetable than an employee, particularly a manual employee in a subordinate position, as any intelligent housewife well knows.

If women decline the support of the state, there is an unfair assumption that they can easily sustain the role of breadwinner and double parent without much difficulty – an assumption not made about men in the same situation. This derives from the equally unfair and unfounded assumption that within intact families where the woman also works she can cope with both functions while her male mate is only expected to manage one. It is reasonable to argue that fathers in these circumstances should take on half the housework and responsibility for the children so as to ensure a less exhausted and therefore happier mother and a more participating father. The argument runs that this will make for more contented parents and therefore happier children. However, to quote one paper on the subject, 'While arguments such as these have a common sense plausibility, the empirical evidence suggests that they are not generally true.' (R1)

It can equally be argued that if large numbers of mothers go out to work and hand over responsibility for their children's daily care to outsiders, they are no different from the father who absented himself from the home in order to work for his family, but now wishes to have the responsibility for bringing up his children as well. But the father who makes such a proposal is in a very difficult position because unless he is prepared to give up work, or work from home, the continuity of care he can offer is largely illusory. He is usually driven to employ or use another woman to provide daily care, at least on a temporary basis, so the mother's *apparent* ability to offer this on a more stable and permanent basis outweighs his claims. If a father overcomes this obstacle, works away from home and brings up his children he still faces a considerable handicap not suffered by a single mother. A variety of studies (R1) make it pretty plain that employers do not look kindly on male employees who share parenting responsibilities, let alone those who undertake them single-handed. They are less likely to get promoted because they are seen as less committed to their careers whereas it is assumed when employing women that they will sometimes be absent to look after their children. Now that it is, quite rightly, illegal to discriminate against women workers on such grounds they enjoy the best of both worlds where men do not.

The attitude of the employer is crucial to the practicality of a home parent father working and looking after his family well. Some are sympathetic and turn a blind eye to marginal time off without deducting pay, others sack those who cannot conform to the rigid requirements of the job because of their children. There is clearly discrimination against manual workers in this context, but the employers' position is at least understandable where work schedules cannot be flexible because they are part of a continuous process on which others depend. There is no escaping the fact that the lone parent father is running in the employment stakes under a considerable handicap and a double one if his situation is known to an unsympathetic employer. A man who finds himself in this dilemma may do well simply to keep quiet about his family responsibilities unless he is very sure of sympathetic understanding not only from his employer but from those of his workmates who may regard him as a rival.

It therefore becomes a necessary and personally enriching process for home parent fathers to redefine success in such a way as to make caring for their children the most important thing in their lives. If they are prepared to do this they can justify their claim, despite social hostility, to equal consideration with mothers for the right to bring up their children.

One of the most unexpected and depressing things to emerge from my survey was the enormous gap between the income of the two main groups of home parent fathers. Half (52%) had after tax incomes of under £7,000 a year.* Not surprisingly as this group involved those living on benefits, but it also included six per cent of our sample who were working part time and/or

*Adhering to the definition of poverty as 1.4 times basic Supplementary Benefit level (ie excluding housing, Council Tax and similar additional reliefs) this would be the current poverty level.

for very low wages. Less expected was that thirty-one per cent of the sample had net incomes of over £12,000 p.a. With such a gulf between better off and poor home parent fathers it would distort the picture completely to discuss their financial situation in terms of an average which would be untypical, so I shall look at the two groups separately. Both groups, however, have to take account of certain common considerations and financial facts before they decide whether or not to take on the responsibilities of lone fatherhood even if they had no choice in the matter as widowers or deserted men.

A great deal is properly heard about the poverty of lone mothers, but the assumption is frequently made that home parent fathers are not affected by a reduction in income to anything like the same degree. The assertion is based on the premise, becoming less valid year by year, that the father is the sole or at least principal breadwinner of the family and so when left with children will not be so badly off. No account seems to be taken of the fact that he will either have to give up work, and thus become just as badly off as an unemployed lone mother, or employ someone to look after his children and therefore eat into his un-augmented or even diminished family income. In the case of lone fathers living solely on Income Support or other benefits or relying heavily on Family Credit to supplement low earnings this assumption is clearly absurd, since what they receive will be exactly the same as a woman in the identical position. There is one exception to this parity. If the lone father happens to be a widower he may be much worse off than a widow with the same child-rearing responsibilities. This arises because there is no equivalent for widowers of the widows allowance for bringing up children. In theory other provision should bring the lone father widower's income up to that of the widow in the identical circumstances, but a substantial body of cases demonstrate that their difference in income can be as much as a hundred pounds a week in the widow's favour.

Widowers are also less likely to be well provided for than widows in another respect. While men often insure their own lives so that their widows will receive a lump sum if they die, they much less often insure their wives to cover against the additional burden of being a lone parent. The wisdom of this precaution, specifically mentioned as clearing the mortgage by two of my widowers, is demonstrated by the fact that half of them were not in debt whereas only a third of the separated avoided it. Income-earning women even less often divert any of their money to insuring their lives for the benefit of their husbands and children.

Before they became lone fathers most of those in my survey for whom comparative data was valid* were earning more than ten thousand pounds a year, but, as the table shows, afterwards the majority earned less.

Income in £000s	0 - 6	6 -10	10 -20	20+
%Before the break	11	18	32	39
%After the break	39	21	25	14

Most strikingly thirty-nine per cent fell below six thousand afterwards compared to only eleven per cent before. When account is taken of the fact that four of the top earners had been on fifty thousand plus and another six on thirty thousand plus the traumatic scale of the change in their fortunes is clear. There were one or two particularly dramatic cases. One man's income fell from £68,000 a year to £9,800 and another's from £50,000 to £6,450.

On average the separated fathers were fifty-seven per cent worse off with reductions ranging from ten per cent to one hundred per cent**. Only two were better off in real terms; one by half a per cent the other by seven per cent. A significant element in the fall was loss of mate's earnings, thirteen per cent had mates who had worked full time and thirty-six per cent part time. Nor do these painful comparisons make any allowance for earnings increases fathers who used to work could have expected from pay rises and promotions.

Interestingly, almost two-thirds of these fathers *felt* better off and another fifth no worse off although only twelve per cent actually were. Two of these said so and one, paying £150 a week for domestic and child care help, felt the same. The results of other surveys suggest that those who felt better off but were not did so because they were in sole control of the family finances and particularly of its expenditure. Some of my fathers may have understated their position. It is unlikely, for example, that the five who had been on benefits for more than two years, all of whose benefit-generating children were still at home, had

*Comparisons were not made for those who had been lone fathers for more than six years. Inflation was allowed for at four per cent per annum.

**Their income was only the sum allowed for inflation or less, ie: £20,000 five years ago should equal £24,000 now, but income was only £4,000 all told.

not received any increments. It seems probable, rather, that they were only expressing how they felt. But most of the optimists were quite aware of the difference between their feelings and reality and when asked to be realistic described themselves as worse off.

To survive nearly two-thirds of the survey fathers were entirely or largely dependent on state benefits*, excluding the Child Allowance drawn by all of them, but under-claimed by two. This was not a situation the majority of them relished. As one widower, William, described it 'I detest going to the Post Office on a Monday to get my allowance. I cringe if there is anybody behind me that I know'. (W13) The general drift of several fathers was 'I don't want to live on benefits. I want help so that I can go out and do a job.'

Simon put the case succinctly, 'I want a job that I can be self-sufficient in and not rely on the state, but I keep getting offered cleaning jobs, warehouse packing, etc which does not earn enough to pay my bills. In a nutshell, although I would do anything for my kids and love them dearly, I find that as a single father we are an ignored minority easily forgotten about, talked around, or just plain insulted.' (S23)

Widowers, only one of whom fell outside the six year limit, were better off on average with a drop in income of only twenty-eight per cent. They receive £910 a year more than their separated fellows although half of them were unemployed rather than the forty-three per cent unemployed among the separated. (Lone fathers are some nine times more likely to be unemployed (44%) than their married male counterparts.) Their fall in income was smaller and one had even increased his income by fourteen per cent in real terms since being widowed.

With so few home parent fathers starting out as lone fathers, in contrast to roughly a third of lone mothers being in that position from the outset, a far higher proportion of home parent fathers suffer a catastrophic fall in family living standards than do home parent mothers. Let fathers' descriptions of their experiences suffice to illustrate the depth and range of that fall.

Michael's life has changed almost totally since he became a single father. 'I owned my own Company, lived in a big house, drove an executive car and had an income of £50,000 a year. I am now almost fifty years old and finding it very difficult to find work of any kind. We live in a house rented from the Council in a very depressed area which is plagued by crime,

*Income Support 20; Family Credit 5; Sickness Benefit 1; Unemployment 2; Disability/Invalidity 3; Guardian's Allowance 1.

violence and drugs. My home has been burgled three times in ten months! I can't afford a telephone and we no longer have a car.

I am still very isolated not having the money or time to socialise. Money is a constant worry. At times we have been short of food. The only heating we have is a small gas fire. We have been cold all winter. I just cope from day to day and although we can just about survive it is very bleak and it's difficult to see how our situation will improve.' (M15)

Neil's ex 'moved out of our house to live with her girlfriend at the end of February 1991 and dumped my daughter on me at the end of April. I had paid her most of our capital because she had our daughter at the time. My solicitor says the law is limited to recoup anything, but I did get custody and £5 maintenance a week. I had a £57,000 mortgage £37,000 of it due to divorce debts. I have an eight-year-old daughter and two shift working. Only an acquaintance having my daughter every other week enabled me to carry on, but it cost me £60 a week. After two years I managed to get a day job which I am on the verge of losing plus the £20,000 salary. I now live in a tatty ex-council two-bedroom flat with £33,000 mortgage but have paid off my debts and saved £2,000. The CSA won't look at my case until 1996. I have lost my living standards and a pleasant way of life yet I did not seek the separation/divorce in the first place. How differently women are treated!' (N11)

Simon's complaint is also a common one. 'It is clear I have fallen far behind in promotion-pay scales since splitting. Part of this is undoubtedly due to the *perceived* lack of mobility and ability to respond. In fact I have offered to go to the USA with my son for four years – not many couples would have done so!' (S16)

Nor is it just those in work and then experienced a big drop in income who suffer. In many ways those who were already closer to the margins of poverty, and therefore without much 'fat' to draw on in a crisis, feel the pinch more. Life on the poverty margin is hard for Henry. (S17) 'Kids' stuff costs a fortune and they grow and wear clothes and shoes out so fast. I have found a great little second hand stall in S... and use it regularly, also the charity shops, but I really love to buy them new clothes.'

And Sam's (S25) plight is similar 'I don't put the heating on no matter how cold it is until I collect my son from school and then as little as possible.'

This economy, and its consequent adverse effect on family health, was reported spontaneously by several of the fathers. The truly amazing thing is how many of these lone fathers tackle the problems of poverty with determination and an ability not to lose sight of their gains. Simon's and Ronald's comments are typical.

'I do sometimes feel I should be doing more for him than I am. But due to lack of money can't. I try and give him as much as a two parent family and more.' (S23)

'I find it very hard financially because the children cannot have all the things they want to like other children, but the children bring me a lot of fun, love and joy.' (K13)

The shameful truth is that we live in a country where many lone fathers (and mothers) would be financially better off giving up their jobs, or refraining from trying to get a job, than they are working and this under a government that extols the virtues of work and lambasts single parents for scrounging off the State. If this were because the level of benefit income of the home parent was so reasonable that he or she felt under no pressure to work it would be no cause for shame, but this is far from the case. As my sociologist friend and former colleague the late Brian Jackson put it 'it means poor housing, sharing bedrooms, basic food, worries over food and other bills, no holidays. In one sample seventy-five percent of children under fourteen never had a birthday party.' (QB1)

The financial plight of lone mothers has often been the subject of public concern and sympathy if not of Government action. That of home parent fathers is no better, but is largely ignored. Those men who have to all intents and purposes enjoyed the services of an unpaid housekeeper, but have been unable to replace her, wholly or partly, by the help of relatives or friends, may have to pay out of taxed income to have their children minded and some of their domestic tasks done while they are out at work. In recent years the majority of married women have been working and earning, admittedly often part-time and sometimes for poor wages, but, nevertheless, supplementing the family income. Women's part-time pay now equals a fifth of family income and two thirds where they are working full time. The average male contribution has fallen from seventy-five per cent in the 1980s to sixty per cent. Women's wages are also going up as a proportion of men's. In an earlier study (M2) one in eight lone fathers gave the loss of wife's earnings as the reason for their drop in income. Today this figure is probably nearer one in three.

For the home parent father this income suddenly disappears just when it is needed most. Moreover, as we have seen, ninety-two per cent of lone fathers can expect no financial contribution towards their children's upkeep from their exes once they have left. On top of this they experience an almost certain drop in earnings due to their inability to do overtime or to pursue their careers or businesses single-mindedly because of their need – and in most cases desire – to be at home with their children. Largely as a result of the greater awareness of the importance to children of sustained parental attention, a quarter of the men in one survey (M2), carried out at a time of rapidly rising wages, who stayed in work suffered a drop in wages because of looking after their children. Two-thirds of the men had no savings and only one-eighth of them more than £300 to fall back on.

Many of those who remain at home or give up work to be at home are often confronted with a second problem. Their lack of skill and experience in shopping, cooking and house care means that initially, from a combination of emotional distress and lack of know-how, they carry out these tasks less economically than did their exes. As income goes down, expenditure appears to go up through ineptitude. To survive, home parent fathers have to learn to shop wisely. The catch is that shopping wisely is not only a matter of knowledge and experience, but a function of the time available which those still working full time will not have. This means they must use convenience foods for speed and these tend to be more expensive. Similarly, when clothes shopping, they do not have the experience to know what is a good buy. Fathers spend more on food and clothing, so expenditure on minor luxuries to compensate the children for dad's shortcomings soon has to fall off. (M2) Lone fathers may do well to ask a sensible woman friend to help them, or better still teach them until they acquire the necessary skills and the accompanying freedom to develop their own tastes. For most of them this will not take too long – I now rather enjoy exchanging tips with my female acquaintances!

The same survey showed some sixty per cent of men feeling themselves worse off because of various combinations of reduction in their own incomes, loss of their exes' incomes and increased housekeeping costs. Surprisingly perhaps, the corollary was that forty per cent said their financial position was better in some way mostly because they were better managers or had better paid work or no longer had a wife who spent too much on herself. This sense of improved economic status, often perceived rather than real, is common to lone parents of both sexes who find themselves for the first time in sole control of their family's expenditure. Clearly not to have the constant worry that a woman will fritter the family income on clothes, cosmetics and casual extravagances or a man dissipate it on booze and betting is for some lone parents a considerable relief. Many women walk out leaving substantial debts behind them in the shape of unpaid bills, large credit card deficits and bank overdrafts (M2) and the debts often come to light for the first time only when they leave home. While much of this is due to sheer selfishness, a substantial minority of women become compulsive shoppers, often buying things they do not really want, to compensate psychologically for domestic or personal unhappiness in much the same way as others become compulsive eaters. In the survey already referred to thirty-seven per cent of home parent fathers said that their incomes had gone up as a result of shedding these burdens.

For the majority of men in the survey quoted earlier finance remained the biggest continuing problem, regardless of social class, though this was more a matter of a sense of continual financial struggle than of desperate poverty. (M2) My own research shows that although isolation emerged as the home parent father's greatest concern, lack of money was certainly a major one expressed with heartfelt anxiety in many cases, but almost always with a determination to make the best of things.

When Karl's (K16) wife left him with their children unexpectedly one lunchtime she was convinced he would 'pack it in' after a few weeks, hand over the house and children and finance her and the family. Eight years later he is still looking after his two daughters, fourteen and a half and nearly eleven, and his son aged thirteen, though he did eventually give up his job three years ago to be at home. He was earning £16,000 a year at the time and now they have to manage on £112 a week and are almost always tight for money – something his eldest daughter, who blames him for the break-up of her family life, resents. Karl buys no clothes for himself, uses charity shops and 'usually runs out of money before I run out of week'. The eldest daughter expresses the usual teenage conflict with her father by running round the corner to her mum, which her mother encourages. Nevertheless, the family seems to be a happy one with 'marvellous and generous neighbours' – they have just given Karl a two year old fitted kitchen. Karl describes his relations with his ex as 'co-operative if not amicable' and she has made no attempt to get the children back. He has also enjoyed great support from the children's school head teacher. He leads a full life by enthusiastically improving his home as a skilled DIY man and cultivating his garden, but is considering going back to work to escape the financial straightjacket. At present the family cannot afford holidays even though they find the Local Authority subsidised ACE Card Scheme – £15 a year for each child to have free access to all local amenities such as swimming pools and tennis courts – a holiday godsend.

Kenneth's (K14) ex left financial chaos behind her when she moved four hundred miles away and although he paid her £2,500 for her share in the equity in their home there is still no formal financial settlement two years later. He is bitter about the fact that she is on Sick Benefit (alcoholism and suicidal depression which also caused the break-up) but in full-time education while he struggles to pay the bills. In fact, he himself has used his period of unemployment to take a two-year degree in geology and courses in both management and computing.

The home parent father, in deciding whether to work or stop at home to look after his family and live off benefits must, in the interests of his children, do some very careful sums before taking his decision, but before he gets out his pocket calculator he must make an even more careful psychological cost-benefit analysis of the pros and cons of staying at home. First and foremost do his children need him there more than they need a good wage packet? This will depend on the ages of the children, the degree of trauma for them arising from the death or departure of their mother, and the nature of the father's relationship with them – close or somewhat tenuous. He should try to put aside his own feelings about working if he can, not an easy thing to do when men are inclined to measure their self-worth by the kind of job they do and the size of the wage or salary they bring home. As one sociologist observed 'without a job there is no future ... a slow death of all that makes a man ambitious, industrious and glad to be alive'. Or as Camus put it 'without work, all life goes rotten'. (M2) Certainly contemporary society seems to think that, while it is acceptable for a lone mother to carry out the prime and essential task of looking after her children while living off the state, a lone father should go out to work. In such a climate of opinion it speaks well of male readiness to adjust values that so many appear to have chosen not to work. Single fathers are twice as likely to be unemployed as single mothers and nine times as likely again as their married counterparts. (LP1) My own survey shows forty-four per cent of single fathers as currently unemployed and fifty-seven per cent still living below poverty levels. This is particularly true for working-class fathers who are more likely to have larger families and, therefore, more likely to be responsible for those children under five who make it so difficult for the lone parent, of either sex, to go out to work.

If children are the principal cause of disputes when couples part, money comes not far behind. The poverty, often long term, which so often accompanies divorce and separation may prove almost as great a handicap to the children of the partnership as the emotional trauma of its disintegration. It must also be recognised that it is also often a major contributory factor in the breakdown in the first place. Some two-thirds of single parent families live at or below Supplementary Benefit level and four out of five below the poverty line. Only one in ten single families are likely to enjoy the average standard of living. (F11/LP1). Eight out of ten lone parents at some stage claim Income Support and lone families are ten times as likely to be below the poverty line as intact ones. The bright side of the picture is that my survey shows that low income does not necessarily have a bad influence on the children of lone fathers.

In fact the children with the best overall outcome had fathers predominantly in the lowest income groups, over half of them below five thousand a year, and a slightly higher proportion of unemployed and manual worker fathers than the survey as a whole.

Remarriage eventually takes almost two-thirds of divorced parents out of the poverty trap, though not by much and less often since the swingeing impositions of the Child Support Agency began to penalise second families more heavily than the courts had done. Amongst all the many criticisms of the CSA it is interesting to note a hidden and largely unknown benefit to which my attention was drawn by a straw poll conducted by one of my interviewees. This suggested that in as many as a third of the numerous cases of unofficial and undeclared payments by men to their ex partners there had been significant increases in the amounts paid as a trade off for avoiding a CSA award and consequent loss of benefits. The negative side of this is that once such collusion has been embarked on the receiver of these voluntary payments, but not the giver, is liable to serious penalties, including prison, for failure to declare them. This not only opens the door to blackmail, but highlights the weakness of a scheme designed to benefit the Treasury not the lone parent or children. It is insulting, as well as unjust in nine cases out of ten, to assume that home parents are drawing benefits from anything but necessity, but if a home parent father cannot handle the loss of self-esteem he feels in being unemployed, and therefore takes his frustrations out on his children, then perhaps he had better opt for work. Before he does so he should seriously reappraise his personal priorities and sense of values.

The foregoing relates to those on or below the poverty line. For the better off home parent father life is easier, if not without its different problems, but at least they can be tackled without the crushing burden of poverty. Nor, apart from Child Benefit to which every parent is entitled, will he be involved in trying to fathom out or depend on the social services system. If he is in a high-powered or demanding job the home parent father will probably find the provision of good quality care for his children more expensive as it may have to be for longer hours and more flexible to cover weekends and overnight absences when he may be away at conferences or on business trips. The hours and demands of a profession or career will probably mean he needs domestic help as well and the costs of working (clothes, car, etc.) will probably be greater than those of someone doing a run-of-the-mill-job to earn a wage. Conversely, some of the 'perks' will significantly enhance his standard of living. Moreover, his job satisfaction is likely to be much higher than that of his manual worker or semi-skilled counterpart. In fact, that will probably be his biggest problem. If he is to be a good home parent father he must not think that housekeepers and nannies can take the place of his ex in providing the love and attention his children need. His children will now need much more of his time and energy than he probably used to give them so he will have to accept that he is handicapping himself in the promotion race. He will, unless he is superhuman, have to devote less time and energy to his career than he used to and, therefore, less than many of his rivals. If he is not prepared to make this sacrifice the separated lone parent should almost certainly not have applied to be the home parent. Both he and the widower have been given an unusual opportunity to reappraise their careers and their life goals, to consider the attraction of rewards not measured in terms of status and money. If they miss the challenges and the limelight of working life they can find compensation in the opportunities for experienced and qualified home parent fathers to contribute to and win the appreciation of the communities in which their new roles will have given them a more intimate part. Even those who still go out of the house to work can become involved in local charities, school governing bodies, village hall committees and a variety of other communal activities where their skills will be useful and where the demands and location of the duties involved will not prevent them from giving top priority to loving and nurturing their children. In the right spirit they can even find themselves enjoying attendance at the netball matches and athletic meetings, the pantomimes and other performances they may once have left to their children's mother!

It is important for a home parent father simply to spend time with his children doing whatever they want to do with undivided attention. This is not easy if he is trying to earn a living and run a home as well. He needs to be able to feel free to earn less by seeking a contribution from the state (or from his ex) towards his children's upkeep so that he has the time and energy to look after them properly. Until, once again, looking after children is accorded its proper priority and respect as a personally and socially worthwhile occupation, men and women who choose to stay at home to do this will be harassed and stigmatised by insensitive politicians and officials. They should ignore the epithets, confident that they are doing the right thing.

15

Ironing pleated skirts

Just as increasing employment opportunity for women has been crucial to their economic emancipation so the large-scale male unemployment of recent years may prove to have been instrumental in the eventual emotional and parental emancipation of men. Many more men have now looked after children, even very small children, and shown that they can do so quite as well as their women who may have had to be away at work, even if only part time, to make ends meet. If the employment pattern should ever revert to that of virtually full employment (unlikely as this is) men may be no more be willing to give up their new family rights than women will be to give up theirs in the job market. It is interesting to note that whereas in 1962 forty-three per cent of men had never changed a nappy, and sixty-one per cent had never bathed their babies, now less than ten per cent have never changed a child and only about a quarter have not bathed a baby. (F8) A survey some years ago showed men doing slightly more than half of the gardening, forty per cent of washing up, twenty per cent of decorating, shopping and cleaning, ten per cent of cooking and five per cent of washing and ironing. (QF8) Another survey (QF8) of middle class fathers, who expressed strongly egalitarian attitudes about family responsibilities, showed that they got up to their children in the middle of the night themselves or shared the getting up just over half the time. They did twenty-seven per cent of putting them to bed and twenty-four of getting them up in the morning, but only thirteen per cent of feeding and dressing, etc. The pattern was not dissimilar for the working class men in this study though they felt they were much more involved than was 'proper'. (F8) Fathers on average spent about seven to eight hours a week doing things round the home and with their children as against women's thirty-five hours.(F8)

My own recent survey suggests that lone fathers, at least if they are to be believed, are now doing a fairer share of home tasks than these earlier surveys would suggest. Although nearly half of them (42%) had never been responsible for keeping house before, when living with their mates they had done a fraction over half the surveyed household tasks (Laundry 35%, Cleaning 40%, Cooking 43%, maintenance and repairs 88%) and, perhaps more surprisingly, over half (51%) the child care. It is possible that earlier surveys, based on women's evidence, have underestimated men's share of these jobs, or gender roles may simply be changing faster than we thought. Even allowing for the exaggeration of self assessment the lone fathers in my survey had clearly been much nearer the ideal 'modern man', yet their mates still left them. Why? Because they *were* modern men? Or was that why they were able more easily to take over the sole parenting role? What they were not good at was sharing the burden of running a home as a lone father – or at least they found it hard to persuade anyone to help them. Only seventeen per cent of my fathers got family help, on average two hours a week if the man who lived with his mother is excluded. Just under ten per cent paid for an average of seven hours domestic help and one man had a full time housekeeper.

In most cohabiting couples when men are involved with their children it tends to be with optional, enjoyable and flexible activities, such as play and outings, which they can take up or drop as pleases them, rather than with the dull routine jobs which have to be performed at more or less set times and places. The extent to which this is a selfish, voluntary attitude or is imposed by the timetable and fatigue of men's employment has not, to my knowledge, been the subject of research. The assumption is that men are idle and bossy and choose to be so. But if a man has to travel and work at set times and places, if the journeys and the work are exhausting, then it is perhaps understandable if he is selective about what he does with his few precious hours with his small children. He will certainly want to spend time with them rather than doing chores. It would be interesting to know if, when the inequalities are reversed, the gender roles are reversed. When the woman toils and the man tends the hearth, does the 'new woman' become equally selective in her involvement? Does she forget the equality for which she fought so long and watch the telly and read the paper while her man gets the dinner? Was she, in other words, fighting for an advantage rather than a principle? Excuses apart, it may be that the 'new father' and the 'modern family' are still to some extent figments of the imagination and that in practice cohabiting fathers still do much less than their fair share of domestic work. What is more surprising is that the available evidence (F11) suggests that women are content with an improvement in male *attitudes* to sharing the domestic burden and willing to ignore what actual practical contribution they make. Perhaps it is more satisfying to have the man feel guilty about his shortcomings than to have him assert himself as an equal partner in domestic and family matters.

Even where both partners were going out to work, in most previous surveys the lion's share of domestic work and child care was undertaken by the mother despite the physical and mental exhaustion this involved. (D2) This is probably not simply a matter of male idleness, though no doubt there is an element of that involved. Men do correspondingly more wage-earning work – the ratio with domestic work is more or less reversed on average – for the simple reason that they are still better paid than women and it therefore makes economic sense for the family unit as a whole for the man to be the primary wage-earner and the woman to be the primary home-maker and child-rearer. As one writer put it 'Fathers remain rather peripherally involved with their children, in the absolute sense, for more complex reasons than a conspiracy to keep women in their place.' (F8)

Although it is diminishing, there is still considerable social pressure for this division of roles to be maintained and both men and women believe men to be less competent in domestic and child care activities. This reinforces the lack of confidence that many men feel in carrying out such work. The world in which they were brought up as children has endorsed this division of labour and they in turn are content to perpetuate it. (F8)

However, the main reason why even women working full time still bear the heavier burden of domestic work and child care is simply that they insist on doing so. 'Increased paternal involvement may threaten to upset fundamental power dynamics within the family ... The roles of mother and manager of the household are the two roles in which women's authority have not been questioned ... Women are being asked to give up power in the one area where their power and authority are unquestioned in exchange for the possibility of power in another area. Many women prefer to maintain authority in the child care arena, even if that means physical and mental exhaustion.' (F12)

Necessary housework, except for someone quite obsessive, is not enough to keep any intelligent and active person occupied for more than a couple of hours a day, so many home parents will find that they need something to keep their minds stretched once they have mastered the intricacies of domestic management. They will soon recognise that the last thing most of the tedious jobs around the home will do is stretch their minds. There is a great range now of distance learning courses ranging from an Open University degree or Open College business studies course to shorter timescale courses relating to various hobbies and leisure pursuits. Many of these from organisations such as the Open University or the National Extension College will give discounts for single parents and it is also sometimes possible to get grants and subsidies for study from the Local Education Authority for the area in which the lone parent lives. A number of useful addresses will be found in Appendix One. It is better still if the home parent father can arrange to get *out* of the home for at least one evening a week to pursue some hobby, sport, course of study or simply to socialise. Twenty-seven per cent of my fathers stressed that the hardest thing to cope with was the deep sense of isolation that stemmed from the social and practical restrictions imposed by their situation. Such isolation is a great breeder of depression and lassitude, such as that experienced by Wilf and Thomas:-

'I am also lonely, miserable, exhausted. I do not exist. I am solely a support for the children and a drudge. I feel I have nothing to look forward to for myself.' (W16)

'You go from one trauma to another, from feeling depressed to feeling happy. Loneliness has a strange effect.' (K12)

The reasons given by Donald and Bernard are fairly typical:-

'All the friends I had before my girlfriend died have distanced themselves from me. Their attitude is they don't know what to say or do so they do nothing and avoid me!' (W17)

'If I go on holiday on my own (with Melissa of course) I tend to feel very isolated seeing lots of families enjoying each other's company and I feel left out.' (B12) So, no doubt, does Melissa!

When men apply themselves to a supposedly female activity that does not demand too much manual dexterity they usually do it as well, and sometimes better, than women themselves – cooking is a prime example. The important thing for the first time home parent father is not to panic but to apply himself to those domestic tasks he has decided are essential in the same methodical and logical way that he would approach a task at work or for some technically based hobby. This is not to say that all lone fathers will be equally adept at every domestic task. Ironing, sewing (not that anyone does much sewing these days), flower arranging (yes, men like flowers too!) and some kinds of cooking may not be so easily mastered by men as they were by the women who used to do these chores for them. I never did learn to iron a pleated skirt properly, but I did learn to buy skirts without pleats or with permanent ones – or simply to leave them unironed!

Many men are tempted to emulate the domestic approach of their former mates, but this is almost certainly a mistake, particularly for working lone fathers, however well intended as a means of minimising the change for the children. Trying to do one hundred percent of the practical domestic tasks after a hard day's work will leave them too short of time and energy to nurture their children and male and female domestic psychology differs. Women are usually persisters, men usually blitzers!

The things to be tackled round the home with which most lone fathers will largely be unfamiliar are too numerous to give guidance on in a lengthy book, let alone a single chapter, hence the rather misleading title of this one. Each lone father's areas of ignorance and ineptitude will differ and on many there will be useful books to guide him, though he may find the expressions and assumptions of basic knowledge in the majority, written for women, exasperating. On the whole it is more efficient as each deficiency becomes apparent to seek specific instruction from friends, family and even exes than to try and master the female skills acquired over a couple of decades in a three-month crash course.

The first thing the home parent father needs to do is to set out his priorities and not feel that he has to do everything. Keeping children and parent nutritiously and sufficiently fed is priority number two, warmth of home and clothing in cold weather number three, monitoring children's and parent's health number four, cleanliness of clothes and hygiene-risky parts of the home such as lavatories, sinks and basins, kitchen work surfaces, beds and so on is number five. Gardening, regular sweeping and dusting, ironing of most clothes and many similar activities are optional extras; nice if you have the time and energy to do them, but to be ignored and neglected, as indeed are priorities two to five temporarily, if there is any risk of them pushing out priority number one – devoting time and energy to loving the children, playing with them, working with them, taking an interest in their deeds and hopes, their ambitions and their fears, their needs and other relationships, their achievements and their failures.

16

Help!

One of the greatest obstacles to a man successfully running a home and family is his 'macho' reluctance to seek the help of friends, acquaintances and neighbours on a personal basis. Women have a lifetime's experience of establishing social networks, principally with other women, based on the school gate, the Friends of the School, the WI, the shopping trip, any one of a hundred other female encounter patterns or simply by 'over the fence' chat. This not only makes it easy for them to ask for help with the children, chores, transport and all the other elements of domestic life that do not always fall easily into place, but it also makes them much more sensitive to the needs of others without having to be asked.

Men do not have women's natural aptitude for social networking. Such networks as they do establish, at work or in sports teams, political groups, charities and so on, are task-orientated rather than person-orientated. If a man asks another for help it is usually in the neutral terms related to the completion of a task which is a commonly accepted goal for all those involved. 'Will you help to get this quote out on time; hold the spanner on the other nut while I turn this one; show me how to swerve the ball to the left?' and so on, not 'I am in trouble, so will you help *me*?' Impersonal objects rather than personal pronouns are the language of male co-operation. A man is often afraid to admit to any personal deficiency or inadequacy that might be implied by asking for help on a man to man – or man to woman basis. The home parent father will have to overcome this inhibition if he is to run a successful household. He will find, in the early days of his lone fatherhood at least, a sympathetic response from the great majority of the women into whose company he will now be thrown provided he is willing to seek help openly. They not only understand the domestic predicament, but feel sorry for him in his situation, even a little admiring, except where 'sisterhood solidarity' has condemned him as a bastard who treated his woman badly. It is important when seeking favours to make it easy for the person being asked to refuse without embarrassment or guilt. If this is done they do not feel constrained and therefore are happy to volunteer to help when it is not inconvenient to them. It is better to have a network of people helping at times that suit them than one or two who are imposed upon until they break away completely.

When the lone father is first on his own he may well be inundated with cakes, offers to do the ironing, outings for the children and a host of other kindnesses – but in most cases it does not last more than a few months for several perfectly understandable reasons. He is seen to be coping better himself, other priorities and objects of sympathy supervene, husbands and lovers become, if not suspicious, mildly irritated at the diversion of attention from themselves. What this initial wave of help and support can do is give a home parent father the breathing space to organise himself, emotionally and practically, and put the assistance he still requires on a more formal footing. This can either be by paying for it in cash from those who offer it on a straightforward business basis if he can afford to do so – so much for ironing, so much for cleaning, cakes and jam bought from the WI stall on a market day – or reciprocally in kind; 'you take my daughter with yours to swimming on a Sunday, I will take your son with mine to football on Saturday; you collect all the children from school on Monday and Tuesday, I'll do it for the rest of the week'. The extent of the help required and the scope of the network needed to supply it will be determined by how much the help and support the father gets from his ex and from immediate family. This depends on where they live and how friendly they are. An ex in Aberdeen or a gran in Blackpool are not much use if you live in Cardiff and one on the doorstep is worse than useless if she would as soon cut a lone father's throat as look at him.

An ex living nearby, sometimes only a few streets or houses away, can be both a blessing and a curse. Proximity means in most cases that there is someone who loves the children who can be called on quickly and readily in an emergency or even just a minor crisis affecting them. If there is any degree of co-operation between the exes, nearness can be at least a practical bonus. It can also be an emotional burden, making it much harder for the home parent to break free and start afresh running his household and family unhindered by any critical glance over his shoulder. If his ex is living with another man right on his doorstep that can make it a great deal harder to control the inevitable feelings of jealousy and revenge or plain heartbroken longing.

Since lack of money excludes the lone parent family from much outside social life it must create its own in different ways, perhaps jointly with others in the same boat. Home entertainment does not have to be lavish and by involving all the children in the preparations for entertaining another family a successful and enjoyable occasion for all can be laid on. A daughter, for example, can delight in playing hostess, a son in looking after guests. Reciprocal hospitality also means that the home parent and his family will get out of the house and have a break from the chores in their turn. Half the lone fathers in one survey (M2) went out less than when they were married (let alone single) and more than a quarter only about the same. It makes sense for home parents to use the time when their children are with their mothers to relax or refresh themselves by indulging in their own favourite pursuits. The children will benefit from the home parent's regeneration when they return.

If the home parent father wants to go out to a pub or restaurant, theatre or cinema he may have to take the children with him. This can often (but not always!) turn out to be a social bonus as well as a financial burden. Given the right encouragement, it is surprising how sophisticated and adaptable even quite young children can become in this context and what excellent company they make. Such outings are also an important part of their education which an isolated and financially hard-pressed lone parent can be forced to neglect. There is no shame in accepting invitations to join them from those better placed financially to entertain by going out. A small gift of flowers from the garden, or a postcard of thanks is ample recompense to most people for the pleasure they can give, and the lone father should remind himself that he may have been asked out simply because his company gives his hosts pleasure! Of course, it can feel demeaning to be constantly on the receiving end of kindnesses which there seems to be no way to repay. The advantage of being helped by others in a similar situation is that support can be two way, but it should not be forgotten either that many people like to help without any prospect of reward or repayment.

Unless they have experienced it, most men have no

conception of the sheer exhaustion and exasperation involved in being under constant mental seige during all a child's waking hours and the constant threat of interruption even when they are asleep. Not to have a private place within one's mind to which one can retreat in peace can be for many a serious deprivation comparable to the torturer's technique of never allowing a victim to sleep – as most mothers could tell them. The lone home father who has no natural breaks should make sure he engineers some for the sake of his own sanity and good temper and consequently for the sake of a happy relationship with his children.

Single parent support groups that genuinely take account of the needs of home parent fathers are few and far between and are usually the result of local initiatives by one or two such fathers. As well as pressing the case for lone fathers to be treated on the same footing as lone mothers they also provide mutual support by way of child minding, exchange of skills and comparison of experiences. Their principal value is in the reassurance they give lone fathers of knowing that others have been in the same predicament and survived and in building up their confidence by calling upon them to provide help as well as to receive it. If there is such an organisation in a particular neighbourhood (I came across about half a dozen in the course of my research) then the local social services office or Citizens Advice Bureau can usually make contact with it. There is as yet no national register or supporting agency for home parent father groups and although organisations such as the National Council for One Parent Families (NCOPF) and Gingerbread claim to be non-discriminatory, they cater, in practice, almost exclusively for women. Quite apart from the volatility of Gingerbread groups – four of the ten I tried to contact from telephone numbers supplied by Gingerbread headquarters that week had already collapsed – the 'wronged woman' atmosphere in some of them can make them unwelcoming and even down right hostile to men. There are exceptions. I found two, out of the six I contacted, with more than the token man (some did not even have that) amongst their membership. These seem to be found where sufficient men have broken through to achieve the critical mass for a self-sustaining and self-perpetuating male sub group, or where the organiser – as I found in the case of the one in Cheltenham – is a true egalitarian who translates a belief in men's rights to be home parents into welcome and support for male members. CRUSE is equally available in principle to both sexes in its provision of support for the bereaved and does have an officer with special responsibility for widowers whom I found helpful. All the same, it is predominantly a women's organisation for women – but then I suppose it was a *widow's* cruse! In none of these organisations for lone parents is the participation of men anything like their eight per cent of share of the national lone parent population.

For a while the lone parent magazine *Singled Out*, launched in 1994 by Mike Lilley, was a good source of contacts and advice for lone fathers; although it concentrated, for understandable commercial reasons, on female interests and concerns it did also write about and for men as well as providing a great deal of practical information of value to home parents of either sex. It became a very useful platform for isolated home fathers to keep in touch with each other and with their common concerns. At £1.95 per issue it was good value for money for a home parent father, but, as the past tense implies, without the backing of a deep purse it folded after a few issues. However, at the time of writing there was a possibility that it might be restarted by one of the bigger publishing groups.

The greatest difficulty in securing personal freedom and avoiding isolation is to find someone in whose care your children can be left with confidence so that an evening out without them is not spoiled by constant worry as to whether or not they are happy and safe. This can be quite a serious problem if you have no close family in your neighbourhood. In the first place paying a baby-sitter usually eats into what is already a very lean domestic budget and secondly it is difficult to be sure that the ones you find are both capable and responsible. You cannot legally leave a child under the age of twelve at home unsupervised by a responsible person, nor can you give anyone under the age of fifteen charge of younger children however mature they may be. (Conversely I know some eighteen-year-olds I would not leave in charge of a jelly baby let alone a child of mine.) Some branches of some of the single parent organisations, such as Gingerbread, do organise mutual baby sitting and child minding for their members. In many towns and villages there are also mutual child minding circles where people earn and spend points by looking after each other's children and farming out their own. The difficulty for the home parent father is that he is usually the only male interested in this kind of exchange and such is the contemporary prurient obsession with child abuse and molestation that many parents are unwilling to leave their children in the care of a man. Nor, unlike the conventional couple, can he be in two places at once both minding his own household and escorting the baby sitter home which is often the condition under which parents allow their teenage children to babysit. Once the home parent has found a pleasant, reliable child minder he should treasure and treat her (it is usually, but by no means always, a her) with consideration, particularly by getting home to relieve her at the time he has said, and reward her as well as he can afford.

Home parent fathers often receive more informal help than lone mothers which may enable them to remain in full employment. The catch is that help is usually offered on the tacit understanding that it will be short term because the father will either employ (or better still marry!) a suitable woman to look after the children so that he can resume full-time money-earning responsibility and leave child care to those presumed to be fittest to undertake it! However, many men give up work or take less exacting work when they become the lone parent so as to be able to look after their children themselves.

Kids' Clubs Network Centres are increasingly common, (over 1200 at the time of writing) now that so many married mothers are working. These are run at many state and private schools, church halls and other communal meeting places. Backed by a forty-five million pound government grant, they cost an average of £3 a day but operate from 2.45pm until 6.0pm during school term and all day in the holidays, thus covering most fathers' travel time as well as working hours. Paying for a competent minder even for this short period can be expensive. There are in theory a number of options open to the home parent wanting day care for a child under the age of five. On closer examination there may be less of a real choice. The state nursery system is overstretched and, for all the talk, it will be some years before a government of any colour achieves the universal provision which it is generally agreed would be desirable. Because no charge is made for state nurseries they are ideal for the impoverished home parent, but there is a catch. Most have long waiting lists and there is no queue jumping for lone parents, so the only way to be sure of a place is to put a child's name down well in advance, yet relationship breakdowns do not usually come with that kind of notice (or if they do we choose to ignore it!). Although nominally for three- to five-year-olds, children are usually well past their third birthday when they start at a state nursery where there will be about a dozen children to every staff member.

The alternative is private care where there are fewer children to each carer, usually between seven and nine, and children can start a little younger – but very seldom younger than two and a half. The problem is simply the cost. Some private nurseries can be as much as £15 a day when run by schools or professional organisations such as Montessori. More usual charges are £5-£8 a day. Also the hours can vary considerably. Some provide only half day sessions, others, increasingly sensitive to the needs of working parents, provide care from 8.00 am to 5.30 or 6.00 pm, but that is a long and tiring day for a small child to be away from its home parent.

In choosing group day care the first step is to find out what is available near enough to home or work to make collecting and delivering children feasible and covering the hours the home parent needs to be away. If money is no problem, the short cut to this is to get a complete list of those in the relevant area from the Nursery Schools Information Line at a cost of £5.95. Information can be obtained free of charge, but less easily, from the early years section of the local social services or from the local education authority. Creches, day nurseries and nursery schools are all headings in Yellow Pages and local libraries also hold lists for consultation on the premises. Word of mouth probably provides the best guidance, so if the home parent knows where the children will eventually attend primary school asking that school's staff and parents for advice is usually the best approach. This will also enable the home parent to find out at what age his child can go to the local primary school. With school budgets now determined by a formula based on the number of pupils, this is getting earlier and earlier and in some cases can be soon after the fourth birthday.

The second thing to assess in the private sector is cost. It is no use the home parent visiting a nursery school that will set him back £75 per week if all he can afford is £25! Child care is not a tax deductible expense of working, though it should be, and for some on benefit assisted incomes a disregard is available to help with care costs (see page 186). When one or two places have been selected 'on paper', they should be visited, preferably for a whole session rather than the quick 'nose round the door' inspection for which a best front can be put on. By concentrating on the relationship between staff and children it is possible to gauge whether the nursery or playgroup is run on a genuinely responsive person to person basis or rather formally. It is happiness and a sense of security the lone parent is looking for at this age not the capacity to turn out university professors or army majors. It is a bonus if the furniture and equipment are new and good and the proprietor or manager charming to parents – but the parent is not the customer. The child is, and customer satisfaction is, in the end, the best yardstick of performance. If after a few weeks a child is not looking forward to going then there is almost certainly a problem, as most children relish the experience after a few days' initial uncertainty. It may possibly just be a clash with some other territorially jealous child who resents the newcomer, but is more likely to be one of general suitability. If this is happening the home parent needs to take time off to spend a couple of hours at the nursery school or playgroup with his child – the best groups welcome this.

If a child is under two-and-a-half then groups are probably not suitable and the personal criteria we have already discussed can be applied to assessing registered child minders who usually take on one two or three children only at an average cost of £3 to £5 a day. The local social services department can help with a list of approved and registered childminders for the very young and what they charge. Whatever the age of the child the important thing is to choose carefully and not be afraid to move a child elsewhere if it is obviously unhappy. For most lone fathers the most usual alternative to other parent care after school remains that of family or close friends and here they do get a little more help than with household chores. A third of our sample were helped by relatives for an average (excluding again the man who lives with his mother) of six and a half hours a week. Eleven per cent get an average of nearly three-and-a-half hours child minding a week from friends. Twenty one per cent pay for help and, apart from three men who have 150 hours a week between them, average 14 hours a week. Excluding the four big spenders, one with a housekeeper, who can lay out up to £150 a week, this costs them £29 a week. At a fraction over two pounds an hour that suggests there is not a little sympathy for their relative poverty among the paid helpers! It is to be hoped that this kind of arrangement will be exempt from any future legislation on a minimum wage.

A good way to identify the practical difficulties that the absence of the second adult in the home is likely to create is for every member of the family to draw up a very detailed diary and timetable of their normal routines when mother was still involved. Then the family can make out a composite schedule of all its activities and identify the gaps and the clashes that will arise now that there is only one home parent. A daughter has a music lesson in one direction at the same time that a son has football practice in the opposite; the family used to eat together at 6pm when dad got home from work because mum worked part time, finished at 3pm, picked up the primary school children and prepared the meal. These arrangements presented no problems when there were two parents to deal with them, but it is not possible to reconcile all the conflicting demands when there is only one parent, without third party intervention or changed routines. Detailed scheduling, by pinpointing difficulties in advance, makes it easier to resolve most of these clashes. Music lessons switched to a Wednesday evening, dad forgoes overtime and gets home by half past five to prepare a later meal for half past six and so on.

There will remain many anomalies which cannot be removed by marginal juggling of times and places. So some tasks, and some pleasures, must be abandoned altogether. This is a necessary solution if only to take account of the limits of one person's time and energy if he is not to have a breakdown or a heart attack. The car will not get washed every Saturday, the gardening will be simplified, dad will give up chess club on a Sunday afternoon even if he still plays squash on a Saturday morning when the children are with their mother. Other things will have to be done by someone else altogether and here it is important to include the children in the reallocation of responsibility. They may grumble, but they are also likely to be secretly pleased to be asked to help. It will encourage them to be more mature, to learn the concept of personal responsibility, and to feel more in control of events. One child will take over washing the car, another getting ready the ingredients for the evening meal and so on. The older they grow the more they can and should help, though it is counter-productive to over-burden them to an extent which takes the pleasure and freedom entirely out of their lives and turns them into drudges or adversely affects their school or college work. These tasks must be allotted even-handedly and older girls should not find themselves taking over their mother's role and doing most of the work. They may well do it without complaining, but their silent resentment will quickly corrode family bonds. The children of single parents will in any case leave home at a younger age on average than those of a stable couple. There will remain things that should be done which, if dad is employed, cannot either be undertaken by him, time shifted or done by the children. For his children's sake and his own the home parent father must learn to ask for help without shame or hesitation from whoever can best provide it.

17

Making ends meet – working

If, having weighed up all these personal factors, the home parent father decides he should work full time (we will look at part time later) then he can set about making the relevant financial calculations. In outline, gross pay plus supplements and benefits, minus taxes, the cost of child care, and the cost of working (travel, special clothes, etc) will give him the level of *net* income he needs to compare with what he would get on state benefits. I have used in this chapter the figures that applied in June 1996 but they, and indeed the various liabilities, may have changed by the time they are read – such is the world of politics!

In calculating his taxable income he deducts first from his gross pay his personal allowance of £3,525 plus his *net* single parent allowance of £1,040 (but no allowance for dependent children). He may also be able to claim mortgage tax relief if he is buying his house. This relief is being steadily reduced and is likely to disappear within a very few years. He may not claim for rent – another of the inequitable anomalies in contemporary Britain. Certain costs in connection with his work, such as special clothing or tools or institutional subscriptions, are also deductible from his gross pay before calculating his tax liability. If he is contributing to a company pension scheme or a personal pension scheme then all or part of his payments may be eligible for tax relief also (automatically allowed for in the payments for a private pension scheme) and the value of company pension schemes, many of which include a contribution from the company itself, should be taken into account when calculating the financial advantage or otherwise of remaining at work or seeking it. On the balance of his income after these allowances have been deducted from the total he will pay Income Tax at the rate of twenty per cent on the first £3,200, twenty-five per cent on the next £21,100 and above and beyond that at the rate of forty per cent. He will also have to make National Insurance contributions at the rate of seven point three per cent of his pay. He can thus calculate his net pay. To get his net income he then needs to add in any benefits he can receive (some of which, such as Unemployment Benefit, are taxable) of which the main ones are his Child Benefit and possibly Family Credit. There are a number of special cases, such as payments to the registered disabled, including his children, which may also have to be included.

However the financial advantages can be more than outweighed by the pressures, as Brian (B14) discovered. His wife had a serious mental breakdown after the birth of their second child, dropped the baby deliberately and once also tried to smother her (then) three-year-old daughter. She went off with the daughter whom the police found a few days later wandering the streets. Now the mother is in sheltered accommodation following a long spell in a mental hospital and Brian collects her every Saturday to spend the day at home with the children, but never without him present. Neighbours are helpful and flexi-time employers reasonably understanding though Brian will not get preferential treatment in the impending redundancies. In part he looks on the prospect of becoming unemployed with some relief as an opportunity to take off some of the pressure that now leaves him too tired on a Sunday, the only free day he has, to do anything with his children but fall asleep in the chair at his mother's house. The children, a girl of seven and a boy of four, and he go out, together with his sisters and their children, two or three times a year and their holiday in 1994 was the first for four years. He also takes the two children to a local Gingerbread Group which 'he could well do without, but the kids enjoy meeting other children'. An experienced accounts clerk, Brian will not be able to get State financial aid when he is made redundant because of his savings so plans to get a job 'filling shelves in a local supermarket' to bring in what he would otherwise get in state benefit and so avoid eating into those savings. This pattern will enable him to spend more time with his children. Brian is forty-two and has been a lone father for three-and-a-half years, but already he looks weary and a bit defeated. He describes lone parenthood as 'best summed up in one word – Hell!'. It is the absence of a harmonious parental couple on which his children might model themselves that most troubles him. 'It was never intended and it is not a natural situation. The fact that my children are not getting the kind of family upbringing that I had fills me with horror, no matter how good a job I do, they cannot experience the inter-relationship of both a male and female living in harmony with each other. Thus I fear for their ability to handle relationships later in their lives.' In practice he is doing a good job as a lone parent and is probably unduly pessimistic about the outcome for his children, but the effect on himself is unmistakeable.

There are solutions other than conventional employment to the problem of how the home parent father can both work and be at home when his children need him. Only a few will be lucky enough to be able to switch from working in office or factory to earning a living at home in a way that entails no absence from home or only a few days each year. The number of people who can earn their living in this way is relatively small. Nevertheless, home working is a rapidly growing sector of the economy as both computers and telecommunications become simpler, cheaper and more effective. The market for handcrafted products is still a good one and the skills of the electrician, plumber or domestic service engineer can also be sold as a freelance on a school hours only basis and still provide a reasonable living. Home Run and Ownbase magazines are a good market place for those looking for home work ideas or jobs. The Health Education Authority publishes a useful guide, *Working Parents Survival Handbook. Working from Home* and *The Freelance Alternative* by Marianne Gray, Piatakus Books, has some helpful tips and the organisation Parents at Work may also be able to help.

Self-employment in general, whether working from home or part time out of the home, that fits in with children's time-tables has one other great advantage – its opportunity, quite legitimately, to avoid taxation. If the work is based at home, a proportion of rent or mortgage, a proportion of heating, Council Tax, repair and other household bills can be set off against income. Telephone, postage, stationery and so on can be almost entirely absorbed, though some plausible part has to be declared as personal expenditure. Mileage for journeys even tenuously connected with work can be charged as expenses at the rate stipulated by the RAC or AA for the vehicle in question up to three thousand miles a year and at a lower rate fixed by the Inland Revenue over that. If the vehicle is old but in good condition this official rate generally leaves a generous margin towards overall income even after setting aside money for a replacement in due course (depreciation) and paying for fuel, repairs, tax and insurance. The largest element in the official tariff is the depreciation rate. This is calculated against a new car which loses most of its value in the first fifteen months on the road. In most cases charging a high mileage is now more cost effective than running a car on the business and being assessed for tax and VAT on its personal use. Other forms of travel and some other expenses can also be claimed. The ordinary employee, who may be obliged to travel by bus or train some distance to work or have to go by car because of the lack of public transport, cannot offset his travel costs against his earnings. This is another unjust anomaly in our tax system. The tax declaration on expenses requires them to be 'wholly and exclusively' in connection with the business, but I wonder how many self-employed people, lone parents or otherwise, are so utterly scrupulous as not to be a little elastic in their interpretations sometimes. The Inland Revenue tends only to pursue those whose claims are clearly unreasonable or absurd and is far too overstretched to chase every possible minor infringement or misinterpretation of the tax laws.

There are also a few full-time occupations, nearly all connected with the education system, teaching, school catering, playground supervision and so on, that fit into the children's timetable. I believe school and college heads and governors should give absolute priority to suitable single parents in making these appointments. Their need is much more desperate than that of the household where the wages provide only a second income.

The alternative is part-time employment, but this is usually so meanly paid, like many full-time occupations available to home parents, especially women*, that in purely financial terms this is often scarcely worthwhile. In any case if the earnings from them exceed £15 per week, 'the disregard', they simply reduce the benefits received by the home parent father pound for pound. Disregarding the disregard is probably the best advice to part-timers whose hours do not bring them within the net of employers' PAYE and National Insurance returns (which would catch them out). This is of course illegal, as is the non-declaration of income -'cash in hand' – from casual work and odd jobbing, but in a society where the very rich cheat the taxman at every turn, live on perks and privileges and rip the ordinary tax payer off at every opportunity, the

* Women's employment break down is: 17% skilled non-manual, professional etc., 58% clerical, retail, skilled manual etc., the rest predominantly domestic cleaning.

poor can scarcely be blamed for a little moonlighting on the black economy. Until we have a decent hourly minimum rate of pay, or better still a minimum income, and a social security system that encourages taking paid work by a graduated reduction of benefits, many home parents have little choice but to risk tax evasion. The financial balance being equal, and if work does not leave the home parent too exhausted to give of his best to his children and home, then the great advantage of part-time work is that it gets him or her out of the house to meet people other than family and neighbours, breaks the sense of isolation of being under seige in one's own home, which can so easily beset the home parent.

One way of defeating the 'part-time work equals low pay' syndrome is to job share. By taking half a properly paid full-time job the rate per hour can be increased substantially beyond the average part-time rate, while still not taking total income above the level at which eligibility for benefits ceases. Job sharing requires both an employer who takes an enlightened attitude to splitting work and responsibility – and he would be unlikely to permit job sharing if he did not – and job partners who can work harmoniously, flexibly and efficiently together. If they are both lone parents and get on well they may even find themselves sharing child care and fetching and carrying to their further mutual advantage. The local Chamber of Trade, Chamber of Commerce or Department of Employment should be able to provide the names of companies and organisations offering job sharing schemes in their respective areas.

Another very flexible, if not very lucrative, way of taking part-time employment is to get on an education course or training scheme for which grants are available. Local technical colleges are the best starting point for enquiries about training. The local authority education department or the Advisory Centre for Education are useful for information on more general educational courses together with advice about how to apply for financial help in undertaking them. The advantage of this approach – apart from the fascinating and challenging age and social mix of fellow students which it can provide – is that, except on emphatically technical courses, most of the home parent's hours of study can be fitted in with family and domestic commitments. Gaining qualification while staying at home to bring up a family greatly increases the chance of making a successful return to the job market when the children are older or have left home. Three fathers in my sample were full-time mature students. Qualifications, such as an Open University degree or Open Business College diploma, gained in this way indicate strength of character as well as knowledge and demonstrate the great self discipline and self motivation sensible employers will be looking for. Christopher's (C12) experience exemplifies the positive approach.

He is a typical tall, fair haired, handsome Englishman with three delightful and vivacious blonde daughters (twelve-and-a-half, eleven-and-a-half and nearly nine) all eager and open to express their views. The children seem very happy and well cared for in his well-kept village semi and conform contentedly to dad's way of running things. He has overcome his initial domestic inexperience and on the basis of a student grant of £5,000, Child Benefit of £1,750 and £1,800 a year of voluntary maintenance payments for the children from their mother runs a comfortable home. The children see their mother most days and stop over one night a week and every other weekend – which makes leisure planning with them a little difficult for Christopher. They get on well with their mother, 'who gave them a great grounding' before she left, and accept their mother's new partner. What makes the situation unusual is that the new partner is a woman and Christopher's ex left because she discovered she was a lesbian (seven per cent of the exes in my survey left for a lesbian relationship and the children in all cases get on reasonably well with their mother's new mate). Unlike most home parent fathers Christopher saw the break coming, partly because he was spending too much time at work, and gave up a £30,000 a year partnership in a small computer firm to be at home. Paradoxically, that accelerated the break-up, but gave him the opportunity to reassess his values and priorities and enrol as a mature student on a degree course in an entirely new field. He gets on reasonably well with his ex, as is perhaps evident from the fact that she was the only one of the exes whose addresses were available in the Fathercare survey who responded to the matching questionnaire.

Christopher already did many things with his children, so because he was already at home he was in a good position to bid to take on their care. His ex also wanted it and only agreed to him having residence on the eve of the court case in which the ex's lesbianism would have been the principal argument why she was unfit to bring up children. Christopher now has his degree so his student grant will shortly end. He has a relationship with a single mother and looks like taking fresh directions in many ways. It seems probable that on the basis of a secure and happy relationship with his children he will make a success of all of them. As he says 'I view bringing up children on my own as easier than when I was living with my ex. We all know where we stand. I have developed an attitude of mind which enables me to get on with things in a positive manner and derive pleasure from it. I get a lot back from my children (most of the time!) and so this makes life easier.'

When a home parent has considered all the options for work and either been unable to get offered them or rejected them as incompatible with his first responsibility as a parent, he is left with no option but to rely upon the state benefits system. If this is the case he needs to make sure he gets the best out of it.

18

Making ends meet – benefits

State benefits already play a critical role in the support systems of many families in the three lower socio-economic classes so relying on them is seen today as much less of a stigma than once it was, but most men still disapprove of the very help they are obliged to accept. Two-thirds of the men receiving benefit do not like doing so. Less than a quarter are not bothered or feel that it is their right. Widowers feel less uneasy about taking state help. (M2) The persistent high unemployment of the past decade, which has now affected at least one in four of the workforce at some stage or other, may have altered attitudes to work, but the work ethic remains strong. A very large proportion of the lone parents in the lower three classes now rely on Income Support, at least initially, to be able to stay at home and look after their children, of whom, on average, they have more than middle-class families. The larger the family the more attractive life on benefits becomes because the difference between what a man can receive from the state and what he can earn gets smaller. A third of men on benefit received it for less than six months and over half made no call upon it after a year. By this time they had begun to make their own arrangements and had returned to work in many cases, partly from their own motivation, partly because of social and official pressure on them to do so. If social or moral pressure is brought to bear on a father before he feels it is good for his children for him to return to work he should resist vigorously. He will usually only be 'lent on' by a benefits officer if he is not exempt from signing on or is not actively seeking work. In any other circumstances he should object and if necessary complain to the superiors of the benefit officers who are harassing him. Generally, however, the genuine case will find them supportive rather than obstructive.

The British social security system appears at times to be devised with the express purpose of making sure that as few people as possible successfully apply for financial support. True, there are vast numbers of free publications about the various benefits and a useful general guide to eligibility is *Which Benefit?*, alias leaflet FB2, widely available free at Post Offices, libraries etc. Although these publications are a little less opaque than they once were they are still pretty abstruse and such are the intricacies and complexities of the benefits system that my advice to every lone parent, whatever their financial circumstances, is to have a thorough session with a benefits specialist. The best contact will be with the local authority's Welfare Rights Office, but help can also usually be obtained from the nearest Citizens Advice Bureau – though not all have benefits advisers. The quality of the CAB's advice in helping people to get benefits must have been good since the Government is now cutting financial support to the central organisation. Local branches are usually funded by the Local Authority and recent reductions in the number of locations and hours of opening, is one of the consequences of pressures on local government spending. In 1996 the Government closed the Department of Social Security freephone help line for individual advice whose friendly and helpful advisers tried to maximise the amount a claimant might get. This petty act of meanness was intended not only to save costs, but to increase the amount of legitimate benefit unclaimed – to the advantage of the Treasury. One of the first acts of any new government should be to close down the 'sneak line' – which encourages people to report neighbours they think may be cheating the system – and reopen the advice line.

Just how greatly such advice is needed is evident from the large sums of unclaimed benefit – well over two billion pounds a year – and the large numbers either unaware of their entitlements or of how to go about claiming them. One fairly sophisticated respondent in my survey (J11), in common at some stage with fifty-seven per cent of those entitled, did not claim the one parent Child Benefit supplement (£6.30 a week) for four years after he became entitled to it. Since only six months benefit can be claimed retrospectively, that oversight cost him more than £1,100! It is only possible to claim more than six months arrears if 'good cause', such as bad advice or wrong information from the DSS, can be shown – a tricky situation since the accused is usually also the judge! Any lone father thinking he may have good cause should get advice from the Citizens Advice Bureau or the local authority Welfare Rights Office. Some of these omissions are because of the overlap with

Income Support, but by no means all. Income Support, and Housing Benefit and Council Tax as well, can contain an element of lone parent additional subsidy from £5.20 to £11.50.

Family Credit can close a gap of over £50 between the incomes of those eligible and those not eligible to one of only about £15.

However, well over a third of the lone parents who are eligible for Family Credit do not claim it, usually because they do not know that they are entitled to it. Others refrain because it automatically triggers a CSA demand to the other parent which may damage precarious relationships with exes or reduce the contact between children and their other parents. One analysis put this as high as fifty-six per cent of those eligible.(P3) As would be expected their incomes are lower on average than those entitled to and claiming Family Credit. Oddly enough, had they claimed, their incomes would have exceeded on average those of families who were claiming.

By contrast Income Support seems to be claimed by almost everyone eligible for it. However, more than two-thirds of these do not report earnings to the DSS, which suggests, improbably, that less than a third earn themselves any additional money. Home owner lone parents should have all their housing costs, such as mortgage interest, met through Income Support. Housing Benefit may be available to help with rent and should be claimed through the local council covering the area of the lone father's current home. Most of those on Housing Benefit are not on Income Support and it is estimated that sixteen per cent of those eligible do not claim. Although disbursed by the local council this benefit is ultimately funded from central revenue. Water rates are allowed for in Income Support and those on this benefit also get full remission of Council Tax. Twenty per cent of those entitled to free school meals are not claiming, though about half these either take packed lunch or go home to dinner. However tactfully administered, the subsidised lunch still carries some stigma and exposes the child to the mockery of its peers and this may account for some parents not claiming.

With so many variations and combinations a book of this kind can only outline the broad principles that govern entitlement to and receipts for the main benefits available. The *summary* alone of the terms and conditions of income support takes up 144 pages of a closely printed A5 booklet.

Child Benefit is currently paid for at the rate of £10.80 for the first child of a married or cohabiting couple and at the rate of £8.45 for the second and each subsequent child. This benefit is normally paid to the mother so the home father must apply to the DSS to get the payments transferred to him as soon as he becomes responsible for looking after the children. This is not always easy as mothers who leave their children may refuse to agree to the transfer and then draw the benefit and spend it on themselves for many months before they can be compelled to make it over. Lone parents at present may claim the additional £6.30 a week for the first child only. Child Benefit is payable for all children under the age of sixteen, or nineteen if they are in full-time education – not very helpful if a child of a poor parent wants to follow a college or university course of three years or more after taking A-levels, though in a few cases the child may be able to claim on its own behalf.

If in order to go out to work a home parent has to place any of his children under the age of eleven in a nursery school, play centre or with a child minder, providing they are registered with the Local Authority as approved, (all these will be only too eager to declare their status) he will be entitled to a 'disregard' of up to £28 per week provided his income is low enough to entitle him to Family Credit. Nominally this is £40 but £28 is in practice the maximum disregard secured because of a 70% 'tapering'. In other words his income can be up to £28 a week higher before his other benefits are reduced. This benefit is *not* a payment so does not help those on the lowest incomes. What the home parent is supposed to do with his twelve-year-old is anybody's guess, the assumption seemingly being made by the authorities that once a child is at secondary school it no longer needs looking after out of school hours. Although once a child is twelve it is no longer against the law to leave it alone without an older (15+) person's supervision, many children of this age, and older, are not yet mature enough to be left safely on their own.

Another quite unjustifiable sex discrimination in payments for children is the Widowed Mothers' Allowance payable to a widow bringing up children (though she is then not entitled to the supplementary element of Child Benefit). No equivalent payment is made to widowers in exactly the same circumstances who are not on Income Support. If savings exceed means tested benefits in both cases a widow bringing up four children can receive as much as £100 a week more than a widower doing exactly the same. Moreover, while a mother receives a maternity allowance, or statutory maternity pay from her employer of up to £52.50 a week for 18 weeks, if the mother dies in childbirth the widower does not receive this payment. This is because the mother is regarded as having 'bought' this entitlement with her National Insurance payments so it is considered to have died with her although the newly born baby still has to be looked after by someone. The widowed father can get the £100 lump sum maternity payment, which is regarded as a family entitlement, but only if his savings are less than £500 or thereabouts. Kafka thou shouldst be living at this hour!

There are basically two patterns of income supplement not just for lone parents, but of particular significance to them. For those working for sixteen hours a week or less (officially!!) and aged over eighteen Income Support will be available on certain broad conditions. The good news is that, unlike a couple, a lone parent does not need to be actively seeking work or even be available for work in order to qualify for this benefit, but a slightly grey area is how the qualifying hours for the self-employed and piece work home workers are to be assessed. Strictly speaking the self-employed should include preparation hours as well as paid hours in their allowable sixteen. However, the onus of proof is on the DSS so the claimants word is almost invariably accepted – to the advantage of the 'flexibly minded' self-employed! Eligibility for Income Support does involve the usual crazy disincentive to prudent financial planning and savings. Income Support will be reduced by £1 a week for every £250 of savings over £3,000 and will not be available at all for those with £8,000 or more. In calculating savings personal possessions – car, furniture, paintings, jewels etc – and the family's main home (unless part of it could 'reasonably be sold off separately') are ignored. Everything else, cash in the bank or in hand, shares, a second home or boat, savings accounts and so on, is brought into the calculation. While it might be thought frivolous to recommend spending savings on national lottery tickets before applying for Income Support, in principle the suggestion is not entirely facetious. It certainly makes a great deal of sense for the lone father before making his application to consider constructive ways of reducing his savings to the £3,000 minimum if he anticipates a sharp drop in earnings because he has decided to stay at home to look after his children or to work only part time.

The most obvious way of getting below this savings barrier is to examine the advisability of reducing any mortgage, hire purchase, lease purchase or other major debt on which interest payments would impose a heavy burden on a smaller income. When looking at these it is necessary to check what interest payments, such as mortgage interest in some circumstances, might be eligible for payment through social security and which, therefore, there would be little point in reducing. The advantage of this approach is that it is unlikely to attract a 'notional capital' assessment, of which more later, although individual social security adjudicating officers have in the past counted such reductions as capital.

For the home parent father either already self-employed or running his own business or planning to do so spending savings before benefit application on capital equipment – computer, knitting machine, tool kit, or workshop machinery, etc – and on raw materials from stationery to wool, timber to spare parts, will usually make sense. So does the advance payment of certain bills – a year's rent, utilities, etc. It is unlikely at present levels of interest that the loss of (taxable) interest on the investment of the capital elsewhere, unless it is a very large sum indeed, would be more than the benefits lost by exceeding the capital savings limit. Again these payments would probably not be deemed 'notional capital'. Nor would money put into special accounts or trusts for children, but if these exceeded £3,000 in total for any child no dependant's allowances would be payable for that child.

For a home parent without these more obvious means of legitimately decreasing capital there are other, much riskier options. The DSS has anticipated most of the following suggestions and reserves the power ('notional assessments') to treat them as if they were actual capital or income of the applicant where it believes money (and in some instances assets) has been spent, given away or not obtained, expressly to reduce a claimant's level of capital or income so as to increase eligibility for certain benefits. This decision lies entirely in the hands of individual adjudicating officers, although there is a mechanism for appeal to an independent tribunal. They vary in their interpretations, but have the power to demand proof, like the tax man, that capital does not exist or has not been evasively disposed of and to disallow a claim until the claimant proves he has not got disqualifying capital or income. If a notional capital assessment is made, then it will be treated as if the claimant had possessed it since the capital was disposed of and the original claim for benefit made. A corresponding proportion of any benefits already paid will be clawed back from the consequently reduced subsequent payments.

The steps considered below are hard to detect and it is equally hard to prove they were taken with deliberate intent to evade the savings limits. Each individual home parent father will have to examine his conscience and assess his discretion before taking any of them. The first is to spend the money on items which will maintain their value for resale or even increase in value at a later date. Pictures, antiques, vintage vehicles, postage stamps and so on. This presumes that the purchaser, or a supportive friend or agent, has the know-how and the judgement to make wise purchases and on acceptance of the fact that a bad mistake or unpredictable change in the market could result in a fall in value, perhaps even a big one. The object of the exercise is to be able to sell these items piecemeal to meet subsequent emergencies or cash flow shortfalls (how grateful I was to be able to auction off some furniture my father had left me in one such crisis). But again the fact must be faced that the crisis and the best time to sell may not coincide and the market may be temporarily depressed at the time a sale has to be made. Modern vehicles, especially new ones, and new furniture are fairly certain ways of seeing an investment fall in value, but if they are, or will shortly be, needed anyway then now is the time to buy them.

A final, but also risky, strategy to be considered is to give the money away! This is not as daft as it sounds initially, provided the recipient is a friend who can be trusted implicitly (money can weaken the sternest resolve). Relatives, other than children are not advisable, as the DSS adjudicators more or less automatically regard pre-claim gifts to them as evasions and make a notional capital assessment. There is no limit to the number of gifts of up to £3,000 in any one financial year that can be made, to different individuals in each case, out of savings without either donor or recipient paying tax on them. The money can then be put into an interest bearing account in the recipient's name and any tax liability on that interest he or she may incur be paid out of that same interest. Then later, when cash may be urgently needed, a reciprocal gift can be made to the lone parent or what he needs can be bought by the friend out of the money saved on his behalf and then given to him.

Care must be taken to see that cash payments are spent at once so that the home parent's savings do not rise above the critical limit again, and that they are not spent on things like basic food and clothes which the benefit payments are intended to cover.

The time which has elapsed since gifts were made by a benefit applicant is also a factor in deciding whether or not a notional assessment should be made, but again this is largely an arbitrary decision by the individual adjudicator. As in many middle-class families particularly there is a tendency to put off what is seen as the humiliation of applying for Income Support it would be sensible to make these dispositions as soon as a job is lost or looks likely to be lost (one of my sample has had eighteen months' notice of impending redundancy) or income reduced below support level and so secure a decent interval between the gift and the application. Strictly speaking the adjudicator might construe this as not an arm's length transaction and therefore a disallowable form of avoidance, but in practice, unless the sums are astronomically large, in which case there was no problem in the first place, he will neither know nor care. A greater risk is that the person to whom the money was given may, deliberately or merely forgetfully, deny the understanding on which the gift was made which, for obvious reasons, can only be a spoken one, and fail to return it. In the absence of written proof (which could itself be proof of avoidance) the money would be irrecoverable.

Alternatively the home parent father could simply lie about his savings, but this is fraud, checks are made and fines, and even prison sentences are imposed. The DSS obtained convictions in ninety-five per cent of the cases it brought in 1993\4. The real irony is that unless tipped off or informed by the claimant the DSS does *not* check capital or savings. However, envy and indignation are formidable informants and one small authority in the north of England alone gets over a thousand phone calls a month from nosy neighbours. It would seem that the Government's invitation to us to spy on our neighbours and the latest special sneak lines were hardly necessary! Only one in a hundred of the cases where fraud is suspected is actually prosecuted. The remainder are treated as over payments and recovered by repayment or reduction in subsequent payments with the financial consequences that entails. Moreover, benefit payments are frequently suspended while an investigation, lasting anything up to six months, is carried out. Ironically, DSS Officers rarely seem to check savings unless the claimant declares *more* than £2,500, so if someone is going to cheat they are less likely to get caught if they go the whole hog and declare little or no savings than if they simply massage a £2,500+ figure a little.

There is little incentive for those wanting to come off Income Support and earn their own living as, in effect, their net hourly rate of pay is often not much more than £1.50. Those on Income Support earn at twenty to twenty-five per cent below the average hourly rate and because of the sixteen hour limit end up with only a fifth of the average weekly pay. Although they can also earn up to £15 a week 'disregard' without their Income Support being reduced, they may still have to pay travel and child care costs which are *not* deductible expenses in calculating benefits. After the disregard is exceeded it makes no difference how much they earn as for every £1 they get £1 will be deducted from Income Support. They have to work for more than sixteen hours a week and come off Income Support to be any better off as well, of course, as having to have a substantial wage or salary. Although they may then be eligible for Family Credit, depending on net earnings and the number and age of their children, this increase in income will probably be offset by loss of other benefits such as free school meals and an element* of housing and council tax benefit.

About one in ten of those receiving Income Support are not entitled to it. Very often this is not deliberate, but because they are unaware of the level of income which can be ignored in calculating eligibility. For this they might be forgiven since the DSS itself admits that it calculates one in eight Income Support claims incorrectly. A sub-sample of those on Income Support and Family Credit in my survey was asked if they had earned more than the disregard at any time but not reported it. Of the twenty respondents circulated with the question eight acknowledged they had earned more than the disregard, six *said* they had not and six did not reply to this question. The inference to be drawn is plain and, as several of them in my survey implied, how else are they expected to survive? Even the Government seems tacitly to admit this as income support is thirty per cent below its own definition of the 'bread line'.

Full-time working parents are not penalised to quite the £1 for £1 hundred per cent of those on Income Support earning

*85p in the pound; 65p Housing Benefit, 20p Council Tax.

more than the 'disregard', but those on Family Credit, Housing Benefit and Council Tax Benefit can find their marginal effective tax rate as much as 92p in the pound. Government policies are thus forcing a great many people both to stay in the poverty trap and not to work. There are certainly some home parents now working who would be better off on Income Support, specially when the additional cost of working in terms of meals, travel, clothes, equipment and so on is taken into account.

If a home parent is on Income Support he may be able to get help from the social fund to meet the cost of the larger items of essential domestic capital expenditure, such as the more costly appliances, and certain other items. However, the lone parent need not hold his breath since virtually none but the most extreme circumstances and the most essential appliances attract such help. Free and cut-priced milk for children under five, help with meeting heating bills in long periods of very cold weather (seven consecutive days at or below freezing – nought degrees centigrade) and with funeral expenses is available to those on Income Support and with little or no savings (less than £500), as are loans both to help them reorganise their budgets and to meet some particular crisis. This help should be applied for through the local DHSS office.

The other straight income-boosting income benefit, Family Credit, is aimed at those working for at least sixteen hours a week and is of most value to employees in poorly paid occupations, whether full-time or part-time, or not very lucrative self employment. It is available to any home parent with children under sixteen, or nineteen if they are in full-time education. The same limits on savings apply as for Income Support. Many people assume this benefit is only for those on the very lowest pay, but a lone parent could be earning as much as £120 a week and still be entitled to £40-£50 a week in Family Credit payment. With four children in various age categories he could be earning over £200 a week and still be eligible for some Family Credit. The form notifying updates in Child Benefit now spells out this entitlement as well in each individual case.

Help, by way of Housing Benefit, is also available with rent payments for those with savings of less than £16,000, according to the home parent's income, the size of his family and the amount of his savings under £16,000. With only one adult in the household the home parent father will also be able to get a twenty-five per cent reduction in Council Tax, regardless of income, savings or number of dependant children, from his local authority simply by notifying it of his solitary status. Those on either Income Support or Family Credit can get free medical prescriptions, eye tests, dental treatment and some other NHS services and items for which a charge is usually made, as can all children under sixteen or under nineteen if in full-time education. Free school meals and help with buying school uniform also is available.

The lone parent who decides to remarry or live with a new mate will not only lose the right to Income Support if either of them works for more than sixteen hours a week, and to the single parent benefit, but will have to make himself available for work – lone parents do not have to – by 'signing on' at the local Job Centre for the Job Seekers Allowance (JSA)* (£37.90 a week for 18 to 24 year-olds, £47.90 for those 25 and over) which replaced unemployment benefit. Means-tested JSA is forfeited if more than 20 hours are worked. Applicants must sign a written agreement actively to seek work of 40 hours a week, retrain if necessary and attend the Job Centre for progress assessment once a fortnight. It is important to emphasise that *anyone* seeking work is entitled to the assistance and advice of the Job Centre whether they are receiving JSA or not. Lone parents may also be able to take work for less than 40 hours. After 13 weeks any job offered, even if not the applicant's usual occupation except in exceptional circumstances, must be accepted and after six months lower pay is no excuse for refusing one either.

Those with paid-up Class I National Insurance contributions get the full amount regardless of other income, such as building society interest, or savings, but get nothing for dependants. If the application is on grounds of financial need, income from other sources will be deducted from the benefit pound for pound. Payment in kind does not count as income, so a box of groceries may be a more valuable payment than cash for doing odd jobs. The JSA will be reduced by £1 per £250 for any savings between £3000 and £8000. Over £8000 in savings means no JSA. However, the back to work incentive is equally available to those on Income Support and those on JSA. After 91 days' unemployment, this provides those returning to full-time work with a lump sump, up to a maximum of £1000, equal to half any benefit deductions made because they had a part-time wage or other income.

*For detailed guidance see *JSA Handbook*, pub CPAG Ltd, 1-5 Bath St London.

The main disadvantage of JSA falls on those for whom attending the Job Centre once a fortnight would be costly or difficult. There is no contribution towards the cost of travelling to the Job Centre nor for child minding during absence from home, but if the absence would be for over four hours then fortnightly attendance may be waived by agreement. The 13-week advisory sessions are still obligatory unless total journey time is over eight hours. Although the applicant may be excused attendance for sickness of two periods a year of up to two weeks, no such allowance is made for caring for sick children. On balance it is highly unlikely that the lone parent will be better off on a Job Seekers Allowance than on ordinary Income Support, but it probably is worth a visit to the Job Centre to find out if this is true in each individual case. Unemployed men are also less likely than women to spend time on Income Support and forty-seven per cent have never been on. Those that have are slightly more likely to have been on it before they became lone parents in contrast to women who are much more likely to go on Income Support at the time of becoming a lone parent, thus seeming to confirm the notion that one of the reasons why a woman leaves a man is because he is not earning enough.

The critical thing with all benefits is to claim everything the home parent father is entitled to without shame and I reiterate the advice to consult the local authority Welfare Rights officers, the Citizens Advice Bureau, or a local Law Centre, to make sure this is done.

Again it might sound extravagant advice, but if a home parent father intends to work other than in conventional employment where PAYE and National Insurance are deducted at source and no or few expenses are allowable, he could well find that an hour (or even half an hour) costing him between £30 and £100 with a local accountant will save him many times that sum each year. There are so many variations in circumstances that only detailed advice can be sure of covering the individual case and ensuring that all a particular home father's advantages are secured for him. To provide comparisons between the relative financial attractions of working and living on benefits, here I shall give only three fairly typical examples (all are assumed to have no significant savings) based on cases in my survey.

Fred, aged 30, has one child aged three, one of six and one of eight. He works full time – 8.30 to 4.30 as a labourer in a jam factory Monday to Friday and earns £3 an hour – £112.50 a week before tax. He travels by bus which costs him £11 a week. His mum lives nearby and comes in to see the kids off to school in the morning, but she works part time as a school cleaner so he has to pay a minder £22 a week to look after the children until he picks them up at 5.30pm. Her charges are low for a registered child minder. He receives £33.60 Child Benefit and he receives Family Credit of £84.46. His ex, who lives on her own on Income Support, gives him £6 a week for the children. So he has in his pocket each week £203.56. His rent is £55 a week, but with Housing Benefit of £24.53 the net cost is £30.47. Council Tax, at seventy-five per cent of the normal rate after a rebate of £3.13 a week is £9.37. He sets aside £18 a week for all the household bills such as electricity (£9.00 a week on average), gas (£6.50 on average) and water rates (£2.50 a week). He cannot afford a car or a telephone, but he takes the children by bus at a cost of £5 to see their mother every Saturday. He is thus left with £140.72 a week to feed, clothe and provide extras and treats for himself and three children.

Jack is 35 and has two daughters aged eleven and thirteen and he works as a groundsman for the local parks department. He bicycles to work to save money. His wage before tax is £140 a week for a thirty-five hour week and he makes another £25 a week evenings and weekends jobbing gardening for the local nobs. A little doubtful about how discreet his patrons may be on such matters, he declares this income on his tax return. In addition to Child Benefit of £25.15, he also receives £48.19 in Family Credit. His net payments after tax from his earnings amount to £210.22. Out of this he pays £35 a week on his mortgage after tax relief at source, and £12.50 life insurance. He also pays a minder £25 a week to meet the girls off the school bus, give them tea and prepare the evening meal five days a week. Absurdly, he gets no relief for his child care costs because the children are over eleven. At weekends they either go with him to the nobs' houses or stay with their mother who has a well-paid job (£28,000 a year) that takes her away during the week. Because she lost the residence battle she refuses to have any contact with Jack and pays him nothing for looking after the children. The CSA has *still* not processed his maintenace application made two years ago. His Council Tax is £11.54 a week and gas, electricity and water rates cost him another £30 a week. He is left with £96.18 a week for everything else.

Ian, aged 45, has been a widower for seven years and has fifteen- year-old twin boys who attend the local high school. As a local radio announcer he earns £13,200 a year before tax, but as he has an understanding employer and colleagues usually works the 8.00 am to 3.00 pm shift five days a week so does not need help at home as the boys are old enough to see themselves off to school and to help around home and garden. Ian gets £25.15 Child Benefit a week and £11.80 Family Credit. After tax and National Insurance he has left in his pocket £12,042.16 a year, ie £1,003.51 a month (£231.58 a week). Out of this he pays £217 a month mortgage interest after tax relief at source and has a very pleasant home because a small but prudent life insurance on his wife reduced the capital debt. He pays £62.50 a month on a life policy for himself that will clear the balance of the mortgage when it matures and he contributes £50 a month to a company pension scheme, half of which is allowable against tax. His Council Tax is £800 a year against which he gets a credit of 23p a week! This, therefore, costs him £65.65 a month. Although the boys' education costs him nothing, school trips, music lessons, sports clubs and so on amount to £150 a month. He is thus left with £458.36 a month for running his home, and to feed and clothe the family, take holidays, have the occasional modest treat and run a rather ancient small car. Finance is tight, but manageable and certainly much easier than when he was first widowed on a lower salary and when the twins were too young to look after themselves. Although his mother-in-law helped with the children he had to use up all the family savings and work one night shift a week to make ends meet so now he feels he has just begun to surface and enjoy life. Because all three men are entitled to Family Credit they, like their children, also have the right to free prescriptions, dental treatment, travel to hospital, vouchers for glasses etc.

By comparison let us see what the three men would have to live on if they gave up work and claimed every benefit to which they were entitled, assuming that they were all to get their rent or mortgage interest paid through Housing Benefit or a mortgage interest addition to Income Support. It is worth emphasising that if any of them were ignorant of their entitlement to Family Credit and associated benefits they would be considerably worse off working than living on Income Support.

Income Support for the lone parent consists of a personal element, currently £46.50 a week, a family element (£10.25) a lone parent supplement (£5.20) and an amount for each dependant child according to its age. With typical complexity child benefit, CSA, court order or voluntary maintenance payments and any earnings above the £15 'disregard' are deducted from the Income Support thus calculated. To complicate matters still further, while rent will be met in full or in part (full in Fred's case) by Housing Benefit paid by the Local Authority mortgage interest (if allowed) is paid by an addition to Income Support. This element is calculated on a formula. If the mortgage and the benefit application were made before October 2nd 1995 then no help is given for the first eight weeks, half the interest is paid for weeks nine to twenty-six and all the interest thereafter. However, if the mortgage was taken out after October 2nd 1995 then no help is given for the first thirty-nine weeks and all the interest is paid thereafter – unless! Unless the lone parent has been left solely responsible for the mortgage payments by virtue of being widowed or abandoned, in which case the pre October 2nd formula applies!

In no circumstances are capital repayment elements or premiums for endowment policies, pensions etc designed to pay off the capital met by Income Support. What tortuous mind thinks up these schemes and who is to determine and with what appeal whether a man or woman has been abandoned or not? Anyway, let's take a look at our three examples – figures in square brackets are not actually paid because they are absorbed into the income support payment.

Benefits (weekly £)	*Fred*	*Jack*	*Ian*
Child Benefit	[33.60]	[25.15]	[25.15]
Housing Benefit	55.00	–	–
Mortgage Interest	–	35	50
Council Tax Benefit	12.50	11.54	15.15
Income Support	109.75	108.70	108.70
Maintenance from ex	[6.00]		
Disregarded Casual Earnings		15[10]	
TOTAL	177.25	170.24	173.85

All three men are just better off, financially, working provided they claim their Family Credit. They remain in the job market, and in Ian's case he is eligible for promotion as well. They also have the male self-esteem factor of being employed. Against this they have to set the quality of care their children are getting compared to what they really need at their particular ages and it is here that Fred may feel he should stay at home since he would be only some £5 a week worse off on Income Support provided that he can cope with the stress of being at home rather than having a job. Clearly his ex is already doing all she can for the children so there is no more to be got from that source. Indeed, if she stopped paying him altogether, but spent the money on, say, clothes or their bus fares, Fred would be no better off at work.

Jack certainly needs to pursue the CSA for maintenance from his ex for the children. He could decide whether or not to work depending on whether or not he is successful and how much he gets – if he has not died of old age while waiting. The applications of those working and not drawing benefits have not yet even begun to be processed, but absurdly if he gives up work his application will move up the queue. His decision will largely depend on his feelings about working and the quality of the care substitute he can get for the children, who are nearing an age where it is of less significance, since he is only about £3 a week worse off on benefits, though if he kept up his life insurance premiums as well he would then be £15.50 a week worse off.

Ian is almost certainly better off working particularly as the boys will soon have left home and he would be unable to afford the life insurance premiums he needs to pay to clear the mortgage in due course.

With a system as unjust, arbitrary, complicated and parsimonious as the one we have just described it is not surprising that the official DSS figure for benefit fraud rises each year. In 1993/4 it was £654 million, only one per cent of the social security budget and less than a third of unclaimed benefits, but still a large sum. Only ten per cent of this is accounted for by organised crime and of the seven thousand six hundred and forty-five people prosecuted I wonder how many were deliberately out to defraud the system and how many were just the ignorant victims of its Byzantine complexity. There are undoubtedly a great many more who knowingly cheat the system and get away with it, calculating that the risk of being caught and punished is preferable to trying to cope on the income provided by the benefits system. There are scroungers, and petty crooks taking the system for all they can get, but my investigations suggest that they are only a tiny proportion of the large number of lone parents who, knowingly or unknowingly, do not play strictly by the DSS rules. It is ironic, if unsurprising, that one of the worst groups for fraud is town hall and social service employees! It is all very well for the Labour Party spokesman to point a finger at means testing (about a third of all benefits are means tested) and suggest investigating hit squads to root out fraud, but he would do better to turn his attention to the poverty and confusion that drives people to cheat the system in the first place.

The greatest benefit any reforming government could bestow on single parents of both sexes would be to simplify the whole system and reconstruct it to ensure that every family has enough to live on without struggling to survive in poverty or feeling compelled to neglect their children in order to work to earn more. It would also need to improve the prospects of post-separation parental co-operation and other parent access by removing the disputatious element from financial settlements. Any couple who have children are tacitly entering into a mutual contract to share in and finance their upbringing within a state that wishes to protect children from the consequences of poverty. All three elements need to be accounted for in devising a simpler and fairer system.

Financial problems and the complexities of earning a living are important matters for the home parent but they are only a means to an end – how the home parent father can best soften the blow for his children of the death or desertion of their mother.

19

Softening the blow – preparing the children

Ninety-nine times out of a hundred children do not want their parents to separate however intolerable the two adults may feel it is to go on living together. Their resistance will be even stronger if one parent, usually the father, does not want the break up either.

A common conscience-easing excuse for divorce in recent years has been that it is better for parents to part than for children to live in a household racked by conflict. Though this is clearly the case where there is extreme physical violence or verbal abuse, the great bulk of the research indicates that children do not want their parents to part, are damaged by such partings, and go to considerable lengths in the early stages to get their parents together again. They resent the arrival of new partners because these constitute a demonstration that the missing parent is unlikely to come back. Such feelings will make a child angry, sad and depressed. (D1)

The potential home parent father trying to get residence must try not to lose sight of the fact that being forced to make choices between parents or be party to their mutual abuse seriously harms many children in the longer run. It may be some consolation to a father who feels he has been gravely wronged as he endures the pain of biting his tongue to know that children have a well-developed sense of justice and will, in due course, make some pretty shrewd judgements on the rights of the matter. They also retain the ability, which so many adults lose, to distinguish between a wrong and a wrong-doer, be furious about the former while continuing to love the latter.

Parents are sometimes understandably reluctant to talk to children about impending separation, but this may have negative repercussions later. Some even think that such a discussion would do more harm than good. Where separation is not planned and may be quite unexpected by one partner this is largely academic. Most children only find out after the event and have a very vague idea or understanding of what is going on, partly because the parents themselves are not always certain. A separation may not be thought to be final by the parents at first as there are often several attempts to 'get together again'. As a result, there may be many ad hoc and temporary solutions to problems about who pays for what and how and with whom the children spend their time. (F7) It is also surprising how many parents do not tell their children about the death of a spouse. They are more likely to get an explanation when a wife has left home. In one study (D1) about one fifth did not say anything. Explanations for departure ranged from those aimed at protecting the children's feelings to those where expressing hatred and contempt for the departed wife was the priority.

Children's reaction to the separation or impending separation of their parents or the death of one of them will differ in different circumstances and at different ages. Children under three do not really understand death, from three to five they see it as a temporary event and only at about seven do they begin to appreciate its finality and its causes. (D1) Whatever the children's ages their need to purge their burden of guilt and loss through grieving is as great as that of the adults most directly affected. They should be drawn into the process at the level appropriate to their understanding. If their mother has died then this can range from a three-or-four-year-old making a card or wreath for mummy to a mature teenager playing a major part in making funeral arrangements and organising and participating in whatever memorial ceremonies, religious or secular, the family chooses to formalise its recognition of death.

If mother has left, then children need to be involved in the discussions about the family's future plans, to feel that they have been genuinely consulted and that their views can influence the outcome. Whether bereavement is through death or separation they will experience a sudden shock of recognition that they do not entirely control their own lives and destinies. Only by full involvement in future plans can they begin to regain that feeling of general control, renewed self-confidence and zest for life and so replace the chaos and uncertainty that the loss of a loved, loving and protecting person creates. Deceiving them 'for their own good' seldom works, but rather adds to their doubts and fears, except in those few cases where the dead or departed parent demonstrably did *not* love her children or care for them but the children did not know it. Where the relationship has been exceptionally tempestuous, particularly where children have been witness to or victims of ungovernable exchanges of abusive rage or violence, the separation may come as a huge relief – as indeed it can for the home parent. But the children, too, may feel guilty or ashamed of that relief and will need to be helped to put it aside by open recognition of the appalling conduct of the departed parent. One of the inescapable lessons of life they have to absorb as they grow up is that there are some truly unpleasant and wicked people in the world and it does no-one any good to pretend otherwise. Great care must be taken, however, firstly to ensure that this verdict is not the subjective product of the father's own hurt, hatred or wounded pride and secondly that it is always expressed in terms critical of the conduct not the person – the association can be left to the child to make to whatever extent is necessary to its own emotional needs. When mother's (or father's) abuse, deceit or violence are the subject of conversation it is good to say plainly that these acts are bad in any circumstances and should be condemned. It is rarely, if ever, a good idea to say that mother (or father) is intrinsically wicked and should be condemned even where this remains the profound conviction of the deserted home parent or the ousted other parent. Indeed, if any plausible explanations, reasons or excuses for the wrong conduct can be offered they should be. The more mature the child the more quickly he or she will make up its own mind whether or not the excuse is valid.

If both parents can tell their children together that they intend to part then so much the better. In this case it is important to work out between them the terms in which they are going to explain both the reasons and the consequences of separation otherwise explanation is likely to degenerate into yet another argument. It is helpful for one parent to write out what he thinks should be said to his child and to discuss and revise this with the other. When this has been agreed as far as possible it should be told to the child by both of them together. In the emotion of the moment all may not go exactly to plan, however a plan provides a useful framework. If a mutually agreed explanation cannot be calmly given to the children then the parents must either take it in turns to tell their side of the story – a course fraught with danger – or, far better, get some third party loved and trusted by the child and reasonably impartial to explain in the first place what is going to happen. The parents can then both concentrate individually on assuring the child of their continuing love.

Most home parents are anxious that their children should understand the reasons and the rights and wrongs for the break-up of their parent's marriage and sympathise, if not necessarily endorse, his point of view. However, it is not a good idea for a home parent to try and state his case at the same time as he tells them of the break-up, or indeed for many months afterwards, when children will be angry, confused and unhappy and so far from receptive or sympathetic. A father's sense of justice may demand that his case be heard, but to keep inflicting the same rhetoric on children can be damaging to their self-image, and counterproductive. One way to resolve the dilemma is for the father to write down his version of events (being as objective as he can, but recognising that none of us can be totally objective!) and invite his ex to do the same. Anyone, and there are many, who finds it difficult to express himself in writing should not hesitate to ask a friend with a good command of written English to write this account for him. When both of the couple have finished, a copy of the two letters should be placed in a single envelope for each child and lodged with a bank or solicitor to be given to him or her when they reach the age of eighteen with a request to keep the information to themselves.

Keeping up as many of the children's established routines as possible can help stabilise the post break-up situation and relieve anxieties to some extent. So can frequent contact with friends and relatives, if necessary at the home parent's own home, so that the fear of disruption is not made worse. The dread of many younger children, from three or four years old until they are mature enough to understand a great deal more about the nature of adult conflict, is that having lost one parent they will lose the other. When one father (J11) was first left on his own he could not even go as far as the garden gate without careful advance explanation to his five-year-old of what he was about to do and how long it would take otherwise she would get into a tearful panic. This applied even when other loved and trusted adults were with her so at first he used to take her everywhere, even to business meetings where she would sit in a corner quietly and happily drawing or colouring while he talked shop. Most people accepted this necessity and accommodated her kindly. Her anxiety diminished steadily and after six or seven months she seemed to accept that dad was not going to disappear as well. Sticking as closely as practical to the customary pattern of family life may also be reassuring to grandparents (particularly in-laws) and other people who love the children and fear they may lose touch with them because of the break-up of the parents' relationship.

How the home parent handles the break-up will greatly influence the outcome for the children, so it is as well to be aware that research seems to indicate that for boys the most distressful element is the nature of the break-up while for girls it tends to be the fact of the break-up itself, although they are not entirely unaffected by the way it happens. (D1) Where the nature of the break up of the family determines the outcome for the children, this can range from virtually no difference when it is caused by death to quite severe damage when it is the result of violent and traumatic separation. But again, care must be taken to recognise that it is hard to decide to what extent subsequent behaviour and performance problems in the children are due to the flaws in the relationship before the actual break-up rather than to the break-up itself. The lesson is that the nearer to normality, from the child's point of view, the home parent can make the severed relationship with the other parent seem, the better the outcome for the child is likely to be.

The commitment to caring for their children themselves clearly meant much to most of the fathers in our survey, almost a third of whom volunteered the information, unprompted, that they thought it 'very worthwhile.' Here are just a few of their comments:-

Matthew: 'Totally satisfying because I know my children are being very well looked after and they live in a very stable environment. Being a single father is not an easy job, but you have to be strong for your children's sake, and do as much for them as you would living with their mother. Being a single father is a round the clock job but I would not change it for anything.' (M11)

Peter: 'I have enjoyed it – it was hard in the beginning because I was not terribly well myself mentally and emotionally, but I have developed a good close relationship with both girls and the last few years it has been very enjoyable. It was difficult because I did not know how to cook, I was not used to shopping on a regular basis, but I have learned and have enjoyed it.' (K15)

Bernard: 'It has its pluses mainly, you are your own boss, your money is your own (or very nearly), you have nobody to answer to. I have also got a lot of pleasure seeing my daughter growing up which I am very glad I did not miss out on.' (B12)

Christopher: 'I get a lot back from my children (most of the time!) and so this makes life easier.' (C12)

George: 'This has been one of the most rewarding jobs I could ever have done, albeit one of the hardest.' (S12)

Ieuan: 'I feel that I am doing well and that makes me feel good.' (S24)

Nigel: 'I take pride in my achievement as a single father bringing up children on my own. My children are my most treasured possession. I never thought that I could get so much self satisfaction by having and looking after children. My home may not be a model home,(but) I tell people that my house is a playground, a toy room, not just a home.' (S32)

Duncan: 'Being a single father is very hard work, physically and mentally more so when in full time employment, but the rewards are high – especially when my son comes up to me and says "I love you so much daddy".' (S26)

Not every father was able to see the positive side quite so clearly as these, but the minority who felt differently was a small one:-

Sam: 'Feelings? Bitter, isolated, discrimination, depression, total responsibility on my shoulders, anger, (for her sake as well as I still care for her) hatred, worry, stress, patronised, "women have managed for years" attitude, lonely, rejection, shunned and desperate. Being a single parent father was a difficult, lonely and thankless task. I don't have any outside assistance ie family or friends, so have to manage the home, kids and finances alone and I can easily become depressed when problems arise, as I feel totally isolated and that no-one is interested.' (S25)

Wilf: 'I do it very successfully to prove my competence ... I am unable to spend the time I want with my children. I am in the house but I am working until their bedtime. I hardly get a chance to talk to them or to help them with their homework properly. This makes us all very unhappy.' (W16)

Perhaps one of the widowers, Ian, and two of the separated

fathers, John and Thomas, best expressed the balanced, swings and roundabouts, assessment of the value of home parent fathering:-

'Life deals from the bottom of the pack. I balance the grief that I experience at the ... premature demise of my wife, with the much greater closeness I have with my sons. I just get on with it. It's my duty – and I love it.' (W15)

'Joy and despair mixed. Mostly joy and recognition that I am enjoying an experience which most fathers are denied – the daily nurture of my child. The despair comes from the knowledge that I had to opt out of my career at the height of my powers with intellect, imagination and energy in full spate because of the restriction of having to be at home at certain hours and the burdens of housework. It makes me feel very sympathetic towards the frustrations of women.' (J11)

'If you have no support at all from friends, relatives or whatever you have the hell of a job – not one that I would volunteer for. A big reward is that you most probably get to know your children for the first time.' (K12)

It is clear that in some cases the removal of the pre-separation stress caused by their parents' conflict and unhappiness may actually lead to improvements in children's behaviour. Lone parents should ask themselves if their children have behaviour problems because their parents are immature and uncommunicative rather than because they are divorced. Or is it that adults with the characteristics that make for poor parents are much more likely to divorce because those same characteristics are the ones which lead to unstable adult relationships? If the children are grumbling, or sulking or moody it may be because the lone parent is grumbling, sulky and moody. (B1) My research strongly suggests that parental attitude shapes child attitude; the happy, optimistic lone father usually has happy, optimistic children.

Two striking influences on the children with the best overall outcome emerged from my survey.

Firstly all the fathers of these children rated themselves as one hundred per cent happier than when they were living with their exes except one who was only seventy per cent happier and one who could not remember after eighteen years apart!

Secondly, *all* the children not only got on well with their fathers, but adopted equally extreme positions towards their mothers. Half of them were a hundred per cent more positive about their mothers than when the family was together, but a third of them were a hundred per cent more negative. A similar picture emerges from looking at the children with maximum scores on any of the four characteristics (happiness, health, behaviour and academic achievement) studied. Three-quarters of them felt a hundred per cent more positive about their dads but two thirds of them equally negative about their mothers. It should be emphasised that this was not a father-inspired response as there appears to be no relationship between the fathers' attitudes to the mothers and the children's. Here I should remind the reader of my reservation that I was unable to check fathers' assessments by a more objective yardstick so these remarkable figures may do no more than illustrate the reasonable supposition that happy fathers make optimistic assessments about their children. However, that would not account for the diametrically opposing views about their exes' relationships with their children these 'happy' men attribute to them. It seems much more likely to me that children like things to be clear cut, black or white, and that if they know where they stand – wherever that may be – they are the better for it. It is even more apparent that where the bond is close between father and child the child does well and that this bond is a more critical factor than is the relationship with the other parent mother.

I checked this supposition by asking the same questions about the children at the other end of the spectrum of well-being. The fifth of them who had the lowest overall scores for health, happiness, behaviour and academic performance were considered in the light of the same influences. The children of all but one of the widowers', who were uniformly unhappy, were in this group. They accounted for forty per cent of it though they make up only fifteen per cent of the population of the survey. Again there were some unexpected results. Only one father rated himself as completely happy and only two others gave themselves positive scores. Four registered maximum misery and overall these fathers' comparative happiness score was a depressing – 4.6 against the upper group fathers +9.6.

The children in the lower group got on with their fathers only a third as well as those in the upper one. The large proportion of widowers in this lower grouping makes a comparison with the higher group of children's relations with their mothers unreliable, but for what it is worth all but one had negative feelings about their mothers, many quite strong.

There is also considerable disparity between the two groups in the length of time the families have been run by lone fathers.

In the upper the average is seven years five months and in the lower two years seven months, if the family with sixteen years' lone fathering is excluded. This finding may carry the optimistic message for lone fathers that, generally speaking, things will get better and children become happier, more stable and achieve more as time passes. Even those who rate themselves badly on these counts can take some heart for three of the worst outcome children had siblings in the best group. Perhaps their fathers should have considered the advisability of letting the unhappy children live with their mother in some cases.

The most noticeable difference of all between the best and worst outcome groups of children is that in employment and occupational status – and it is not the difference right-wing critics like to think. Whereas in the better group forty-three point eight per cent had an unemployed father who was, therefore, presumably at home looking after them, only thirty-one point six per cent of the children in the lower group enjoyed this situation. In the upper group one third of the fathers were manual workers; in the lower none. Indeed, in the lower group fifty-seven per cent of the fathers were professional and managerial, thirty-six per cent skilled and seven per cent semi-skilled. It is hard to escape the conclusion that the fathers of the children who were doing well put their children first while of those in the lower group virtually all still largely put their jobs and careers before their children.

The loving and reasonably competent home parent father who minimises conflict with his ex and sees that she has plenty of contact with the children has already achieved the most important things for the well-being of his family, but there are other measures which can be taken to improve the outcome of separation or maternal death for them. Reactions to separation vary widely but it is surprising how short-lived the overt distress of children whose parents separate can be, particularly if both parents continue to have a loving and close relationship with them. What inner torments may still continue is often harder to establish, but the bulk of research shows that in all but a handful of cases the effects of divorce which persist into adulthood are probably only slight. (D1)

The home parent father can expect in his children the normal symptoms of bereavement, or loss – shock, numbness, disbelief about the death or parting, sadness, longing, anger and pain – that he is experiencing himself. Or the children may be feeling guilty that they are *not* reacting as expected or that they could not prevent the death or disaster or that they are alive and have survived it. Eating and sleeping patterns may be disturbed, concentration may become difficult and they may sometimes feel physically sick and exhausted or unwell. In this situation they need to be reassured that these feelings do not mean that they are going out of their minds or that when they forget about what has happened and become involved in their other activities they are doing anything wrong. Without burdening them with responsibility, they should be allowed to become involved in the practical consequences of what has happened so that they too can grieve and come to terms with it. Older children may find it helpful to talk to the family doctor or psychiatric nurse or to call the CRUSE bereavement helpline in the case of death.

Youngsters may bottle up their grief because they fear they will cause distress or not be understood, so may need help to realise that there is nothing wrong with crying and showing emotion. The home parent can perhaps do this by allowing his own grief to show, though he must be careful not to unload his burden onto their young shoulders. A hug is often all that is needed. It is not always easy for the lone father to support his child at a time when suffering great personal distress himself and he may need to find someone else to help in this process of comfort. A teacher, neighbour, friend who pops into the house a couple of times a week after school for a chat, a cup of tea and a laugh can do much to restore life to normal. Friendships made or strengthened in these circumstances can be invaluable to adults and children alike.

Outside supportive members of the immediate family and close friends, the surest ally for the home parent father of children over four or so should be their school. Here, in term time, a child will spend more waking hours each day than he does at home with a team of, usually, dedicated and caring professionals whose aim is the all round development of the children. School can be a useful means of liaison and contact with other sources of help for children and can often advise parents on how to go about getting the support they need. This may cover anything from financial assistance to psychiatric counselling.

One of the first things a home parent father should do on finding himself with the sole responsibility for his family is to let each child's head teacher and form teacher know that it has suffered the loss of its mother. The relevant members of staff will then know that they should both give that child additional support and make some allowance for poor behaviour and performance, while not allowing it to disrupt the lives of other children. The last thing a grieving child needs is the disapproval and reprimands of his teachers for the inevitable shortcomings that will arise out of such circumstances. This will only make him feel that the whole world is agin' him and does not care at a time when a little additional kindness from a role model can do much to heal the hurt. The communications will then become two way, with the teacher feeding back to the parent necessary information about the child beyond the normal exchanges of ordinary school life. The teacher will be able to give the parent a yardstick of the child's progress in relation to the average for its peers. If educational problems develop, as well they may for a while, then additional help, and if necessary, 'special needs' teaching can be provided. The home parent father must also be responsible for making sure that the school communicates fully in parallel with the other parent if she is still in contact with the children. Not only is it important for the child's sake that the other parent mother should not feel left out, but she still has a legal right to know.

There is sometimes prejudice against lone fathers in schools and one or two in my survey and others have reported hostility from individual teachers, but this is the exception and if it occurs should be reported at once to the head or a governor. Children now have other class members who are also single parent so they and their teachers are more aware and sensitive to these situations. However, unless they are already the friends of the home parent father it is probably better not to involve a child's teachers in the parent's own problems. By being child-focused and detached from the parent they can be seen by the child as an alternative source of comfort and counsel and it is children not adults that they have been trained specifically to deal with. School can so often be, in the right circumstances, a sanctuary for children either from the conflicts of antagonistic parents or from the disorder of a home parent father's early attempts to run a household. Incidentally, school dinners, mocked as they often are, can also provide a welcome and cost effective means of making sure that a child has at least one good meal a day for a father who is finding it difficult to cope.

Paradoxically, the much greater prevalence of disintegrated families and awareness of the problems of children from them itself carries a slight risk that teachers' expectations of such children may be lower and this in turn is likely to diminish their actual performance. Once an initial period for adjustment has passed, it is up to the home parent to see that this is not allowed to happen by discussing both the family's situation and the individual child's performance frankly with the teacher. In this context girls seem to adapt to their new circumstances in much less time than boys. (M2)

About two-thirds of children experiencing the death or defection of a parent will show a drop in their work standard, inability to concentrate, day-dreaming and so on, some of them become sad and depressed, others aggressive and disobedient. These moods and behaviour changes will inevitably disrupt their friendships with their peers, who usually don't understand the cause of them, and that in turn will make the child feel even more isolated and depressed. Even when they have plenty of friends they will often say that nobody likes them, that they are stupid and so on, even when they are doing well. This is when they need the reassurance of praise, but not unrealistic or exaggerated praise which they will know to be false. The home parent father can do a lot to make sure that his children's friendships continue to be cultivated by having their friends round to his house and by doing things with them. With younger children specially it is a good idea to invite the mothers also to reassure them about the home parent father's competence and trustworthiness.

Good peer group relations are even more important in the single parent family since there are no in-family safety valves for the inevitable tensions between parent and child. Peer group relations in these circumstances may change in character and the unhappy child of the lone parent becomes, because of its very vulnerability, a tempting target for bullying. The signs of such victimisation can usually be spotted early by the child's parent if they have not already been picked up by a teacher.

Bullying takes many forms, so the evidence of it may be cuts and bruises, broken possessions or a child apparently continually losing money. Some may not want to go to school or work, lose interest in outside activities, become tearful, jumpy, depressed or anguished. Some turn to drugs, some may even attempt suicide. Bullying needs to be taken seriously and the child needs to see that the parent is doing so. The home parent should involve school or employer and if necessary the parents of the bully, or bullies for gang bullying which is the commonest form. Because bullying needs to be dealt with promptly it should be reported as soon as recognised to the head teacher (or employer if the youngster is already at work, where as much bullying takes place as in schools). The child itself is unlikely to complain directly for fear that 'sneaking' will be added to its list of defects by the other children and its life made even more unbearable by the bullies. However, serious adult intervention is usually enough to warn off the bully and no head wants such behaviour in their school. An appeal to the chivalrous instincts of one or two of the ringleaders – usually, but by no means always, boys – may also bring about a change of heart. Nor should the home parent father overlook the possibility of the not uncommon phenomenon of sibling bullying and if it arises should intervene sharply to put a stop to it. In the lone parent family it is even more important than in the intact family not to show undue favour or disfavour to an individual child except on special occasions or in special circumstances. Hardest of all, the home parent may have to face up to the possibility that his child is the bully not the victim. He or she will still need love and support. Unhappiness and inability to cope with life can often be compensated for by taking it out on others and the bully is in as much need of help as the bullied, though a lot less likely to get much sympathy. The organisation Kidscape is a good source of advice and help over bullying.

It would be exceptional if, after losing their mother through death or her defection, children were not disturbed, depressed, unhappy, and badly behaved, at least for a while. The lone father, struggling with his own emotional problems, can console himself that in ninety-nine cases out of a hundred he and his offspring will not only survive but flourish once more.

20

Children in trouble

Children will usually have emerged from the obvious traumatic effects of parental separation within two or three years. This can seem a long time to a worried home parent father and even longer to his child, but is not unusual. There is some evidence that the long-term (delayed) effects of bereavement may be greatest in children whose parent died when they were toddlers. It is not known whether there is any specific period during the first five years when the susceptibility to stress is particularly great. (M1) Because children are afraid of losing their other parent it is necessary to recognise that what had previously been quite routine separations, like going to school or to bed, can become times of considerable anxiety. This type of emotional disturbance, even in older children, can result in regression and immature behaviour as the child reverts to conduct prior to the break-up. Again, the regressive behaviour should be relatively short lived if the home parent father is providing a secure, affectionate and stable home.

After separation many children show quite marked physical symptoms. Long bouts, two or three days at a time, of frequent and severe vomiting and stomach ache with a dull headache which appear to have no physical cause are not uncommon. They entail having to nurse the child and concentrate on it very closely for that time and thus allay the child's fear of losing the attention or presence of its remaining parent. These very real physical symptoms, which cause child and parent equally real distress, may last on and off for as much as three or four years, but should gradually decrease in severity and frequency as security returns. It is particularly difficult for the lone parent, with no-one with whom to discuss symptoms or to reassure him, to decide just how ill a child may be – symptoms always seem to be worst in the middle of the night when a false alarm would be at its most embarrassing. Most GPs are understanding about such anxieties and prefer to be consulted early on than run the risk of overlooking a serious physical cause. They clearly recognise an important part of their function as being parent calming as well as child curing! However, they do not always make it sufficiently clear that the disorders are probably psychosomatic and what preventive measures are necessary as far as they are practicable. I suspect this to be a general shortcoming of hard-pressed, time-short doctors.

With teenagers the problems can seem even more traumatic and at their worst involve drink, drugs, smoking, under age sex, vandalism, crime and other anti-social behaviour. Where these occur they are often no more than brief deviations on the route to a child becoming a responsible social being and are usually short lived. The most common experimental deviations are with drink, drugs and smoking. To see teenage children through the process of coming to sensible terms with these potential addictions it is first necessary to be informed about them, their effects and consequences and to have a clear idea where the parent himself stands in relation to their use by himself or his children. The home parent father is very likely to drink alcohol, possibly to smoke* and even to use drugs so what does he intend to do by way of example? Is he prepared to modify his own use to conform to his idea of what is appropriate for his son or daughter? If he is not, prohibitions and dire warnings about the consequences of abuse are unlikely to have much effect.

In many families the children may learn to handle drink in a social context in small quantities when they are still relatively young so that it does not become an obsession when they are older. Solitary drinking really is a problem, but cannot usually be concealed for very long. The signs to look for are unexplained bottles and cans about the house, or a child who feels constantly tired, has headaches, stomach pains, mood swings, aggression, or loss of interest in life generally. Again, if a child is always broke and money, and even household items, frequently mysteriously disappear there may be a drink (or drugs) problem. If confronted a child may be very unwilling to discuss the issue or truculently assert its right to drink or take drugs when and where it wants. If any of these situations arise, help should be sought immediately either through the local authority drugs and alcohol abuse unit, (in the telephone book under the Local Health Authority) or from one of the charities specialising in these problems. Details of the leading ones are in Appendix One.

*The Easy Way to Stop Smoking by Allen Carr gives adolescents a clear picture of the consequences of smoking without scaremongering

Drugs can present an even greater problem than drink for a number of reasons. Parents, particularly older parents, are far less likely to have any personal experience of them, so are much less likely to recognise the signs of their use or appreciate the effects and attractions they can have. The use of alcohol or tobacco by those under the age of eighteen and sixteen respectively is not itself illegal. Under those ages, selling, or giving them to children, other than on private premises, is. The use of drugs and their possession is illegal, thus carrying the possibility not only of embroiling the youngster with the law, but also drawing him (or slightly less frequently her) into the criminal world of drug pushing and the other crimes necessary to finance a drug habit. The risk starts much earlier than many parents realise with drug pushers seeing school playgrounds and the after-school routes home, even at primary schools, as prime target areas. Many drugs, possibly even cannabis it seems now, can cause serious physical and mental damage and involve other serious health risks, such as contamination with HIV or hepatic viruses through the use of shared needles. Perhaps even more difficult to counter than the serious and not infrequently fatal health problems caused by drug taking is the fact that the drugs scene is part of the new sub-culture of the young which has in the past decade or so grown into a detached world almost unrelated to the adult world and impossible for anyone over twenty-five to communicate with. This is a dangerous and socially destabilising phenomenon of which little notice is yet being taken, but, as it comes to engulf more and more children in its dangerous ethos, may have to be treated as a threat to society no less grave than epidemics such as AIDS.

A problem child in a family can, if the home parent is not careful, divert a disproportionate amount of his precious attention to the detriment of the other children. It is very hard to take a balanced view and act rationally when there is no-one to share the load with and neighbours and other parents may be pointing the finger and saying 'There! That's what happens when fathers bring up their children'. The answer is for the lone parent to trust his own judgement and not worry that others may think that he is making too much – or too little – fuss.

Because the anti-social public conduct of teenagers and even pre-adolescents can so often impinge disconcertingly on the life of a home parent who is a law-abiding and responsible citizen it can obscure the no less significant, and from teenager and parent point of view equally destructive, private signs of a child's inner problems. Deceit, rudeness, petty theft, destructiveness and fighting, singly or in various combinations, are common among adolescents and among older pre-adolescent children either as they identify with or are influenced by their peers and those a little older than themselves or in self-assertive rebellion against their parents, teachers or others in authority. Indeed, it is arguable that without some self-assertion, even if only in a minor way, adolescents are unlikely to develop independence, self-confidence and their own personal identity in adulthood.

Most home parents find their children more demanding, aggressive and angry after divorce, but the great majority also find that their own relationship with them improves and that in doing so it alleviates the problems of the children themselves. That is not to say that anti-social conduct of any kind should be condoned or ignored in the hope that it will just go away. It may simply pass, but if resolved in this passive way will then have failed in its underlying subconscious purpose as a distress signal. Acquiescence will also leave the impression in the child's mind either that such behaviour is not reprehensible in itself or that the parent in question does not care about the child.

'Why did you do that?' 'What's the problem?' Tactfully timed and phrased questions of this kind will often elicit tears, confessions and confusion, as much from relief at being able to talk about the problem as from shame. Sometimes direct questions can be counter-productive and this is hard to anticipate. An angry response is usually a signal that it is best not to press them – at least for the time being. Patient attention to a rambling and apparently irrelevant narrative may be the only way to find out what the problem is. Once established, the threefold response needs to be love, understanding and condemnation of the conduct – in that order! The first needs to be overtly expressed more often than many parents realise and sometimes in the face of apparent rejection of both words and gestures of affection. Though a child may seem to reject them at the time, he or she may find the fact that such gestures were made comforting in retrospect.

The second can be very hard to achieve. To understand an adolescent – or indeed a child – it is necessary firstly to listen very carefully to what they are actually saying, without comment, question or interruption except where this is clearly invited or required, however halting and inarticulate the expression of the ideas may be and however absurd they may seem. It is a great temptation from the vantage point of greater age and experience to intervene, to impose conclusions, to interrupt and fill the groping pauses in the narrative. This not only indicates that the adult is not truly listening at all levels, but can undermine the trust and confidence of the adolescent and infuriate him or her as well. After a sequence of such experiences they may very well cease to try and communicate with the parent at all. Nothing makes a child more cross than the common adult habit of finishing off sentences, often incorrectly, when it gropes for words. 'Shut up and *listen*, dad!' the child may quite rightly say and the adult should learn to apologise and 'shut up' – most of the time. A good home parent listener will enable his child to talk to him about *nearly* anything and everything at any time. What last secrets remain locked in anyone's mind we can never know nor should we wish to do so if we do not want them to be mere shadows of ourselves. It is a good idea sometimes to listen to oneself when talking to a child as well, on a tape recorder if necessary, in order to analyse from the subcarrier of tone and pitch the underlying message the child is getting together with the one our words are supposed to convey. 'Don't shout at me, dad' may seem an odd response to a request or prohibition voiced at perfectly normal volume, but the child is picking up that suppressed shout*.

The third element of response is a tricky one as it requires a clearly expressed distinction between care for the child and condemnation of the conduct. Outright negation is not enough. What is needed is an explanation why the behaviour is wrong, hurtful to those near and dear, and ultimately self-destructive, given at the same time as the categoric and unequivocal prohibition the child is usually silently looking for. Only in those very rare cases where a child turns out to be genuinely amoral will this triple approach not have at least some long-term effect.

It is easy and understandable to be made very angry by much teenage anti-social, anti-familial behaviour and hard to resist the temptation to shout or even hit back. It does not hurt an adolescent, or a child, to learn that its parent can be hurt, provoked, angry or even be unfair and unreasonable at times, in other words that he or she is a fallible human being. However, the lesson is best learned if taught within the bounds of reason.

*I quote and am grateful to my daughter Emily for these insights.

Certainly physical violence (other, perhaps, than a spontaneous sharp slap to a small child not yet capable of reasoned argument) achieves quite the opposite result. There is a kind of Newtonian third law of psychological motion 'every (wrongful) action has an equal and opposite reaction'. There is substantial research evidence to show that teenagers convicted of various crimes had been beaten or smacked more often than their unconvicted peers. (F8). This may not be a case of cause and effect, but it is a strong enough possibility to bear in mind and enough to justify standing the old adage on its head and concluding 'apply the rod and spoil the child'.

A lone father must also be frank with his children, but in language appropriate to the state of their understanding and age. If he does not tell them the truth they will cease to trust him and may find this more distressing than dealing with a situation, however embarrassing and difficult, openly and honestly. These exchanges are not one dose cures, but a continuing course of treatment!

Sex is a particularly important area about which to keep lines of communication open with children from a very early age if they are to be able to confide in their home parent when it matters. Many children are reluctant to admit that they don't know some things relating to sex and it is up to both parents, even when separated, to ensure that they do know the facts at an appropriate age (usually much younger than one thinks these days) about contraception, pregnancy, sexually transmitted disease and, most importantly of all, the emotional implications of sexual relationships. If they are likely to be sexually active they should see their doctor or a family planning centre which, as well as providing contraceptives, can also help them with other problems related to their sex lives. Both NHS and reputable private family planning centres (see Appendix One) are staffed by professionals whose role is to give practical advice and help, not to make moral judgements – though these may not necessarily be a bad thing. There is no substitute on the emotional and moral side for a well-informed parent in whom a child has sufficient trust and confidence to discuss any personal problem whatsoever.

All these tribulations will probably pass quite quickly, but if they do not then, without rising to the bait by losing his temper or bursting into tears, the home parent must lay down the rules firmly and confidently. If the problem continues or gets particularly serious he may be able to get advice and help, at quite short notice and without saying who he is if he does not wish to, from the duty officer at his local social services department or probation service. The anxiety for many single fathers about this approach is the fear that they will be considered unable to cope and that their children may be taken into Local Authority care. The anonymity of the 'phone call can guard against this provided the caller dials 141 before calling the number to prevent a 1471 number check back.

Two teenage cries for help in particular can either be indicative of a serious problem with drink or drugs or an equally serious underlying psychological problem; running away and attempting suicide, or threatening to do either of these things. Both should be taken seriously. The trend for suicide in Great Britain and Northern Ireland has been down in the last few years after rising for more than a decade, but it still accounted for the lives of 97 males under the age of twenty (seven under 14) and 26 females (three under 14) in 1995. (OPCS) It also has to be remembered that only indisputable suicides are recorded as such and others may be classified as accidental death.

In 1994/5 some ten thousand children under sixteen, the legal age for leaving home, were reported (C9) as running away, ie being away from home without parental permission for a twenty-four hour period or more. A great many more are not reported because they return home within twenty-four hours, nevertheless their breaking away should ring alarm bells.

If a child of any age runs away, however briefly, so great is the relief when it returns that the home parent all too readily closes his eyes to what may have been the underlying cause until the child does it again – and by then it may be too late. Running away must be treated seriously the very first time it happens. Even if it is only threatened it must not be ignored. If a home parent fears that his child may have run away – and the younger the child the less leeway there should be before a late return triggers action – the first thing to do is check with all the obvious people who know where the child might be; the other parent (most likely if living nearby) relatives, parents of best friends, neighbours. If that draws a blank the police should be called. They would much rather be set on the trail quickly and find it a false alarm than have undue delay put a child's safety and even its life at risk. If children are under sixteen the police will bring them home when they find them unless they would be in danger, from a violent parent for example. If they are over sixteen they cannot be forced to return though the parent with residence will always be informed that they have been found. Some teenagers over sixteen do not want to come home, but do want to let their parents know they are safe. They can do this through the Missing Persons Bureau with which parents should keep in touch if their children have been missing for some time. (See Appendix One)

Suicide is an extreme form of running away and any mention of it, however jokingly, needs to be taken seriously. The way the topic is raised should give the home parent an indication of the best mode in which to deal with it. The more lightly or obliquely the subject is raised the more acutely the parent will have to listen to the underlying messages in what is being said. Even if the parental overtures and sympathetic enquiries are brusquely, even angrily, rebuffed the very fact that they have been made will reassure the youngster that his parent cares. If the home parent remains worried he should contact the Samaritans for advice and in the case of older teenagers even suggest, directly or indirectly, that they might like to get in touch themselves. Samaritans listen, rather than advise, but Childline and Kidscape do give advice. For longer term help there are youth counselling advice and information centres for youngsters between the ages of thirteen and twenty-five in many areas and contact can be made with them through a GP or Citizens Advice Bureau. A list of other helpful organisations and publications will be found in Appendix One. The threats and dark hints about suicide may be no more than attention seeking, but they may be because the future seems too bleak to enter or it may be that the young person can only see death as the way out of some crisis – pregnancy, debt, drug addiction, a criminal offence, discovering their own homosexuality or even that most devastating of teenage experiences, their first broken heart. The parent who has kept open good lines of communication and a loving heart can usually show another escape route. Lone parents need to be extra sensitive to these problems and supportive of their children who may have already experienced a sense of failure and rejection as a result of the break-down of their parents' relationship.

If suicide is actually attempted it is usually by drugs overdose. If this is suspected the child should be taken without delay to the nearest hospital casualty department – if there is one left within reasonable distance from you – or an ambulance should be called. Some drugs can cause serious damage to vital organs even without loss of consciousness so urgent treatment is still required. Giving the casualty department doctor or ambulance personnel the bottles or boxes of any drugs you think have been taken, complete with their residual contents, will help the hospital identify the nature and quantity of the drugs involved and so speed up treatment. Unless the home parent knows exactly what and how much has been taken and has been appropriately trained he should not attempt on the spot emergency treatment in most circumstances, but get the child into professional hands as quickly as possible. Inducing vomiting, for example, is not always the best emergency treatment though it often can be. If it is likely to take more than a few minutes for the ambulance to arrive, a telephone call, once it has been summoned, to the local GP or hospital may provide guidance provided the parent is quite certain what has been taken.

When the immediate emergency has been dealt with the first priority is to prevent a recurrence – second attempts at suicide usually follow closely on the heels of the first. Through the family GP the support of a psychiatric team can be enrolled after a suicide attempt. It is critical that the child is not left to cope with the same situation that caused the problem in the first place. Sensible but not paranoid precautions, such as securely locking away all dangerous medicines and edged weapons, can be taken, but nothing can prevent the determined suicide except to remove the reasons for the desire to die. That will depend very largely on how sensitive, loving and dedicated a home parent the child has – male or female.

21

Am I good for them?

There is no evidence to prove that with children over the age of two single mothers will generally make any better lone parents than single fathers or that their children will do better than those of lone fathers in any respect. The most significant ingredient in determining the future development of the child of a single parent is the character and ability of the parent.

While few fathers are likely to want to return their children to an ex there will be times when they find themselves at least considering it: sheer exhaustion, the feeling that the struggle is hopeless to prevent them adopting their mother's bad habits, repugnant beliefs or morality, frustration at not being able to devote more energy to work or to get work at all, poverty and practical ineptitude can all engender depression, despair and thoughts of surrender. Whatever the temptations the one thing calculated to do real harm to the children would be to hand them over for any of these reasons. They would see it as a second and worse betrayal than when their mother left.

Plagued by guilt, a father may feel that he is no longer providing the best possible care for his children and that their mother or some other female relative might do better. It is unlikely that she would and a father would have to be convinced beyond doubt, and indeed have detached, and probably professional, third parties convinced beyond doubt, of the necessity for such a change to justify it. But there are a few circumstances in which it might be the right course of action in the children's interest. Where a father becomes physically or mentally incapable of effective caring, where conflict with a teenage child has gone far beyond normal adolescent rebellion, or where a child consistently expresses a desperate longing to live with the other parent (rather than just using the idea as a threat in the family power struggle) then a change of residence *may* be appropriate. If a father genuinely concludes that it is better for his children to be transferred to the care of their mother, in parting with them he will be doing perhaps the hardest and most unselfish thing he has done in his life – particularly if his ex is still hostile to him. Such a decision should be made as the result of a three way negotiation between father, mother and child in which the older the child the more it sets the agenda and guides the decisions. The presence of a sympathetic friend or professional counsellor during such negotiation may prove helpful to everyone, and the father may well also need help afterwards in what is in effect another bereavement, particularly if his ex lives far away and he is unlikely often, or even ever, to see his child again. However, if the decision was taken in consultation with the child, to meet the child's needs and wishes and in its obvious best interest, the chances are that the close bond established while lone parenting will remain and contact be maintained.

Rather than a change of residence it is much more likely that what is required is a greater willingness by the father to share the burdens of parenting, ideally with his ex if that is feasible, otherwise with such family, friends and neighbours as are willing and able to take on some of the duties. A genuine break from the cares of children and home may be all that is needed to regenerate enthusiasm and energy for home parents. Once the children have been made secure in the knowledge that their home parent father is permanent and reliable, probably after about two or three years, a short holiday without them may be all that is needed for complete rejuvenation. The children's pleasure in his return will also do wonders for his self esteem.

There is no escaping the *general* truth of Professor Halsey's dictum that 'while there is no utopia in intact families, nor is there evidence to contradict the poor average outcome of children who have experienced family disruption and lone parenthood by comparison'. (QLP1) In the run up and process of divorce children do usually show disturbed behaviour and for some time afterwards. School work falls off and the setback this gives means that the children are likely to leave earlier and less well-qualified and with fewer opportunities for higher education. The children of divorces are slightly more likely to have less well-regarded jobs, lower earnings, earlier marriage and divorce and increased frequency of psychological and psychiatric problems. I emphasise the very general nature of the poorer outcome for lone parent children for two reasons; firstly the average outcome is only *slightly* worse and secondly it need not necessarily be so. It is natural for the single father constantly to ask himself: 'Is my child in good health, properly nourished, clothed and housed, being well educated and socially integrated and growing up a happy, responsible and normal person?' Reasonable questions, apart from the fact that there is no such thing as a normal child or, rather, that the acceptable range of normality, so called, is very wide indeed and embraces the great majority of lone parents' children.

Most lone fathers worry about the impact of the break-up on their children and whether its consequences will be permanent. It is necessary to face up to the fact that they may, although they are unlikely to be as serious as the father fears and may be much preferable to the alternative of the children being brought up by their mother. Unfortunately, it is not possible to test the alternative so it is a necessary act of faith for fathers to believe they will make the better carer if they are to fulfil their responsibility for bringing up their children effectively. Care and anxiety are inseparable from being a good father, and doubly so from being a good single father, yet excessive worry makes a poor parent. The surest guideline is to follow instinct, to do what love and common sense dictate.

The most obvious evidence of a child's progress and normality, or otherwise, is its behaviour, so we will look first at the patterns of conduct likely to follow the death or desertion of its mother, how these should change and what can be done to help them develop along constructive lines.

When a child behaves antisocially, self-destructively or even in a criminal way, when it suffers from ill health or appears backward in school the instant and natural reaction of the lone parent is to presume he or she has fallen down on the job, is a failure as a parent. This is seldom true and by taking the right remedial action (or inaction) the adverse tendency can usually be reversed fairly soon. Research (F7) suggests that while the long-term damage from divorce is a matter of concern it affects only a minority of children and that children's responses vary very greatly. The lone parent may reassure himself on several counts. Firstly that in problem children there has been a substantial contribution from pre-divorce tension and not necessarily from the presumed effects of the divorce itself. (F7) Secondly, although not all children show persistent effects, early *paternal* deprivation also has a significant influence on a child's personality development. (F1) Thirdly, low father participation in a child's life appears to have some link with adult crime. (F8) And finally, 'A comparison of children's behaviour in lone father and married father families showed no significant differences, except a slight tendency for more lone than married fathers to describe their children as having difficulties in peer relationships. (F11) The home parent father may justifiably reassure himself that any difficulties his child is experiencing would have been as great – possibly greater – if its mother alone was bringing it up.

It may be deduced that the loss of a father probably has a greater influence and can do more damage (F5) than the maternal deprivation so frequently studied. I read of one moving example in which 'one child spent his time rocking in his chair listening to records his father had left behind and making repeated efforts to contact him on the toy telephone'. (D2) Arguably, the home parent father's child has the better option.

Nor should the initial effect of purely material changes be overlooked. There is usually a drop in living standards, often a change in house and home, sometimes of school and friends. Children get a sense of powerlessness from the way the shape of their lives is determined by the events surrounding divorce and separation. Because these unpleasant experiences are at the hands of the people they look to for stability and support they can become angry and distressed. This is particularly true if they are not given a clear picture of what is going on. Children can get a very distorted idea of what is happening in a parental break-up and need opportunities to talk about their fears and fantasies in order to exorcise them. The younger the children the more likely they are to experience the difficulties and in a way the more difficult it will be to explain things to them both in language and concepts which they can grasp and accept. Symptoms of this disturbance in younger children are clinging behaviour, fear of the dark and a whole chain of excuses for not going to bed or to nursery school or panicking when the parent is out of sight. At this age children believe that their relationships are permanent and indestructible. When this suddenly proves not to be the case everything becomes uncertain. A stable and predictable pattern of living will gradually dispel these fears in most cases.

Family life can become disorganised and unpredictable as father learns to cope, practically as well as emotionally. His emotional and behavioural self control and consistency of life patterns are the key to re-stabilising the children's lives, but these take time to achieve and in the meanwhile most children will show some signs of disturbed behaviour. It is easy to exaggerate these, but if children show signs of behavioural problems the home parent father should think back to when he and his ex were together and it was obvious to the children that there was conflict between them. What were behaviour patterns then and do the present ones differ in either kind or degree from that?

As with most conditions the hardest thing is diagnosis. What is abnormal, disturbed, delinquent and so on? With teenagers particularly it is 'difficult to decide whether a young person's moods and behaviour are simply normal reactions to everyday stresses and new feelings and situations or signs that things are going wrong.' (YP1) At different stages of development children behave in different ways so it is easy for an over-anxious parent to confuse natural, age-related behaviour with abnormal behaviour if they have never had any intimate experience of these changes before. Moreover, the dividing line between ordinary problems and disturbed behaviour can be a thin one. If there is a mental health problem it certainly needs to be dealt with early, but it is possible to provoke the very thing feared by premature and excessive reaction to the ordinary displays of temperament that are part of the process of maturing. Broadly speaking there are three indicators that there is something affecting a child which calls for professional advice and help. If there is a combination of several kinds of extreme behaviour, if the behaviour persists unremittingly for some length of time and if the child is failing to cope with other areas of life such as school work, peer, parent and sibling relationships, or eating and sleeping either excessively or too little.

Very small children when distressed may resume infantile behaviour which they had left behind such as bed wetting, thumb sucking, temper tantrums and so on. Because small children are exploring and developing their means of communicating, especially language, they will often say things randomly, inconsequentially and on the spur of the moment so individual instances of bizarre or unusual comment need not be taken too seriously. As with other signs, it is the persistence and the range of out of ordinary remarks that gives the warning, but oddity is as likely to be a sign of exceptional talent as of a problem. Smaller children will often find it difficult to put into words what is troubling them. If they like to draw or paint asking them to make a picture of what is the matter can enable them to express themselves. A dramatic or frightening drawing may quickly identify a problem the child does not have the vocabulary or verbalising skill – or the courage – to put into words. When they are a little older the stress will be manifest in bad behaviour at school (and much poorer than usual work standards, though this can be a warning sign at any age) and unwonted aggression against play fellows and classmates and even hitherto favoured teachers. Nor are siblings and parents exempt. (M1/D1) The wounds of maternal loss often reopen again when an older sibling leaves home more or less permanently for college, work or marriage.

It is easier for children to handle stresses one or two at a time. So as long as they are growing up in some areas there is no need to worry too much about others. They will come right later. Growing up too slowly or persistent all round clinging to childhood may indicate a problem as can maturing too rapidly. Young girls particularly can look more grown up than they are or feel and it is easy to assume mistakenly that the child who seems to be reacting well is the one who expresses little anger or disturbance. In fact, this may be the very opposite of the truth. (D1) In some respects children of divided families are much more mature than the average for their age. While this is gratifying and helpful in many ways it can tempt a lone parent into treating them as more grown up than they are and asking too much of them. There is no denying, however, that divided homes usually make for adaptable children who soon develop gifts of tact and diplomacy which will stand them in good stead in later life.

22

Father and child

One or two studies have implied that a child is better off living with its lone parent of the same sex than with the opposite sex parent. 'Boys who lived with their fathers were more mature and more sociable and displayed higher levels of self-esteem than boys who were in their mother's custody. For girls the opposite was the case: they were less demanding, more independent and more mature when in the custody of their mothers. Girls who lived with their fathers were seen as less co-operative and less honest than in their mother's custody. Similarly the boys in paternal custody were more honest and more co-operative than the boys in maternal custody.' (F7/F9) Other research (F12) indicates higher levels of anxiety in females reared by a single father whereas the rate of delinquency for boys is lower than that for boys in single mother homes. If true, this suggests that half of all one parent families ought to be father-led not just eight per cent. However, perhaps all this just begs the question; are we perpetuating gender stereotypes by assigning *expected* characteristics to them? We should not forget that gender roles are in a state of flux for boys and girls as well as for adults and that the differences in behaviour from stereotypes are just differences not necessarily deviations or perversions or indicators of disturbed personalities. The population of lone father families and the amount of research on them is still too small for any certain conclusions to be drawn. More recent studies suggest that today the outcomes for children related to gender alone do not greatly differ. Any sample studied must be careful to allow for the bias due to the fact that a significant proportion of current single fathers find themselves in that role because desertion or drug and alcohol abuse by the mother have thrust it upon them.* The children of such mothers are likely to show disturbed behaviour regardless of other factors such as fathercare.

It seems to me, on the basis of personal observation and experience as well as *some* research referred to at the start of

*But only 11.5% in my survey.

this chapter, that the reverse of such conclusions may equally well be true. In many respects there is a stronger bond between parent and child of the opposite sex because they are not quasi-sexual rivals for the attention of a third party. However, same sex bonds may grow stronger as the child grows older and seeks a role model for its maturing adult self. For balanced sexual development and the cultivation of social skills with both same sex and opposite sex peers the influence of both parents produces the best results. At puberty, therefore, close, prolonged and frequent contact with the other parent, or a substitute of the same sex as the child, for whom it feels affection and respect, is important for the daughters of home parent fathers – as it is for the sons of home parent mothers. For lone parents of either sex who have not found a new mate the absence of this balancing factor needs to be compensated for.

At puberty the physical changes are usually very apparent, though the rate and timescale at which they occur differs greatly and can start as early as ten or eleven or as late as sixteen.

The invisible emotional changes that stem from the physical are in many ways more important for the home parent father/child relationship though perhaps child is scarcely an appropriate, if legally correct, term any more. Girls at the menarche, the onset of their first period, have a watershed between receding childhood and imminent adulthood, which marks a more decisive transition than is experienced by boys. It can quite significantly affect their relationships with their fathers, more so if the father is a lone parent. The menarche puts them into the same camp as their absent other parent mothers and because it means that they can now conceive and bear children draws attention to the sexual difference with their fathers – males with the potential to fertilise. Both parties have to learn to develop a new relationship in which control and deliberate flirting on the one hand and controlled response on the other play a significant part. 'The father may feel threatened by the onset of his daughter's puberty and he may become angry and restrictive with her. The girl, frustrated and disappointed by her father's treatment, may flout his authority and 'act out' through sexual behaviour.' (F5)

With boys, the capacity to beget children gives them access to an adult male set of interests, indeed preoccupations, which can enable them to identify even more closely with their fathers and develop that specifically male camaraderie which begins when little boys like to watch and help their fathers do things – and the fathers encourage their presence – and culminates in the self-sacrificing intensity of the relationship network of a sports team or a military unit. In such circumstances men usually subordinate personal considerations to a common cause in a way most women seem to find quite alien.

At puberty children become very sensitive so parents must be tactful about any teasing and keep off topics connected with the process itself, such as appearance, about which a child will be touchy. Girls in particular will often seek reassurance about how they look. Most of them never completely grow out of this! Boys today are not entirely exempt from the need either. Preoccupation with their sexuality is not abnormal for children at puberty although this can be exasperating for an adult who has attained a more balanced perspective. The home parent should try to remember the novelty, intensity and excitement of his own first discovery and exploration of his sexuality and make allowances for his child accordingly. It is easy to forget the fierceness of early adolescent attachments, usually, but not only, to members of the opposite sex. Heartbreak can feel very real at that age and should be consoled not dismissed with 'you will get over it' – even though the parent knows that they almost certainly will fairly quickly. If the child does not get over it then that may be another warning sign of a reluctance to cope with the new family situation.

Most children, as part of growing up, experience attraction to people of the same sex and most grow out of it. Adopting homosexual attitudes can be one way of rebelling against parental authority and of implying criticism of the parents' failed heterosexual relationship. It is up to the home parent, in close co-operation with the other parent if possible, gently and tactfully to help an adolescent child pass through the homosexual phase to normal heterosexuality in such a way that should the transition not come about – it will in at least nineteen cases out of twenty – the door is left open to loving acceptance of the homosexual child. The home father may find it more difficult to be detached and objective when his ex has left him for a lesbian relationship, as was the case for seven per cent of the men in my survey. It may be that a child turns out to be naturally homosexual and whatever the home parent father's own feelings it is most important that he makes it clear that he loves and accepts his son or daughter as an individual regardless of their homosexuality. The same applies, of course, if a daughter gets pregnant or a son fathers a child while they themselves are still children. Love and support need not be confused with approval. There are local organisations offering support to pregnant teenagers and young mothers (but again noticeably not to young fathers). The CAB should be able to help or the Trust for the Study of Adolescence. Advice on homosexuality can also be obtained from these and other organisations. (Appendix One)

Of rather more likely interest than such traumas are the ordinary ailments of childhood and the occasional possibility of more serious illness. Is my child under the weather? Sickening for something? Seriously ill? Having me on? These are questions the home parent father will ask himself many times before his children are of an age to be responsible for their own health. There are a number of good simple guide books to family health. There are also more complex health encyclopedias, but too close a study and dependence on them can lead to a serious case of proxy hypochondria! Most childish sickness is transient and swiftly over, though the capacity of some children to melodramatise the slightest symptom may give the impression of imminent demise. I have seen several girls give Oscar-winning performances of being at death's door only to be miraculously cured a few minutes later. Consciously or unconsciously, sickness and pain can be used by a child to refocus parental attention on itself and in the immediate aftermath of a family break-up or bereavement this is often the case. Problematically, there is no added immunity at this time from real physical illness. Indeed, a child may even be more susceptible so childish complaints of pains, sickness and other symptoms have to be taken seriously even when they consistently occur on a Monday morning just before school or prior to or just after a visit to the other parent. With serious symptoms, or persistent minor ones, the doctor should be consulted and fully briefed on any recurring patterns or associations.

There are some symptoms, or rather combinations of symptoms, which should be taken more seriously than others and if any particular symptom persists then it should not be ignored. Even if it points to no immediate danger it can be evidence of a general condition that could greatly reduce a child's pleasure in life. In the first instance, unless the child's symptoms are clearly serious, a phone call to the family doctor or a chat with the local pharmacist or GP practice nurse, can help to indicate the best course of action. When in doubt the child should be taken to the doctor's surgery or, if the surgery is closed, the doctor called in. Unless the call is clearly frivolous the doctor would rather be called sooner than later and understands that the parent is not qualified to assess the seriousness of a child's symptoms. It is often mistakenly thought that young people do not suffer from depression but this is not only common among teenagers but also can sometimes be found even in primary school children. This may be no more than the fluctuating moods caused by emerging hormones, but it may be more deep-seated.

If the doctor does prescribe treatment it is important for the home parent father to know exactly how the medicine is to be taken and to control its administration for all but near adult children. He must also know what effects and side-effects to expect and make sure the doctor is aware of any other medicine or treatment the child is receiving which might be contra-indicative. Liaison with the other parent is obviously critical in this context. The fact that it was the doctor that prescribed does not always mean that a hard pressed GP is not grateful for reminders and it is better that the home parent should ask than worry. If children are being treated for a short-term illness with antibiotics, antihistamines or other drugs which may affect their behaviour or preclude some activities, or if they take long-term medicine for such conditions as asthma or diabetes it is important to let the school (head teacher, form teacher and school secretary) know and to drop them a reminder note when the child changes form or year or moves to another school. Having consulted the doctor it is a mistake to expect miracles and instant cures. He is sometimes fallible and sometimes simply baffled like any specialist in any other field and should be looked on as a friend and partner with you and the child in a team concerned for the child's health, not a scapegoat. One of contemporary societies most destructive trends is people's perpetual search for someone to blame, or even sue, if life does not conform to their exact expectations when sometimes a more stoic acceptance of misfortune might be more appropriate. A lone parent child will gain nothing from being encouraged in such negative attitudes.

The most important thing the home parent father can do for his children's health is to see that they get plenty of exercise, are appropriately clothed and housed and are properly fed on a balanced diet. It is tempting to assuage guilt and quieten the pangs of pity by feeding your child with sweet things, but sweet words are what it needs most and food follies will do it harm rather than good. This temptation is compounded by the fact that many men have little confidence in their ability to cook well, particularly if time is short in which to do so. Men actually make very good cooks and even if the home parent father does not become a great chef a high level of competence can be attained by applying the kind of logic and time management in the kitchen he would apply to his job. It is a good idea, specially if a father is just learning the culinary ropes, to mix easy-to-prepare routine meals served most of the time with special meals – Sunday dinners, meals on high days and holidays – in whose preparation children of all ages can participate. Fortunately, the most nutritious food is often the simplest; plenty of fruit, vegetables and salads with good protein sources such as meat and cheese, bread and potatoes for physical energy and sensible drinks such as fruit juice and milk will ensure a healthy diet. Depressingly, it seems that the march of Macdonalds is irresistible and many families, particularly those with domestically unskilled parents, are compulsive consumers of junk food with the result that many mothers are bad or negligent cooks. As one home parent father complained "She wasn't a good manager or cook at all. I don't think she could boil water right ... even no proper dinner on Christmas Day – she would be out'.(M2) In such families mother's departure may even mean an improvement in diet. In others, where the mother has been a skilled, conscientious and imaginative cook it will be some while before father's culinary efforts begin to approach the same standard, but he can at least feed the children sensibly from day one. This does not mean no junk food, sweets, soft drinks, the treats that most children love, but that they should be just that, treats, not part of the every day diet. Obesity is a disease and one that has reached epidemic proportions in Britain.

In the weeks and months immediately following a bereavement or parental separation it is sometimes hard to distinguish children's ordinary illness or malaise from the effects of the change. The picture is further obscured by the somewhat different ways boys and girls react and home parents' response to them. These differences come on top of the different patterns of male and female development in normal intact families, some of which we have looked at earlier.

In part these differences of response between boys and girls are innate, but they are also conditioned by parental behaviour of which the home parent father should be aware. A father's differentiation between children of different sexes starts at birth. He will hold a baby girl more snugly than a baby boy. If he is bottle feeding, he will stimulate the boy child, by movement of bottle and baby, more than the girl whom he treats more passively and he will be more persistent with a boy than with a girl. (F9) A child largely learns its gender role up to three years of age. 'By the time their children are two years the father/son relationship is frequently very close, a camaraderie quite unlike the feeling about daughters. Girls very often experience the kind of situations which accentuate male power over them, the fairly firm guidelines about how they should behave. In contrast, fathers let boys get away with more mischief, being in the majority of cases less strict than mothers'.(F8)

As the children grow older fathers will respect daughters' privacy, especially from adolescence onwards when it is reinforced by sexual taboo, more than that of their sons – ingeniously measured in one study (F9) by the frequency of knocking on bedroom doors! The same study suggests that fathers discourage daughters developing confidence and ambition by interrupting them, helping them before they really need help and by encouraging them to concentrate on being pleasant and helpful to others. 'Boys and girls receive very different messages from their parents, especially their fathers: for boys the message is do well; for girls it is have a good time. Fathers can positively affect their daughters' cognitive development; often they simply fail to do it!'. (F9)

The different approach of fathers generally, and to the two sexes specifically, continues throughout a child's development. However, observation and research (F9) suggests that the home parent father can modify his behaviour to take account of the absence of the feminine touch and that it is not irrevocably determined by his genes or conditioned by his upbringing. If a father demonstrates warmth and nurture (characteristics which have been hijacked by the feminists, but are by no means exclusive to women) sons in particular seem to make better adjustments to their sex roles. (F12) While compensating for the lack of yin the home parent father does not want to abandon those yang characteristics which are valuable in shaping his children's character. The ability to play with them more like another child than an adult (particularly valuable if the home parent has an only child), the tendency to let quite young infants explore and take risks (where mothers impose clear and very limited boundaries) and so to develop a spirit of independence (F9) are both characteristically male approaches which have beneficial results. Lone fathers who treat their girls a little as if they were boys in this respect do not seem to diminish their femininity thereby, though lone mothers do often considerably emasculate their boy children by their wrapped in cotton wool approach. The inference is that home parent fathers should not be inhibited about approaching both child rearing and home running in a typically masculine way, applying logic and ratiocination, but that they also need to be aware that their children need feminine perception and sensitivity and modify their approach accordingly. In other words there is no reason they should not enjoy and provide the best of both parental worlds.

For a whole variety of reasons boys seem to lose out more than girls when a parental relationship breaks down, even if the home parent is their father. Girls get more attention in the immediate aftermath (F16) perhaps because of the straightjacket of stereotyping. Although boys are less able to cope with the stress (D1) they are expected to be tough and brave and so get less sympathy from the adult world. If they are to have the relief of being able to express their pain and sorrow without shame they need to see the paternal role model uninhibitedly doing the same. They will often find it hard to describe how they feel, let alone discuss it with anyone else, though if dad has developed that early comradeship with his sons in an open way in which weaknesses and ineptitude are mutually admitted, the boy when older may better be able to talk about his feelings to his father. Sadly, this early male bond is more usually based on an ideal which specifically excludes confessions of weakness or failure in a society where openly to show tender feelings is still often considered unmanly. (F1)

Boys, like their fathers, will usually cope with the pressures on them after a break-up by putting a great deal of energy into physical pastimes. In most cases, unless the disturbance runs very deep, this male safety valve proves a perfectly valid and effective solution, but in case it does not the lone father does well to make sure that sons have a sympathetic female ear available to them which can listen to tales of woe and weakness without judgement, scorn or disapproval.

The cliches of the macho-male and the neurotic female, like most cliches, contain an element of truth. Boys tend to externalise their problems in aggression and anti-social behaviour when they come from families with a high level of conflict whether disrupted or intact. Girls tend to internalise their problems and their behaviour difficulties tend to be expressed as depression, anxiety or withdrawal. The consequences of this suppression may only really surface many years after the parental break-up. The compensating factor for girls is often their ability to form intense relationships with a small group of their peers amongst whom problems are much more freely discussed from a very early age than is the case amongst parallel groups of boys.

Often, children supported with love and understanding can mature rapidly and develop a sense of responsibility and diplomatic skills which would not normally come to them until much later. The transition to independence and adult activity comes earlier in the children of single parents because to some extent the children have to fulfil an adult role in the life of the remaining parent. Provided they do not *have* to grow up too quickly because the inadequacies or emotional demands of their fathers make premature, and usually anxious and depressed, adults of them, this maturity beyond their years can bring them distinct advantages at school and work. I observe that the usually less mature children of the same age gladly accord to the lone father child the role of leader in their activities. There is a temptation for lone fathers, however, to lean too heavily on their young daughters for emotional support and companionship which is not such a good thing – though preferable to the patronising and over-protective attitude, evident in some intact families, which can retard a girl's development and undermine her self confidence. As one daughter put it 'My father taught me to be independent and cocky, and free-thinking, but he could not stand it if I disagreed with him. I do not know how that can be resolved'. (F10) Or, as more grandly put by Elizabeth Barrett Browning 'My mind is naturally independent and spurns that subservience of opinion which is generally considered necessary to feminine softness ... I feel within me an almost proud consciousness of independence which prompts me to defend my opinions and to yield them only to conviction!!!!!!'. (QF10)

There are similar pitfalls with an only child and for the home parent father the only daughter presents the greatest temptation to elevate her prematurely and harmfully to the full status of adult companion. (C2)

I think it has been shown in the course of these twenty-two chapters that while the bonds between child and adult – or better still adults of both sexes – are an important element in its healthy development, with whom they may happen to be formed is largely irrelevant. Children have few presuppositions about the roles the various adults in their lives should play. Nor do they have the kind of idealised platonic notion of family that so many adults seem obsessed with. (FF1) This is hugely encouraging to the home father who finds himself with both the responsibility and the desire to provide his children with the primary bond in their lives, but it does have a painful corollary. The nurturing of an adult personality requires the progressive slackening and eventual untying of the majority of those bonds. The lone father who has come to rely too heavily on those bonds for his own emotional satisfaction and support may find letting go does not come easily.

The home parent father may start becoming more uptight and possessive about his child in this situation, laying down unduly severe rules about what they do and where they do it and with whom. Even more likely, in a lone father's case, is that the anxiety that he will not be able to cope with the daily routines – everything from making sure his children have brushed their teeth to doing their piano practice – will result in him constantly badgering them about these things. The child told not to forget to do this or that will often reply 'I am, dad' and although the task might not yet have been begun it is telling the parent by this inaccuracy that it has not forgotten and does not need to be reminded. Even when children have forgotten they may still find it self-protectively necessary to say 'don't nag, dad!'. How easy it is to make children the victims rather than the beneficiaries of parental anxieties in the lone parent family. The home parent must teach himself from the outset, therefore, not to become so wrapped up in his children that he makes it hard for himself – and just as hard for them – to find new interests or cultivate other relationships. If he does not have these to give balance to his outlook on life he may find it impossible to let go of his child as it grows older.

To make letting go easier nature has provided children with an ever sharper vision as they grow older to detect parental feet of clay. As one of them explained 'There comes a moment when you begin to detach the father from his moral camouflage, to realise that his displeasure is not always disinterested, that even when he pretends otherwise he can be ordinarily angry, genuinely unfair'. (F10)

The father, in turn, must gradually adopt a less omniscient stance. The older a child gets, the less infallible and unshakeable he has to be and he will find it a great relief no longer to have to play the part of sheltering 'sturdy oak' (F6) and suffer the contradictory surges of overwhelming love and occasional keen hostility that this role begets. He has to face up to the fact that sometimes his children are demanding and unlikeable, maybe even more than he thought, or thought he was supposed to think they were.

Children are not always able to express the disagreement which is symptomatic of the development of their own personalities as tactfully as most adults do. The child who tells the home parent to 'get real' or 'to get a life' is only saying that it disagrees. Insults are shorthand for differences which children may find difficult to put more precisely and politely into words. The home parent represents an adult world which adolescents want to join, but whose authority over themselves implies that they are still children and not yet adults. They therefore resent and reject that authority. As children get older, it becomes more important for lone fathers not to take up arms against every rebellion, to try to be flexible on minor things so that firm markers can be set down with conviction, and usually without too much opposition, on the things that are really important. It can be a rough time for everyone. This makes it tempting to the exhausted home parent to tell the child he does not care what they *do*, but this may be interpreted as not caring about *them*. If the home parent father does get angry, when he has cooled down he must be sure to let them know that the real cause was anxiety for them not concern for himself. We all need to be told that we are loved and important to others and never more so than when we are growing up. These declarations are essential ground work for enabling children to turn to their home parent (or, indeed, their other parent) if they really do need help.

This book has inevitably largely been one of generalisations so it is necessary to come back to the starting point that the circumstances of no two lone fathers and their families are alike. As a previous study of lone parent families pointed out 'There is neither a single outcome, nor explanation for the outcomes of children who have experienced family disruption and who live in one parent families. Nor do the outcomes occur at a single point in time'. (WPP3) In other words the fate of their children is to a great extent in the hands of the lone parent who brings them up on a daily basis. The cynic might say that in many respects we survive in adult life despite our parents not because of them. However, the truth of the matter is that a conscientious, well-informed and loving home parent father *can* give his child a flying start and overcome the undoubted handicaps imposed on his children by the break-up of their parents' relationship.

What, then, constitutes the best formula for successful home parent fathering? As far as contact with the other parent is concerned an all or nothing approach seems the most likely to benefit the children. Either they should not have contact with their mothers and be free to make a fresh start as lone parent children only (and, of course, to fantasise about the ideal mythical mother) or they should have face to face contact, supported by other indirect means, on an average of more than two days a week and preferably at between four and seven.

Money if anything seems to be a handicap rather than an advantage, though not of course to the father nor in terms of the practical opportunities it can purchase for the children. Its pursuit can distract the lone father from what has now become his primary function as a child rearer. The experience of working-class men used to manual work and close family networks seems the best basis for approaching lone fatherhood and those who do not have it would do well to take a leaf out of these lone parents' book.

Very important in securing a good outcome for the children from lone parent upbringing is the attitude of the father. Happiness and optimism rub off!

Perhaps most important of all is the creation and sustaining of a close bond between father and child. This has been considered the prerogative of mothers, but can demonstrably be created as effectively by fathers with highly beneficial results for the child.

My survey and the stories of my fifty-two home parent fathers support the claim that single fathers can and do make at least as good a job (and sometimes as poor a job) of looking after their children after the break-up of the parental relationship as mothers do. They are, therefore, equally entitled to be considered for and awarded that responsibility.

However, while they remain a neglected minority, treated only as an irrelevant sub division of lone motherhood or of general fatherhood*, they will remain invisible and therefore unable to secure that right in sufficient numbers to make it no longer a matter of surprise. Newspaper and magazine editors, publishers and television programmers have often said to me 'surely it is not nearly so bad or so substantial a problem as you claim?' It is.

The only way to remedy the considerable injustice and deprivation suffered by men who bring up or would like to bring up their children (and by the children themselves) is for those who are already doing so to come forward as forcibly as their female counterparts and claim that right on behalf of all fathers. It is not enough for fatherhood to be treated as a minor department of single parent organisations and government departments run by women for women and which define lone parenthood almost exclusively in female terms. The solution may be for an entirely separate advice and campaigning charity to be set up for lone fathers and fathers alone.

Since it is evident that fathers are as capable as mothers of bringing up children successfully on their own, and that many more would do so if given the chance, a fundamental change in law, attitudes and opportunity is required to give them an equal right with mothers to do so. Much of what men gain thereby will benefit women, too. There can be no justification for the cruel discrimination from which men now suffer in relation to their children and the distribution of family assets and income when marriages and cohabitations end with parental separation. All men, and any women genuinely interested in sexual equality, need to mount an unrelenting campaign to secure men's equal right to be home parent fathers.

*One lady to whom we spoke who was writing a book on fatherhood dismissed lone fathers as such a small minority as to warrant only a PhD thesis or perhaps a very short chapter in her book!

Appendix One

List of Addresses
Bereavement\Separation

CRUSE (National Organisation for the Widowed & Their Children),
Cruse House,
126 Sheen Road,
Richmond,
SURREY, DW9 1UR.
0181-940-4818

Divorce, Conciliation and Advisory Service,
38 Ebury Street,
LONDON, SW1W 0LU.
0171-730-2422
(Fee Charging, Non Profit Making)

Relate (Ex Marriage Guidance)
Little Church Street,
RUGBY, CV21 3AP
01788-732241

Lone parenting/Access

Gingerbread,
16-17, Clerkenwell Close,
LONDON, EC1R 0AA
0171-336-8183

Families Need fathers
134 Curtain Rd
LONDON, EC2A 3AR
0171-613-5060
0181- 886-0970

Mothers Apart From Their Children (MATCH),
BM Problems,
LONDON, WC1N 3XX.
(Tel unknown)

National Counsel for the Divorced & Separated (NCDS),
PO Box 19
LEICESTER, LE2 3ZE
0116-270-0595

National Council for One Parent Families
255 Kentish Town,
LONDON, NW5 2LX.
0171-267-1361

Contact a Family (for parents of disabled children)
170 Tottenham Court Road,
LONDON, W1P OHA
0171-383-3555

Scottish Council for Single Parents,
44 Albany Street,
EDINBURGH, EH1 3QR.
01310-556-3899

Access and Child Contact Centres,
United Reform Church,
Goldsmith Street,
NOTTINGHAM, NG1 5JT
0115-948-4557

National Family Conciliation Counsel,
34 Milton Road,
SWINDON,
Wilts.
01793-618486

National Family Conciliation Council,
155 High Street,
DORKING,
Surrey, RH4 1AD
01306-882754

Parent Network
44-46 Caversham Road,
LONDON NW5 2DS
0171-485-8535

Parentline
Endway House,
The Endway,
HADLEIGH,
Essex SS7 2AN
01702-559900

Childrens Problems

NCH Action for Children Care Line, Freephone Service,
85 Highbury Park,
LONDON N5 1UD
0171-226-2033

Association of Child Psycotherapists
120, West Heath Road,
LONDON NW3 7TU
0181-458-1609

Young Peoples Counselling Service,
Tavistock Centre,
120 Bellsize Lane,
LONDON NW3 5BA
0171-453-7111 Ext. 337

NSPCC
42 Curtain Rd
LONDON EC2A 3NH
0171-825-2500

Trust for Study of Adolescence
23 New Road,
BRIGHTON BN1 1W2
01273-693311

The Childrens Society
Edward Rudolf House
Margerty St
LONDON WC1X OJL
0171-837-4299

Childline (*mainly* for children)
Freepost 1111
LONDON N1 0QW
HQ 0171-239-1000
Counselling 0800-1111

Bullying

Kidscape
152 Buckingham Palace Rd
LONDON SW1W 9TR
(large envelope & 2 1st Class stamps)
0171-730-3300

Legal

Solicitors Family Law Association,
14 Gough Square,
LONDON EC4A 3DE
0171-836-8400

Childrens Legal Centre,
The University of Essex,
Wivenhoe Park,
COLCHESTER,
Essex CO4 3SQ
01206-873-820

The Child Abduction Unit,
Lord Chancellor's Department,
81 Chancery Lane,
LONDON WC2 1DD
0171-911-7094

Reunite: National Council for Abducted Children
PO Box 4
LONDON WC1X 3DX
0171-404-8356/7

Scottish Courts Administration,
26-27 Royal terrace,
EDINBURGH, EH75 AH.
0131-556-0755

Court Urgent Business Officers
(Urgent legal applications out of hours)
Midland & Oxford 0121 200 1234
Northern 0161 832 9571
South Eastern 0171 936 6000/7264
Wales 01222-396925
Western 01272-743-763

Legal Aid Board
85 Grays Inn Road,
LONDON WC1 X8A
0171-813-1000

Missing Persons Bureau
Roebuck House
284\6 Upper Richmond Rd West
LONDON SW14 7JE
Office 0181-392-2000
Freecall Helpline 0500-700700

General

National Association of Citizens Advice Bureaux,
Myddleton House,
115-123 Pentonville Road,
LONDON N1 9LZ
0171-883-2181
For local offices see Yellow Pages

British Association of Counselling,
37A Sheep Street,
RUGBY,
Warwickshire.
01788-778328

Alcohol Concern
Waterbridge House,
32-36 Loman Street,
LONDON SE1 0EE
0171-928-7377

Drug problems Freephone
Dial 100 and ask for freephone drug problems. You will be given local sources of help

National Stepfamily Association
Chapel House
18 Hatton Place
LONDON EC1N 8RU
0171-209-2460
Counselling 0990-168-388

Samaritans – see local phone book
National number 0345-909090
Charged at local rates

MIND (Mental health problems)
Granta House
15\19 Stafford Broadway
LONDON E15 4BQ
0181-519-2122

National Extension College
Brooklands Avenue
CAMBRIDGE
01223-316644

Holidays

SPLASH,
19 North Street,
PLYMOUTH,
Devon.

O.P.F.H.,
Kildonan Courtyard,
BarrHill,
GIRVAN,
South Ayrshire,
KA26 0PS
01465-821288

HOP
51 Hampshire Road,
DROYLESDON,
Manchester,
M43 7PH
0161-370-0227

HELP,
52 Chequer Avenue,
Hyde Park,
DONCASTER,
South Yorks,
DN4 5AS
01302-365139

Single Parent Travel Club,
37 Sunningdale Park,
Queen Victoria Road,
New Tupton,
CHESTERFIELD, S42 6DZ
01246-865069

Working from home

Parents at Work
45 Beech Street,
LONDON, EC2Y 8AD
0171-628-3578
0171-628-3565

Ownbase
68 First Avn
Bush Hill Pk
Enfield
Middx, EN1 1BN
(Tel unknown).

Home Run
Cribau Mill,
Llanvair Discoed,
CHEPSTOW,
Gwent, NP6 6RD
01291-641222

Home Employment Services
Bureau (guide book)
100 Grays Inn Rd
LONDON, WC1X 8AU
Send sae and 2nd class stamp.

Childcare

Advisory Centre for Education
1B Aberdeeen Studios
22/24 Highbury Grove
London, N5 2EA
0171-354-8321

Family Rights Group
(advice on children in care)
The Print House
18 Ashwin St
London, E8 3DL
0171-923-2628

The National Association of
Gifted Children,
Elder House,
MILTON KEYNES,
MK9 1LR.
01908-673677

Parents Against Injustice
(Wrongful accusations of child
abuse)
10 Water Lane,
BISHOPS STORTFORD
Herts, CM23 2JZ
01279-656564

Kids'Club Network

Bellerive House,
3 Muirfield Crescent,
LONDON, E14 9SZ
0171-512-2100
0171-512-2112

West Wales

Lisa David
Economic Development Unit,
The Business Resource Centre,
Parc Amanwy,
Ammanford,
Dyfed, SA18 3EP
01269-590222

Midlands

James Hempsall
PO Box 531,
Leicester, L32 8PZ
0116-238-7122

North

Harvey Gallagher
5 Charlotte Square,
3rd Floor,
Rear Offfice,
Newcastle-upon-Tyne,
NE1 4XF
0191-261-1954

Money

Benefits Freephone advice line
0800 666 555 Now defunct so try
Your Local Authority (phone book)
Welfare Rights Officer

National Debt line,
Birmingham Settlement,
318 Summer Lane,
Birmingham, B19 3RL
0121-359-8501

Child Support Agency
Enquiry Line 0345-133133
Regional Offices in phone book

Child Poverty Action Group
1-5 Bath Street,
LONDON, EC12 9PY
0171-253-3406

Appendix Two

Fifty-Two Fathers – A survey (1995)
Sample and questionnaire

Methodology

Organising an objective and accurate survey of such an elusive population as the home parent fathers of the United Kingdom (excluding Northern Ireland) proved a challenging task but, with the exceptions I shall describe, I believe the sample obtained to be a representative one.

A home parent father is here defined as a man living on his own (or until very recently on his own in three cases) providing the principal home for his dependent children and with whom they spend fifty per cent or more of their time when not in school. A dependent child is defined as one under eighteen years old living at home or if over eighteen (five children), who is disabled, unemployed or still in full-time education and financially dependent on its father.

During the winter of 1994 and '95 and the spring of 1995 the questionnaire which follows was distributed to some twenty-eight individual lone fathers and to twelve groups consisting of or containing lone fathers. Twenty-seven of the individuals and eight groups, providing between them a further twenty-eight respondents, replied. Of these fifty-five replies three were rejected on the grounds that the parent did not have the majority of the care of his children or were in some other way invalidated. In one other case a lone father's last dependent child, which he had brought up single-handedly for the past fourteen years, had only just left home so his response was taken as valid. This gave a sample for the survey of fifty-two home parent fathers, of whom eight were widowers, and one hundred and three dependent children.

As each respondent returned his questionnaire it was acknowledged and he was thanked and those who had been separated or divorced were asked to comment on any contact with the CSA. If they had not volunteered their ex's address they were given an explanation of why it was needed and asked again. This elicited only three more addresses, but also in some cases explanations as to why the address had been refused or that it was not known. Of the forty-four non-widowers twenty gave their exes' addresses and seven said they did not know (interestingly the children of three of these still had contact with their mother). The remaining seventeen either specifically refused to give the address or have been deemed to have refused by virtue of not responding to a second request. Two of the initial respondents, who came via group contacts, could not be followed up because one did not give an address or telephone number and remained anonymous. Another, who gave only a telephone number had lost the use of that telephone line by the time a follow-up call was made. Their responses to the initial questionnaire have however been used.

Following the initial return fifteen respondents were written to or telephoned for clarification or completion of specific replies and this resulted in some additional information, but not all that was necessary. Therefore, in June 1995, a further supplementary questionnaire (see below) was circulated to all fifty contactable respondents to establish two general points that had arisen spontaneously in a sufficient number of conversations to suggest useful lines of enquiry. Tidying up questions were added where this was necessary. Forty Seven replies had been received by 10th July 1995 when the data file was closed. Contacting single fathers has not been easy, hence the fairly lengthy span of the survey, but the data, as far as possible, has been related to a date of the 1st January, 1995.

The anonymity of the subjects has been preserved, but for consistency of cross reference they can be identified by the prefix letters, B – Bristol (4); C – Cheltenham and Gloucester (3); K – Kingston on Thames area (6); M – Manchester and district (5); T – Telford (1); N – Northolt/Harrow (2); R – Reading (1). Lone fathers identified from the media or on an individual basis or known to me personally are indicated by the letter J (3). Slightly under a third of those whom I contacted on the this personal basis replied. The largest single source of respondents came from a short paragraph in the magazine *Singled Out*, specifically aimed at single parents, which described the book and invited people to get in touch with me. These are indicated by the letter S (22). This may have introduced some opinionative bias into the sample in that readers of such a magazine may be more aware of and feel more strongly about the issues affecting single parents. The bias is probably not an important one in view of the good representation of those segments of the community that are least articulate. Three of the widowers came from the groups described above, three through *Singled Out* and the remaining two through CRUSE. To encourage replies and avoid economic bias the questionnaires were all sent out with pre-addressed and reply-paid envelopes. Twenty-nine per cent of my sample were personally interviewed in their homes, at work or on neutral ground. A further twenty-three per cent were briefly contacted by telephone.

Dismayed as I have been at the way the situation, opinions and attitudes of so called 'absent' fathers have usually been interpreted through the study of what their exes have said about them, I wished to avoid falling into the same trap so decided to distribute a matching questionnaire to the exes of the forty-four divorced or separated men in my study. This fell foul of two unexpected obstacles. Firstly, as we have seen, there was the difficulty of obtaining addresses, but the second difficulty came from the twenty other parent mothers themselves. Seventeen did not reply at all. Two wrote defensively angry letters at the inference they had drawn – there was certainly no implication of it in the accompanying letter – that they were being blamed for leaving their children. Only one completed and returned the questionnaire. Perhaps it is reasonable to infer from their reluctance to respond a strong sense of guilt and shame among the other parent mothers. No conclusions can be drawn from the single matching questionnaire reply, but it is interesting to note in passing that it coincided very closely with the views expressed by the lone father except in blame for the break-up and financial fairness, where the ex thought the husband had been more generous than he thought himself, and in the amount of domestic work undertaken in the joint household, where she thought he had over-claimed his share by a third.

I should have liked to pursue this matching process further, but could afford neither the time nor the money to do so. The same constraints led to what I regard as the only other significant defect in the methodology. I should like to have been able to interview a substantial cross-section of the children and their teachers to check fathers' perceived ideas of their happiness, educational progress, etc. I hope some properly funded future survey may be able to make the comparison between parental perceptions and less biased objective ones by outsiders with a close knowledge of the children and thus to establish how reliable parental opinions may be. However, since it is perceptions not facts that determine parental conduct and attitude, the findings of this survey based on fathers' opinions should prove useful, whether or not the paternal opinion is a completely accurate one.

The sample

The sample, in the event, has proved quite a well-balanced one with only one significant under representation. Only one of the fathers surveyed came from an ethnic minority. This group is under represented partly because it is a hard one to contact through conventional media and organisations and partly because the social structures of many ethnic minorities absorb their single fathers without needing to turn outwards for help or advice. When I initially closed my sample on 30th April 1995 I had only five widowers including unmarried men whose mates had died (<10%) as opposed to the fifteen per cent which the Office of Population Census and Surveys (OPCS) 1991 sample indicated as the appropriate proportion of the single father population. I therefore tried to recruit more widowers, both to give better balance to the basic sample and to give me a larger sub-sample with which to make comparisons. Because the status of widowers does not involve conflict with a non-resident other parent they are more readily absorbed into society both by the family networks of both sets of parents and by their friends and neighbours, which makes them hard to contact. Nevertheless, our widower sample with the three additions recruited in May\June is probably large enough to draw some tentative conclusions from.

In geographical terms Northern Ireland has not been included and figures are therefore related to either Great Britain or to England and Wales alone. Scotland, with only one respondent, is under represented in the sample, but otherwise, as Table Four shows, the geographical spread and the balance between urban (27) suburban (15) and rural (10) presents a reasonable cross section of British society as does the educational background and the employment pattern (see Tables Four and Two) though a somewhat loose definition of professional and managerial occupations results in a slight imbalance (38.5% of the sample) in that direction. I thought at first that this might be because these middle-class fathers were better equipped for the battle to secure residence of children, but the fact that only one of the nine contested court cases is from this group contradicts that supposition. Perhaps these men are more confident and in better circumstances to bid for residence though, as we shall see, they do not make any better a job of it. Forty-two per cent of the survey fathers left school at the minimum age. Twenty-one per cent stayed on but did not have further formal education or qualifications and thirty-seven per cent had some form of higher education. Forty-five per cent were unemployed and fifty-five per cent (including 6% students) employed. The unemployed consisted of thirty point five per cent manual workers, forty-seven point eight per cent skilled or semi-skilled and twenty-six point seven per cent professional and managerial. The employed respondents broke down into three point four per cent manual forty-four point nine per cent skilled or semi-skilled and fifty-one per cent professional and managerial. Clearly home parent fathering and doing a manual job are harder to reconcile than lone fathering and skilled or professional occupations.

Between them our fifty-two home parent fathers had a total of one hundred and three dependent children ranging in age at the time of bereavement or separation from six weeks to twenty-two years. Of these there was one child living with the ex from a family where the siblings had been divided between the parents. The fathers had a further thirteen children now living independent lives. Of the dependent children nine in six families were from the fathers' previous relationships and in one case a father was looking after a child from his ex's previous relationship along with his own. This very varied pattern typifies the confusion with which many children will have to cope in the family patterns of the future.

The questionnaire concluded with two open-ended questions designed to get home parent fathers to express their views and experiences both of social attitudes to them and their role and their personal feelings about being single fathers. These replies are quoted widely throughout the text.

Had I had better financial resources my survey could have been more comprehensive, thorough and complete and I hope that a much larger scale study may now be funded by a charitable or academic institution to follow up what I have here begun. Nevertheless I believe this survey to have been valid and accurate within its limits and the conclusions drawn from it legitimate.

Questionnaire
Code F1

Fathercare Questionnaire – 6 Pages

Introduction. Your replies to these questions remain absolutely confidential and will not be revealed individually to anyone other than the author and his research assistant. We may ask you to grant us a personal interview later.

The other parent of the children you are looking after is referred to throughout as your 'ex' whatever the marital status of your relationship. Where there is a straight choice eg Yes or No just tick the appropriate box. Elsewhere fill in the spaces..... If the question does not apply to you leave it blank.

Thank you for taking the trouble to complete this questionnaire. When the book is published we will, of course, send you a copy.

Personal details:

Date of Birth .... Year .... Month ....

Did you

(a) Leave school at the minimum leaving age ....

(b) Continue with school or vocational training. ....

(c) Study for a degree or similar qualification (HND etc) ....

What is your present full time job? ....

Or present part-time job? ....

If unemployed usual occupation ....

If unemployed for how long? Years .... Months ....

List all your children, oldest first, in the chart below giving their sex (B = Boy, G = Girl) their age in years and months (eg 13.5) who their mother was (C = current partner; X = most recent ex partner; P = any other previous partner) and where they live now (H = at home with you; M = with their mother; I = independently)

Below the line (1a etc) list in the same way any children living with you of whom you are not the father.

	Sex	Age	Mother	Live		Sex	Age	Mother	Live
1	.	.	.	. .	5	.	.	.	
2	.	.	.	. .	6	.	.	.	
3	.	.	.	. .	7	.	.	.	
4	.	.	.	. .	8	.	.	.	
1a	.	.	.	. .	3a	.	.	.	
2a	.	.	.	. .	4a	.	.	.	

Page 2

Rating on a scale of -10 to +10 (-10 = very much less, 0 = same, +10 = very much more) whether each of your children now, compared to when your and your ex lived together, are more or less:	CHILD 1	2	3	4	5
Happy					
Healthy					
Well-behaved					
Doing well at school					
Get on with you					
Get on with their mother					

Rate on a scale 1 to 10 how far you and your ex agree or disagree (0=totally disagree 10=completely agree) about:

Access	....
Education	....
Upbringing	....
Religion	....
Financial arrangements	....

On a scale -10 to + 10 (-10 = very much less.+10 very much more, 0 = same) are you and your ex more or less

	You	Ex
Happy	....	....
Healthy	....	....
Financially well off	....	....

Have you a new partner living with you now? Yes No

How long have you been living together? Years .... Months ....

On a scale of 0 (very badly) to 10 (very well) rate how your previous children and new partner get on together. ....

On a scale of 0 (very badly) to 10 (very well) rate how your children get on with their natural mother

Now	....
Before you parted	....

On a scale of 0 (very badly) to 10 (very well) rate how your children get on with their mother's new partner if she has one ....

Ex's name and address if known ....
....
....
....

Ex's Date of Birth	Year	Month ....
Were you married?	Yes	No
Are you divorced?	Yes	No
Are you legally separated?	Yes	No

How long did you live together?	Years	Months ....
How long since you parted?	Years	Months ....
Who left the family home?	You?	Your ex?
Was your ex your first live in partner?	Yes	No
Were you your ex's first live in partner?	Yes	No
Please list the reasons for your relationship breaking up		
Did you try formal mediation at any time?	Yes	No

Since you parted have your relations with your ex

improved? ....

stayed the same? ....

got worse?. ....

Rate how well you and your ex now communicate from 0 (no communication at all) to 10 (complete communication whenever necessary) ....

Rate the degree of hostility between you from 0 (total hostility/hate) to 10 (friendship/love) ....

Domestic experience:
Have you ever run a home before? Yes No

When living with your ex what share of the domestic work did you do (0 = none, 10 = all of it) under these headings:

Cooking ....

Cleaning ....

Laundry ....

Maintenance\Repairs ....

Child care ....

How many hours' help a week do you get with (a) domestic work (b) child care from:

relatives	a	b ....
friends	a	b ....
paid help	a	b ....

If paid help how much a week does this cost you? £ ....

How much money do you get each week
"in your pocket" after tax etc from:

Wage or salary	£ ....
Income Support	£ ....
Child Benefit	£ ....
Unemployment Benefit	£ ....
Voluntary payment from ex	£ ....
Court order payment from ex	£ ....
CSA payment from ex	£ ....
Contributions from relatives	£ ....
Other (please specify)	£ ....
Total current *annual* income after all tax and other *state* deductions	£ ....

Total annual income of family as a whole after all tax and other state deductions *before* your ex left £ ....

Are you currently in debt?	Yes	No
Do you own or rent your home?	Own	Rent
Have you a mortgage ?	Yes	No
Is the home you live in the one you shared with your ex?	Yes	No

What payments do you make (give as a weekly sum) to your ex for:
Herself £ ....
Your children £ ....

What lump sum, if any, have you paid your ex for:
any equity in your home £ ....
any pensions or other rights £ ....

Rate how other major property was divided between you and your ex (0 = You got none of it 10 = you got it all)
Car(s)
Major items of furniture
Significant savings
Other(please detail)

Do you feel you are better or worse off financially than when you lived together?
Better?
The same?
Worse?

Before you parted was your ex working?
Full time?
Part time?
Only at home?

Rate the financial arrangements made for fairness on a scale 0 (totally unfair) to 10 (completely fair)
For You? ....
For Your Ex? ....
For Your children? ....

How often (ie daily, once a week, never, etc) does your ex

(a) see your children? ....

(b) have them to stay overnight? ....

(d) have them for a holiday? ....

(e) write to them? ....

(f) get letters from them? ....

(g) telephone them? ....

(h) get a phone call from them? ....

Have you a phone? Yes .... No ....

Has your ex a phone? Yes. .... No ....

How long would it take your children to travel between your home and your ex's?

On foot? ....

By bicycle? ....

(If you own one) By car? ....

By public transport? ....

Do your children still see as much of your ex's close relatives as they did before you parted?

Her Parents? Yes .... No ....

Her brothers\sisters? Yes .... No ....

(If any) her other children? Yes .... No ....

Did you and your ex agree about who your children should live with voluntarily? Yes .... No ....

As a result of a court order? Yes .... No ....

Or did it just happen? Yes .... No ....

How much do you blame yourself for the breakdown of the relationship with your ex? Rate out of 10 (0 = not at all; 10 = completely) ....

Describe people's attitude to you as a single father bringing up your children (use another sheet of paper if you want to)

Page 6

Describe your own feelings about being a single father bringing up your children (use another sheet of paper if you want to)

(Page space given here)

Name .... Address ....

Tel No ....

....

....

Supplementary Questions:

Are you a member of an ethnic minority (ie not English, Irish, Scots or Welsh by descent in the last three generations)?

Did you own a car in January 1995?

Are you currently in a stable relationship with another adult in which, apart from living together, you regard yourselves as a couple?

Did your ex ever use or threaten serious physical violence against you? (ie a knife or throw heavy objects etc)

Did you ever respond to attacks, threats or abuse with physical violence?

Or initiate it?

Appendix Three

Table One Lone Fathers:

	Age	AEx	Dif	Mar\Co	Sep\Dt	Caus	Sta	Arr	No	Pt\qt	
B11	34	29	05	07.00	02.11	AM	m\d	H	3	11x	y
B12	51	37	14	07.07	//.//	AM	m\d	V\C	1	11x	
B13	35	39	- 04	12.00	01.07	I\F	m	V	1	12x	
B14	42	31	11	07.00	03.06	M	m	H\V	2	11x	
C11	44	46	- 02	19.04	00.11	A	m	H\V	2	11x	
C12	40	35	05	14.00	01.00	AW	m\s	V	3	11x	
C13	54	51	03	25.00	05.00	O	m\d	V	1	11x	
J11	61	38	23	07.06	05.11	I	m\d	V\C	1	22x	yo
J12	43	43	01	17.06	02.04	AW	m\d	V	2	12sx	y
J13	51	47	04	20.00	07.00	O	m\d	V	2	11x	
K11	40	37	03	14.00	06.00	I	m\d	V	2	11s	
K12	43	38	05	13.00	06.04	I	m\d	C	2	11x	
K13	49	XX	XX	17.00	04.00	AM	m\d	C	2	22x	y
K14	51	38	13	08.06	04.00	M	m\d	H	2	22x	
K15	49	47	02	14.00	06.00	AM	m\d	H	2	12x	
K16	51	36	15	08.00	08.00	AM	m\d	C	3	11x	
M11	33	29	04	07.08	04.06	I\A	cos	C	4	11x	
M12	53	38	15	03.00	09.00	F	co	H	1	22x	
M13	42	49	- 07	18.00	01.09	I\A	m\d	C	2	11x	
M14	50	46	04	19.00	07.00	M\F	co	H	2	11x	y
M15	51	50	01	25.00	03.06	F\AM	m	H	1	11x	
N11	48	48	00	12.03	04.02	AW	m\d	H	1	12s	
N12	42	36	06	02.00	16.00	F	m\d	V	1	11s	
R12	42	37	05	09.10	03.06	I	m\d	C	4	11s	y
S11	36	40	- 04	12.06	05.03	A\I	m\d	V\C	1	12x	y
S12	28	22	06	02.06	02.06	A	m\d	H\V	4	21s	
S13	39	34	05	01.00	06.00	I	co	V\C	1	12s	y
S15	33	25	08	05.00	01.08	I\A	m\d	V	1	11x	
S16	39	37	02	09.10	04.10	M\I	m\d	V\C	1	11x	y
S17	34	30	04	10.07	02.08	F	m\d	H	2	21s	
S18	55	36	19	07.00	06.05	I	co	C	5	22x	y
S21	42	42	00	15.06	00.05	I\A	m\d	C	2	12x	y
S22	33	30	03	01.00	04.03	M	co	H	1	11x	
S23	48	31	17	11.06	00.03	A	m\d	H	3	11x	y
S24	27	24	03	04.00	02.00	M	m\d	V\C	2	11x	
S25	37	31	06	08.00	02.00	AM	m\d	H	2	21x	y
S26	42	32	10	03.06	02.03	I	co	V	1	12x	yo
S27	42	41	01	14.00	02.01	I	m\d	V	1	11x	
S28	30	35	- 05	02.02	09.08	I	cos	H\C	1	12s	
S29	40	38	02	19.00	01.01	AM	m	V	2	11x	
S30	48	40	08	07.02	11.02	F\I	m\d	C	1	21x	y
S31	38	37	01	10.03	07.02	AM	m\d	C	2	11x	y
S32	36	33	03	07.08	05.11	AM	m\d	H	3	11x	y
T11	41	32	09	05.11	04.02	M	m\d	C	2	21x	y
W11	45	42	03	09.00	06.08	D	m\o	H	3	21	
W12	55	38	17	03.00	03.00	D	m\o	H	1	11	
W13	35	31	04	06.00	00.09	D	m\o	H	2	11	
W14	40	35	05	00.07	01.08	D	m\o	H	2	11	
W15	52	45	07	14.00	05.01	D	m\o	H	3	21	
W16	45	46	- 01	09.06	04.08	D	m\o	H	2	11	
W17	35	30	05	03.00	06.00	D	co	H	1	22	
W18	44	40	04	24.00	01.03	D	m\o	H	4	11	

Table One Legend

Age = Age; Aex = Ex's age; Dif = age difference; Mar\Co = duration of marriage\cohabitation; Sep\Dt = time since death or separation;

Cause = End of relationship caused by the following categories: AM = Another Man; AW = Another Woman; A = Adultery; I = Incompatible; D = Death; F = Financial; M = Mental illness
alcoholism etc.

Marital status:- m = married; d = divorced; co = cohabiting; s = legally separated; o = dead

Arr = Arrangements for children in the following categories:
H = It just happened; V = by voluntary agreement between the parents; C = by Court Order;

No = the number of dependent children

Pt\qt:- Pt = how many cohabiting relationships including the one under study each parent had had. The first digit is the ordinal for the father the second the ordinal for the mother. qt = who
left the family home, x = the ex other parent mother; s = the subject home parent father.

Mediation. The letter y at the end of the row indicates that mediation or counselling was sought jointly by the parties. The suffix o indicates that it was sought by the father only.

TableTwo

Lone Fathers Education\Occupation\Income\Children

	Ed	Emp	IncB	IncA	Source	Feel	No\ Ages Child
B11	c	U SkMan	05.29	05.29	2\3	W	B10\G8\B7
B12	a	E SkMan	00.00	08.11	1\3	B	G12
B13	a	E SkMan	14.80	11.00	1\3\5	W	G8
B14	c	E Pro	14.09	14.09	1\3	W	G7\B4
C11	c	E Pro	15.00	12.59	1\3	W	B17\G14
C12	b	S Pro	30.00	08.60	1\3\5\6	W	G9\G11\G13
C13	c	U Pro	07.86	05.82	4\9	W	IB27\IB23\G22
J11	c	E Pro	60.00	09.60	3\9	W	4xIB\G11
J12	c	E Pro	xx.xx	19.02	1\3	B	B16\G14
J13	a	*E Pro	Refused—————				W B20\G18
K11	a	E Man	07.80	07.80	1\?	S	PB19\G14
K12	a	*U Man	07.80	05.17	3\4	S	PG14\PG11
K13	a	U ?	04.48	04.48	2\3	W	PB9\PB7
K14	c	U Sk	18.00	05.30	2\3	W	PB12\PG11
K15	c	E Pro	30.56	30.56	1\3	B	G20\G17
K16	a	*U Sk	06.37	06.37	2\3\5	W	G15\B13\G11
M11	a	U Man	07.80	06.03	2\3	S	2xG7\G9\G10
M12	a	*U SSMan	Nk	05.23	2\3\9	B	IPx2\B12
M13	a	E SSMan	xx.xx	04.70	2\9	W	IG18\B12\B9
M14	a	*U Man	04.68	04.68	2\3	B	B8\B10
M15	b	U Pro	50.00	06.45	1\2\3\7	W	IB24\G11
N11	a	E Sk	30.00	15.00	1\3	B	G12
N12	b	*E Sk	NA.00	16.00	1\3	B	B18
R12	c	U Pro	50.00	05.09	2\3	W	B12\B10\B7\B4
S11	a	U Sk	06.50	04.22	2\3\8	W	B9
S12	a	U Pro	18.00	05.11	2\3\7	W	B3\G4+ 1aB4 1aB5
S13	a	U Man	Na	04.78	2\3\9	B	B9 + B4 with ex
S15	b	E Sk	10.92	11.96	1\3\9	B	B3
S16	c	E Pro	68.00	31.00	1\3	W	B9
S17	a	U Pro	14.80	04.50	2\3	W	B6\B9\IPB16
S18	b	*S Sk	20.80	08.45	3\9	W	G7\B9\G11\B12\G13
S21	b	E Sk	16.80	13.9	1\3	W	G10\B12
S22	c	E Pro	05.00	05.00	1\3\8	S	B5
S23	b	U	Sk	22.00	05.99	2\3	W B3\G9\B10
S24	b	E SSMan	Na.	10.34	1\2\3\8	B	G3\B5
S25	a	U SS	22.60	05.40	2\3\5	W	B8\PB15
S26	c	E Sk	09.50	11.25	1\3	B	B4
S27	c	E Pro	27.00	22.80	1\3	B	B16
S28	a	*E Sk	03.64	04.75	1\2\3	B	G11
S29	b	E Pro	22.50	20.50	1\3	W	B10\G7
S30	a	*E SS	09.00	07.50	1\3\8\9	W	IG19\B16
S31	b	*U Man	20.02	06.79	2\3\8	W	G17\B15
S32	c	S Pro	10.00	06.93	2\3\9	W	1aB16\G12\B8
T11	c	U Sk	06.00	04.81	2\3	W	G4\G6
W11	c	*U Sk	12.25	06.47	2\3	W	B15\B12\B10
W12	a	U Man	10.00	04.28	2\3	B	B3
W13	c	E Pro	18.80	13.2	1\3\9	B	G1\B4
W14	c	U Man	10.00	06.91	2\3\9	W	B9\G11
W15	a	E Pro	20.00	23.6	1\3\8	S	Bx3 10
W16	c	E Pro	15.07	20.05	1\3\9	S	B11\G8
W17	b	U Sk	06.50	02.80	2\3	W	G8
W18	a	E Sk	15.20	09.56	1\2\3	B	IB24\IB21\B18\ G15\1aB15\1aG14

Table Two Legend

Education:-
a = left school at minimum age; b = continue at school; c = higher education degree HND etc

Occupation:-
E = Employed (26), U = Unemployed (23) * = more than 6 years, S = Student (3) Sk = Skilled non manual; Sk Man = Skilled manual; Man = Manual; Pro = Professional and managerial; SS = Semi-skilled; SSman = Semi-skilled manual.

Income:
IncB = Income before ex's death or departure. For comparative purposes where this was more than six years ago subjects have been excluded. In the remaining cases the given income has been increased by 1 per cent for every three months to account for inflation and rising wage levels.
IncA = Income at the time of completing the questionnaire. The numbers following represent the sources as follows:
1 = wage\salary; 2 = Income support\Family credit; 3 = Child Benefit; 4 = Unemployment Benefit; 5 = Voluntary payment from ex; 6 = Court order payment from ex; 7 = CSA payment from ex; 8 = Other such as sick benefit, disability allowance etc.

Subjective feelings about financial circumstances:-
W = feel worse off; S = Feel the same; B = feel better off.

The final column represents the subject's children:
G is a dependent girl, B is a dependent boy. The prefix I indicates a natural child now living independently. The prefix la equals a dependent child who is not a genetically related child ie Step-children taken on within the past six months or ex's children by another father who still lives with the home parent. The prefix P is a home parent's child by a previous partner. + = natural child living with ex. The numbers following B or G indicate the age of the child rounded to the nearest year.
B = 49; G = 41; IB = 10; IG = 2; PB = 6; PG = 3; laB = 4;
laG = 1; IP = 2; + =1.

Table Three

Relations with Ex and Domestic

	Rl	Cm	Ho	Dm	Co	Cl	La	MR	CC	ar	af	ap	br	bf	bp	Lpw
B11	w	06	05	Y	05	05	04	10	05	--	--	--	08	--	--	---
B12	s	08	00	N	05	05	02	08	03	--	--	--	--	--	--	---
B13	w	05	02	N	02	00	02	08	08	02	--	--	15	--	--	---
B14	w	06	05	Y	05	03	03	10	03	01	--	--	02	--	08	20
C11	s	07	04	N	03	02	02	09	04	--	--	--	--	--	--	---
C12	s	08	05	Y	08	08	08	10	08	--	--	--	--	--	--	---
C13	s	05	06	N	02	02	02	10	05	--	--	--	--	--	--	---
J11	i	08	07	Y	01	01	00	06	03	--	--	--	--	04	--	---
J12	s	08	09	N	04	06	05	10	03	--	--	--	--	--	--	---
J13	s	08	08	Y	07	03	03	04	02	--	--	06	--	04	--	30
K11	i	10	10	Y	05	00	00	10	05	--	--	--	--	--	--	---
K12	w	05	03	N	00	06	00	10	06	--	--	--	--	--	--	---
K13	i	05	00	Y	10	10	10	10	10	--	--	--	--	--	--	---
K14	w	00	00	N	02	01	00	06	03	--	--	--	--	--	--	---
K15	s	02	04	N	01	01	01	05	04	--	--	04	--	--	--	20
K16	w	05	03	N	05	02	02	10	05	--	--	--	--	--	--	---
M11	w	10	00	N	10	05	05	10	05	--	--	--	02	01	--	---
M12	s	00	00	N	02	02	02	10	07	--	--	--	--	--	--	---
M13	w	00	00	Y	05	05	05	10	07	--	--	--	--	04	--	---
M14	w	00	00	Y	04	04	04	10	08	03	--	--	--	--	--	---
M15	w	00	I	N	06	03	03	06	06	--	--	--	--	--	--	---
N11	w	10	05	N	00	00	00	10	05	--	--	--	--	--	--	---
N12	i	00	02	N	07	08	07	10	06	--	--	--	--	--	--	---
R12	w	00	00	Y	05	01	01	08	06	08	--	--	05	--	--	---
S11	i	04	06	Y	05	03	02	08	08	--	--	--	04	--	--	---
S12	w	00	02	Y	05	09	10	10	05	--	--	--	--	--	--	---
S13	i	10	10	Y	01	01	01	01	01@	Lives with mother						
S15	w	01	01	Y	04	03	02	10	06	--	--	--	--	--	50	55
S16	w	01	00	Y	07	09	05	10	08	--	--	--	--	--	18	35
S17	w	00	00	Y	04	03	05	10	05	--	--	--	--	--	06	04
S18	X	00	NA	Y	10	05	07	10	05	--	--	--	--	--	--	---
S21	w	01	01	Y	04	04	04	10	06	--	--	15	--	--	15	40
S22	w	02	04	Y	08	08	08	07	08	01	--	--	01	--	18	27
S23	w	00	10	N	05	05	05	10	05	--	--	--	--	--	--	---
S24	X	00	I	N	00	05	00	10	05	02	--	--	05	--	--	---
S25	s	01	07	N	03	03	00	10	08	--	--	--	08	--	--	---
S26	i	09	06	Y	09	02	04	10	04	--	--	--	10ex		21	35
S27	s	09	05	N	01	06	05	09	05	--	--	--	01	--	--	---
S28	w	00	03	Y	07	08	07	09	08	--	--	--	15	04	--	---
S29	w	05	05	N	00	00	00	10	01	Hse keep			05	--	--	100
S30	i	08	08	Y	01	00	01	10	04	--	--	--	--	--	--	---
S31	w	01	00	Y	01	03	02	10	05	--	--	--	--	--	--	---
S32	w	02	02	N	06	06	07	10	07	--	--	--	10	--	--	---
T11	w	00	04	Y	05	05	05	10	04	--	--	--	--	--	--	---
W11	NA	>>>>>		Y	05	03	01	06	05	--	--	--	--	--	--	---
W12	NA	>>>>>		Y	04	05	05	10	XX	--	--	--	--	--	16	15
W13	NA	>>>>>		Y	07	05	03	08	07	02	--	--	15	02	65	150
W14	NA	>>>>>		Y	10	10	10	10	10	--	--	--	--	--	--	---
W15	NA	>>>>>		Y	04	03	03	08	05	--	--	04	--	--	40	150
W16	NA	>>>>>		Y	04	00	01	01	03	05	--	06	05	--	09	64
W17	NA	>>>>>		N	05	07	07	09	06	--	--	--	--	--	--	---
W18	NA	>>>>>		N	04	04	01	09	05	--	--	--	--	--	--	---

Table Three Legend

R1 = relations with ex since separation, w = worse, i = improved, s = same, x = not given.

Co = Communication with ex on a scale 0 = none 10 = complete.
Ho = feelings for ex on a scale 0 = complete love 10 = absolute hate.

Share of domestic tasks performed before death or separation on a scale 0 = none, 10 = all.
DM = run a house before Y = yes, N = no.
Co = Cooking; Cl = Cleaning; La = Laundry; MR = Maintenance and repairs; CC = Child care.

Help with domestic work in hours per week:-
ar = relatives; af = friends; ap = paid help.
Help with child care in hours per week:-
br = relatives; bf = friends; bp = paid help.
Lpw = total cost per week of the above.

Table Four – Lone Fathers by occupation etc and domicile

	Occupation	Ex	Unmp	Domicile	
B11	Gen Builder*	F	08.0	Bristol	(U)
B12	Leading Trackman	H		Bristol	(U)
B13	Instrument maker	F		Bristol	(U)
B14	Accounts asst	H		Bristol	(U)
C11	Coll Lecturer	P		Highnam Glos	(R)
C12	Computer managerS	H		Cheltenham	(U)
C13	Aero design eng*	H	00.6	Cheltenham	(U)
J11	Writer\TV directr	H		Talybont Powys	(R)
J12	Architect	H		Monmouth	(R)
J13	Journalist	P		London	(U)
K11	Bus driver	H		Kingston on T	(S)
K12	Engineer*	H	06.4	New Malden Sry	(S)
K13	XXXXXXXXXXXXX*	P	04.0	New Malden Sry	(S)
K14	Draughtsman*	P	04.0	Surbiton	(S)
K15	Doctor (GP)	P		Thames Ditton	(S)
K16	Production audit*	P	03.0	Morden Sry	(S)
M11	Manual worker*	F	04.6	Manchester	(U)
M12	Driver*(Invalid)	H	11.6	Manchester	(U)
M13	Driver	P		Manchester	(U)
M14	Fk lft trk driver*	H	10.0	Manchester	(U)
M15	Writer\trainer*	F	02.6	Bury Lancs	(U)
N11	Fk lft trk Eng	P		Northolt	(S)
N12	Fk lft trk Eng	H		Harrow	(S)
R12	Co Director*	H	01.6	Wargrave	(S)
S11	Chef*	P	05.3	Stoke on T	(U)
S12	Transpt Manager*	H	02.6	Peterborough	(U)
S13	Labourer* (invalid)	H	16.0	Pontypridd	(U)
S15	RAF desk NCO	H		Coltishall Nflk	(R)
S16	Software consult	F		Sunbury on T	(S)
S17	Retail Manager*	P	02.8	Sheffield	(U)
S18	Refrig EngineerS	H		Canterbury	(U)
S21	BT Tech Officer	P		Reading	(U)
S22	Farmer	P		Bacton Nflk	(R)
S23	Motor Mechanic*	F	00.3	Welwyn Gdn City	(U)
S24	Motor Mechanic	H		Putney	(S)
S25	YT Supervisor*	F	00.4	Blyth Nthmb	(U)
S26	Blding estimator	H		Huntingdon	(U)
S27	Sales Manager	P		Mansfield	(U)
S28	School technician	H		Whttlesey Cambs	(R)
S29	Commercial Direct	P		Farnham Sry	(S)
S30	Post Off Clerk	P		Wiston Leics	(S)
S31	Buldg worker*	F	05.6	Northampton	(U)
S32	Land SurveyorS	P		Penrhiwceiber	(U)
T11	Dom Sevice Eng*	H	04.7	Woodbridge Sflk	(R)
W11	Chef*	H	06.8	Amingham Staffs	(R)
W12	Factory worker*	F	03.0	Telford	(U)
W13	Structural Eng	H		Newcastle on T	(U)
W14	Farm worker	disab*?	08.0	Newquay Cornwall	(R)
W15	Journalist	H		Edinburgh	(U)
W16	Systems analyst	H		Surbiton	(S)
W17	Wireman*	H	03.6	Kingston	(S)
W18	Admin Asst	P		Wellington Somst	(R)

Table Four Legend

Ex = Wife working H = at home(25) F = Full time (9) P = Part time (17)
?(1) not known. NB 5 said homemaker.
* = Unemployed (23) e.g. 02.8 = 2 yrs 8 mths unemployment
U = Urban (27) S = Suburban (15) R = Rural (10)

Table Five

Lone parents' health etc and agreement on children

	Ac	Ed	Up	Re	Fn	Avg	Ha	He	Wo	xHa	xHe	xWo	NpMonths
B11	08	06	07	xx	06	---	07	07	02	03	07	06	N
B12	10	09	10	xx	xx	---	07	08	06	xx	xx	xx	N
B13	10	10	05	10	10	09.0	-t	-t	-t	-t	-t	-t	N
B14	00	10	10	07	10	07.4	-t	-5	-5	xx	xx	xx	N
C11	10	10	04	07	02	06.6	-4	00	-4	10	xx	xx	Ng
C12	09	09	08	xx	09	---	05	00	-5	00	-5	-5	N
C13	10	xx	10	xx	10	---	05	00	-5	05	00	-2	Ng
J11	10	06	06	10	08	08.0	-3	-3	-8	00	01	-8	N
J12	10	08	08	07	10	08.6	07	07	04	04	00	-7	Ng
J13	10	10	10	10	10	10.0	-5	-5	-5	05	05	03	N
K11	10	10	10	10	10	10.0	10	10	-5	10	10	-5	Y.?
K12	03	00	00	00	00	05	00.6	00	-t	05	00	05	N
K13	05	10	10	00	00	05.0	10	10	-t	00	05	00	N
K14	No Contact					---	10	00	-t	xx	xx	xx	Ng
K15	10	10	10	03	05	07.6	10	10	10	xx	xx	xx	N
K16	10	10	06	10	05	08.2	10	00	-t	xx	xx	xx	N
M11	10	10	10	10	00	08.0	00	00	10	xx	xx	xx	N
M12	No Contact					---	xx	xx	xx	xx	xx	xx	N
M13	No Contact 00					---	-2	-2	-t	05	-2	09	N
M14	00	00	00	00	00	00.0	10	08	-t	No Contact		N	
M15	00	06	06	05	06	04.6	-6	03	-6	03	-3	10	N
N11	00	00	00	00	00	00.0	10	05	10	00	-10	-10	N
N12	10	10	06	10	05	08.2	10	00	10	-5	00	00	N
R12	00	00	00	00	00	00.0	-5	-5	-t	-5	-5	-10	N
S11	10	01	02	02	01	03.2	05	09	-t	-t	-10	10	N
S12	00	xx	10	xx	xx	---	10	05	-t	xx	xx	xx	Y.6
S13	10	10	10	10	10	10.0	10	-5	10	10	-5	10	Ng
S15	02	02	02	na	na	---	10	03	05	-t	-8	-10	N
S16	09	06	04	08	01	05.6	09	-5	-8	xx	xx	xx	N
S17	00	00	00	00	10	02.0	-5	00	-t	10	00	10	N
S18	No Contact 5 yrs					---							N
S21	04	06	06	04	07	05.4	-5	05	05	-5	00	-5	N
S22	03	08	05	xx	00	---	05	02	02	xx	xx	xx	N
S23	08	10	08	10	00	07.2	-t	10	07	05	-5	-10	N
S24	10	No Contact				---	05	08	07	xx	xx	xx	N
S25	04	05	05	05	02	04.2	-4	-2	-8	00	02	06	N
S26	10	03	05	01	07	05.0	07	03	02	03	03	05	N
S27	08	09	09	10	03	07.8	06	00	02	04	-2	xx	N
S28	No Contact					---	10	10	10	xx	xx	xx	N
S29	07	10	10	10	00.-07.4		-t	-5	-t	10	00	00	N
S30	08	06	04	10	00	05.6	07	03	-6	05	-3	00	N
S31	00	00	00	00	00	00.0	05	03	-8	xx	-3	07	N
S32	00	10	10	10	00	06.0	10	10	-t	00	00	10	N
T11	00	00	00	00	00	00.0	10	10	-t	08	-10	-10	Ng
W11	--	09	08	10	06	08.3	-6	-2	-6	-----------			N
W12	--	10	10	10	10	10.0	xx	xx	xx	-----------			N
W13	--	07	05	08	04	06.0	-8	-8	02	-----------			N
W14	--	10	07	10	05	08.0	-5	00	-6	-----------			N
W15	--	07	08	07	08	07.5	-2	00	00	-----------			N
W16	--	10	09	09	09	09.3	-8	-1	01	-----------			N
W17	--	NA>>>>>>>>>>>				---	-1	00	-t	-----------			N
W18	--	10	10	10	09	09.8	00	00	-2	-----------			Y.4

Table Five Legend

On a scale -10 to 10 agreement between the parents on:-
Ac = Access; Ed = Education; Up = Upbringing; Re = Religion; Fn = Finance. Avg = average on all five only.

On a scale -10 to 10 compared with before death or separation:-
Ha = father's happiness; He = Health; Wo = Financial well being. xHa = mother's happiness; xHe = Health; xWo Financial well being. -t = -10 in this table.

New relationships. The final column N = no cohabiting or relationship in which the home parent and another adult regard themselves as a couple. Ng = such a relationship but not cohabiting.
Y = such a relationship cohabiting.

NB anyone cohabiting for more than six months before the questionnaire was dropped from the survey sample.

Table Six - **Childrens' attitudes**

	Ha	He	Wb	Sc	Gy	Gm	Np	Mn	Mb	Mp	add
B11\1	05	10	08	06	10	10	10	10	10	10	Ref
B11\2	07	10	07	06	10	10	10	10	10	10	"
B11\3	05	10	06	05	10	10	10	10	10	10	"
B12\1	10	10	06	05	10	09	xx	xx	xx	09	G
B13\1	-5	00	00	00	00	00	xx	05	10	05	Ref
B14\1	00	-3	00	ty	-3	03	xx	07	10	xx	G
B14\2	too young ----------------------					--xx	07	na	xx	"	
C11\1	05	01	00	ty	06	-4	xx	07	02	02	Ref
C11\2	-3	00	-2	-1	02	??	xx	08	08	02	"
C12\1	00	00	00	00	06	01	05	05	05	06*	Ref
C12\2	00	00	00	00	06	06	05	05	05	06*	"
C12\3	-3	00	00	00	06	02	05	05	05	06	"
C13\3	00	00	00	ty	-2	02	08	08	08	07	Ref
J11\1	-2	-1	00	02	05	-3	xx	07	10	05	G
J12\1	-2	06	00	-1	00	00	09	10	10	08*	G
J12\2	-2	00	-2	04	-2	-2	09	10	10	08*	"
J13\1	00	00	00	00	00	00	xx	08	07	05	Ref
J13\2	00	00	00	00	00	00	xx	08	07	05	"
K11\1	10	10	10	10	10	10	na	10	10	10	Ref
K11\2	10	10	10	10	10	10	na	10	10	10	"
K12\1	10	01	01	10	10	-5	na	05	05	08	G
K12\2	08	01	01	10	10	-5	na	05	05	08	"
K13\1	10	10	05	10	10	10	xx	05	05	00	Ref
K13\2	10	10	05	10	10	10	xx	05	05	00	"
K14\1	03	00	01	03	03	-t	xx	no contact			NK
K14\2	03	00	01	03	03	-t	xx	no contact			"
K15\1	10	10	10	05	10	10	xx	05	07	04	G
K15\2	10	10	10	05	10	10	xx	05	07	04	"
K16\1	07	00	-2	00	00	00	xx	10	10	03	Ref
K16\2	07	00	02	00	00	00	xx	10	10	03	"
K16\3	07	00	02	00	00	00	xx	10	10	03	"
M11\1	00	10	10	xx	10	00	xx	xx	xx	xx	Ref
M11\2	00	10	10	xx	10	-t	xx	xx	xx	xx	"
M11\3	00	10	10	xx	10	00	xx	xx	xx	xx	"
M11\4	00	10	10	xx	10	00	xx	xx	xx	xx	"
M12\1	No contact								05	xx	NK
M13\1	-3	00	00	00	-1	-2	xx	03	10	xx	G
M13\2	-6	-5	07	07	10	-t	xx	03	10	xx	"
M13\3	-6	-5	07	08	10	-t	xx	03	10	xx	"
M14\1	10	10	08	08	10	-t	xx	00	03	00	Ref
M14\2	10	10	08	08	10	-t	xx	00	03	00	"
M15\2	05	03	05	05	05	-5	xx	00	03	00	"
N11\1	05	00	00	0S	05	00	xx	0S	07	0S*	G
N12\1	00	00	-2	00	-2	-t	xx	xx	xx	xx	NK
R12\1	02	02	02	0S	00	-S	xx	xx	xx	xx	G
R12\2	03	-2	02	0S	02	-2	xx	xx	xx	xx	"
R12\3	-S	-S	00	-5	00	00	xx	xx	xx	xx	"
R12\4	02	-5	00	00	00	00	xx	xx	xx	xx	"
S11\1	05	05	00	08	08	-4	xx	05	08	xx	G
S12\1	10	00	05	ty	00	-t	10	00	05	na	G
S12\2	10	00	05	ty	00	-t	10	00	05	na	"
S13\1	10	10	06	10	10	10	xx	10	??	xx	G
S13\2	too young ----------------------------						- 10	??	xx	"	
S15\1	05	00	05	na	06	-7	xx	02	03	xx	Ref

Table Six continued

	Ha	He	Wb	Sc	Gy	Gm	Np	Mn	Mb	Mp	add
S16\1	03	05	00	05	00	00	xx	09	07	xx	G
S17\2	-5	05	09	05	09	-t	xx	00	08	10	G
S17\3	00	00	05	10	10	00	xx	00	10	08	"
S18\1	10	10	10	10	10	-t	xx	00	01	00	NK
S18\2	10	10	00	05	10	-t	xx	00	01	00	"
S18\3	10	10	10	10	10	-t	xx	00	01	00	"
S18\4	10	10	00	05	10	-t	xx	00	01	00	"
S18\5	10	10	10	10	10	-t	xx	00	01	00	"
S21\1	00	05	05	05	08	00	xx	06	08	01	G
S21\2	00	05	05	05	08	01	xx	06	08	01	"
S22\1	10	10	00	ty	00	09	xx	09	00	xx	Ref
S23\1	-5	05	-5	-8	05	-8	xx	-5	10	-8	G
S23\2	-t	05	-5	-5	05	-9	xx	-5	10	-t	"
S23\3	-5	05	-5	05	05	-5	xx	-5	10	na	"
S24\1	05	03	00	05	xx	??	xx	??	02	??	NK
S24\2	07	03	04	ty	xx	??	xx	??	02	??	"
S25\1	08	02	00	01	00	00	xx	05	05	xx	NK
S2S\2	-8	04	-1	00	06	-1	xx	0S	05	xx	"
S26\1	05	00	00	ty	05	00	xx	06	05	xx	Ref
S27\1	00	00	00	00	-1	-2	xx	07	08	04	Ref
S28\1	10	10	08	10	08	-t	xx	no contact			NK
S29\1	-1	00	00	00	01	-2	xx	05	10	03	G
S29\2	00	00	00	00	01	-2	xx	05	10	03	"
S30\3	01	02	03	05	03	00	07	07	07	02	G
S31\1	05	04	10	10	10	-5	xx	01	08	00	Ref
S31\2	08	04	10	04	10	-t	xx	01	08	00	"
S32\1	05	00	08	00	10	00	xx	05	0S	05	Ref
S32\2	0S	00	08	00	10	00	xx	05	0S	0S	"
S32\3	08	00	-5	00	05	00	xx	05	05	05	"
T11\1	09	10	09	10	10	01	xx	01	01	xx	G
T11\2	10	09	09	10	10	01	xx	01	01	xx	"
W11\1	00	00	00	00	00	na	xx	na	09	na	na
W11\2	00	00	00	00	00	na	xx	na	09	na	na
W11\3	00	00	00	00	00	na	xx	na	09	na	na
W12\1	na mother diedwhen child 6 weeks old									na	na
W13\1	05	-6	05	00	07	na	xx	na	07	na	na
W13\2	0S	-6	-2	0S	07	na	xx	na	07	na	na
W14\1	0S	00	00	05	00	na	xx	na	10	na	na
W14\2	05	00	00	05	00	na	xx	na	10	na	na
W1S\1	00	00	00	00	0S	na	xx	na	09	na	na
W15\2	00	00	00	00	0S	na	xx	na	09	na	na
W15\3	00	00	00	00	05	na	xx	na	09	na	na
W16\1	-t	-8	00	00	00	na	xx	na	10	na	na
W16\2	-5	00	-2	-3	00	na	xx	na	10	na	na
W17\1	-4	00	-5	-1	04	na	xx	na	xx	na	na
W18\3	-8	00	00	-t	00	na	xx	na	10	na	na
W18\4	-5	00	-2	-1	00	na	xx	na	10	na	na

Table Six Legend

Comparisons on a scale -10 to 10 for children now and before ex's death or departure:- Ha=Happy; He=Healthy; Wb=Well behaved; Sc = getting on at school; Gy = get on with father; Gm = with mother; on a scale 0 to 10 how children get on with:- Np = father's new partner; Mn = mother now; Mb = mother before; Mn = Mother's new partner. Add = Address; Ref = Refused; G = Given; NK = Not Known; xx = no response; ty = too young; -t = -10 in this table.

Table Seven – **Contact between children and other parent mother**

	a	b	c	d	e	f	g	h	ft	bke	car	ptr	P	S	OC
B11\1	120	64	34	7	0	0	p13	p0	i	i	150	x	Y	Y	Y
B11\2	same														
B11\3	same														
B12\1	364	156	52	x	x	x	px	px	10	04	002	005	N	N	N
B13\1	024	024	12	21	y	y	p52	p52	i	i	120	150	N	N	N
B14\1	52	000	00	00	00	00	p52	p0	i	i	020	060	Y	Y	N
B14\2	same														
C11\1	000	000	00	00	00	00	py	py	30	10	005	N	N	N	N
C11\2	156	06?	00	00	00	00	py	py	30	10	005	N	N	N	N
C12\1	052	156	26	21	00	00	p365	py	i	i	010	i	Y	N	N
C12\2	same														
C12\3	same														
C13\3	350	000	00	00	00	00	py	py	15	05	003	n	Y	Y	N
J11\1	208	156	26	14	02	02	p18	p156	i	40	012	060	Y	Y	N
J12\1	156	000	00	14	00	00	p208	p156	20	i	002	N	N	N	N
J12\2	same														
J13\1	052	000	00	00	00	00	p104	p52	i	i	*	060	N	N	N
J13\2	same														
K11\1	364	052	y	y	00	00	p364	p364	45	10	005	060	Y	Y	N
K11\2	same														
K12\1	104	048	17	14	y	00	py	p0	i	i	*	240	N	N	N
K12\2	same														
K13\1	026	012	12	00	00	00	py	py	y	i	i	y	N	N	N
K13\2	same														
K14\1	000	000	00	00	00	00	p0	p0	i	i	480	480	N	N	N
K14\2	same														
K15\1	012	006	00	07	02	02	py	py	60	40	015	i	N	N	N
K15\2	same														
K16\1	104	052	52	00	00	00	py	py	i	i	030	060	Y	Y	N
K16\2	same														
K16\3	same														
M11\1	000	000	00	00	00	00	x0	n24	i	i	*	030	Y	N	Y
M11\2	026	013	26	00	00	00	x0	n24	i	i	*	030	Y	N	Y
M11\3	034	017	17	00	00	00	x0	n24	i	i	*	030	Y	N	Y
M11\4	same														
M12\1	No contact of any kind														
M13\1	012	006	00	00	00	00	p0	p0	10	02	001	na	i	Dead	
M13\2	same														
M13\3	same														
M14\1	000	000	00	00	00	00	p0	nx	i	60	020	120	N	N	N
M14\2	same														
M15\1	000	000	00	00	yx	00	p0	n0	i	i	*	060	N	Y	Y
M15\2	same														
N11\1	052	000	00	00	00	00	px	px	20	x	*	x	N	N	N
N12\1	000	000	00	00	00	00	x0	y0	x	x	*	060	Y	N	Y
R12\1	061	000	00	49	00	00	n12	p0	x	x	045	x	Y	Y	N
R12\2	same														
R12\3	same														
R12\4	same														
S11\1	104	012	06	00	00	00	p52	p52	15	10	005	015	N	N	N
S12\1	000	000	00	00	00	00	x0	n0	i	i	300	780	N	N	N
S12\2	same														
S13\1	364	20	00	00	00	00	n0	po	10	05	*	i	N	N	N
S13\2	same														
S15\1	024	012	12	07	00	00	n0	n0	i	i	p	180	N	N	N

Table Seven Continued

	a	b	c	d	e	f	g	h	ft	bke	car	ptr	P	S	OC
S16\1	111	52	52	07	52	06	p6	p156	i	i	060	120	N	N	N
S17\2	000	000	00	00	00	00	p0	n0	03	02	*	i	Y	Y	N
S17\3	same														
S18\1	000	000	00	00	00	00	x0	p0	i	i	180	300	N	N	N
S18\2	same														
S18\3	same														
S18\4	same														
S18\5	same														
S21\1	000	000	00	00	00	00	x0	p0	60	30	013	025	N	N	N
S21\2	076	026	26	00	00	00	p78	p78	i	i	013	025	N	N	N
S22\1	101	075	26	49	00	00	n12	p0	i	i	240	na	N	Y	N
S23\1	017	000	00	00	04	52	x0	p0	i	i	030	120	N	N	N
S23\2	same														
S23\3	same														
S24\1	000	000	00	00	00	00	x0	p0	x	x	x	x	N	N	N
S24\2	same														
S25\1	052	026	00	00	00	00	p52	p26	25	10	005	i	Y	Y	N
S25\2	same														
S26\1	364	182	26	49	i	i	i	i	20	10	005	i	Y	Y	Y
S27\1	111	048	12	07	00	00	p130	p78	i	i	040	090	Y	N	N
S28\1	000	000	00	00	00	00	n0	n0	i	60	*	030	N	N	N
S29\1	026	012	12	00	00	00	p12	p12	i	i	*	i	N	N	N
S29\2	same														
S30\3	170	078	26	14	26	26	p130	p130	i	60	020	090	N	Y	N
S31\1	006	000	00	00	00	12	p0	p04	i	i	480	i	N	N	N
S31\2	same														
S32\1	005	005	00	00	01	01	12	p0	i	i	*	540	Y	Y	N
S32\2	same														
S32\3	same														
T11\1	000	000	00	00	00	00	p1	p0	i	i	*	660	Y	Y	N
T11\2	same														

Table Seven Legend

a = No of days a year see each other
b = No of nights spent at mother's house
c = No of weekends spent at mother's house
d = No of days holiday a year spent with mother
e = No of letters a year mother to child
f = No of letters a year child to mother
g = No of phone calls a year mother to child
h = No of phone calls a year child to mother
i = impractical or irrelevant
x = unknown
N= not possessed etc + No of calls etc
p = phone owned + No of calls etc
Y = yes but quantity\frequency not known

Journey times between mother and child in minutes:-
ft = on foot; bke = by bicycle; car = by car; (*Father has no car) ptr = by public transport.

Contact with Ex's Family. P = Ex's parents; S = Ex's brothers and sisters; OC = Other Close relatives eg children by former marriage.

Table Eight – Financial Settlements

	debt	home	Payx	Payc	Equit	Pens	Car	Frn	Sav	0th	Fy	Fx	Fc
B11	v	Rny	000	000	000	000	na	10	na	na	xx	xx	xx
B12	n	Rnn	000	000	000	000	00	00	00	00	xx	xx	xx
B13	v	Oyv	000	003	000	000	10	05	00	00	05	05	xx
B14	Y	Oyy	000	000	000	000	10	10	10	00	10	10	10
C11	Y	Oyn	000	000	10k	1\2	10	09	10	00	08	10	02
C12	y	Oyy	000	000	24k	000	05	08	05	00	05	06	06
C13	y	Oyy	000	000	35k	000	05	05	05	05	10	10	10
J11	n	Oyn	000	000	23k	000	05	04	05	00	05	10	05
J12	n	Oyn	025	008	48k	000	00	06	08	00	09	07	10
J13	y	Oyn	000	000	000	000	xx	xx	xx	xx	07	10	08
K11	y	Rnn	000	010	000	000	10	00	00	00	00	00	10
K12	n	Rny	000	000	000	000	10	10	00	00	00	05	08
K13	v	Rnn	000	000	000	000	00	00	00	00	00	00	00
K14	Y	Oyy	000	000	2.5	000	xx	xx	xx	xx	00	??	00
K1S	n	Oyy	000	000	not yet - -		00	07	00	00	xx	xx	xx
K16	y	Ony	not yet settled - - - - - -				xx	xx	xx	xx	02	08	05
M11	n	Rnn	000	000	000	000	xx	xx	xx	xx	00	00	00
M12	y	Rny	000	000	000	000	10	10	10	10	xx	xx	xx
M13	y	Oyy	000	000	08k	000	05	03	na	na	00	10	00
M14	n	Ony	000	000	000	000	10	10	10	10	10	10	10
M15	y	Rnn	000	000	000	000	07	07	07	07	00	10	00
N11	n	Oyn	000	000	30k	06k	na	02	05	na	00	00	00
N12	n	Oyn	000	000	000	000	na	00	00	00	03	08	06
R12	y	Rnn	000	000	000	000	05	00	00	na	00	05	00
S11	Y	Oyy	000	000	000	000	10	10	00	na	10	10	10
S12	Y	Rnn	000	000	000	000	na	00	00	na	00	00	00
S13	y	R(yorn)	000	000	000	000	00	00	00	00	xx	xx	xx
S15	n	Rny	000	000	000	000	00	10	.5	xx	xx	xx	xx
S16	y	Oyy	000	000	000	000	05	08	00	00	09	04	05
S17	y	Rny	000	000	000	000	10	00	00	na	00	00	00
S18	y	Rnn	000	000	000	000	05	05	00	00	00	10	00
S21	Y	Oyy	not yet settled - - - - - -				10	10	10	10	08	??	??
S22	v	Rnn	005	000	000	000	05	05	na	na	00	08	??
S23	y	Oyy	000	000	000	000	10	10	na	na	07	07	07
S24	n	Oyy	000	000	1.3k	000	10	05	na	na	05	10	05
S25	n	Oyy	000	000	000	000	10	08	00	na	04	06	03
S26	y	Oyy	000	021	na	na	na	na	na	na	03	09	09
S27	n	Oyy	000	000	15k	000	00	05	05	na	03	07	09
S28	y	Rnn	000	000	000	000	00	00	00	00	xx	xx	xx
S29	n	Oyv	000	000	not yet set		00	08	05	na	03	10	00
S30	n	Oyn	000	000	000	000	10	10	na	na	05	07	00
S31	y	Oyy	000	000	000	000	na	02	05	na	00	10	00
S32	y	Oyy	000	000	000	000	10	10	10	10	00	10	00
T11	n	Rnn	000	000	000	000	10	08	00	na	10	00	00
W11	Y	Rnn	everything -										
W12	n	Ony	everything -										
W13	n	Onv	everything -										
W14	y	Oyy	everything -										
W15	n	Oyy	everything -										
W16	n	Oyy	everything -										
W17	Y	Rny	everything -										
W18	y	Rny	everything -										

Table Eight Legend

Debt = debt other than mortgage; Home:- O = owning, R = Renting followed by n\y for mortgage and n\y whether present home was the matrimonial home.

Payx = maintenance payments to ex
Payc = maintenance payments for children with ex
Equit = payment for equity in the home
Pens = payment for share of pension rights

On a scale 0 = got nothing to 10 = got all in the division of:-
car, frn = furniture, sav = savings, oth = other.

Father's opinion as to fairness of these financial arrangements for:-
Fy = father, Fx = Ex, Fc = children

xx = no opinion offered or subsequently elicited.

Table Nine

Analysis of unemployment by duration\occupation\income and number of children

Unemployment

	Duration	Occup	Inc	Ch	Notes
B11	8.0	Sk	5.29	3	
C13	0.6	Pro	5.82	1	
K12	6.4	Man	5.17	2	
K13	4.0	Sk	4.48	2	
K14	4.0	Sk	5.30	2	
K16	3.0	Sk	6.37	3	
M11	4.6	Man	6.03	4	
M12	11.6	SS	5.23	1	Invalidity
M14	10.0	Man	4.68	2	
M15	2.6	Pro	6.24	1	
R12	1.6	Pro	5.09	4	
S11	5.3	Sk	4.22	1	
S12	2.6	Pro	5.11	4	
S13	16.0	Man	4.78	1	Invalidity
S17	2.8	Pro	4.5	3	
S23	0.3	Sk	5.99	3	
S25	0.4	SS	5.4	2	
S31	05.6	Man	6.79	2	
T11	4.7	Sk	4.81	2	
W11	6.8	Sk	6.47	3	
W12	3.0	Man	4.39	1	
W14	8.0	Man	6.91	2	Disabled daughter
W17	3.6	Sk	2.80	4	Partner with similar income

NB several quite specifically say they are homemakers and chose unemployment to be so.

Table Nine Legend

Pro = professional or managerial; Sk = skilled; SS = semi-skilled; Man = Manual.

Table Ten Legend

Rl = Relationship with ex compared to before break, w = worse, s = same, i = improved.

Co = Communication with ex, 0 = none, 10 = complete as necessary for children etc.

Ho = Hostility towards ex, 0 = absolute hostility, 10 = complete love.

Blm = Self-assessed share of blame for break up on a scale 0 = no blame at all 10 = all blame.

Vio = Violence experienced. V = violence from ex, R = retaliation, C = ex attack on child spontaneously referred to, I = violence also initiated.

Cse = Cause of break up A = adultery; AM = ex prefers another man; AW = ex prefers another woman; M = ex's mental problems (inc alcoholism and baby blues) I = incompatibility; F = money; O = no reason given. (See Table one)

Ch Av = Childrens overall average "score" for change in happiness, health, behaviour and academic performance since break up. (See Table six)

Ch Arr = How children came to be with father. H = happenstance; V = voluntary agreement with ex; C = Court order.

Table Ten

Father\ex relations

	Rl	Cm	Ho	Blm	Vio	Cse	ChAv	ChArr
B11	w	06	05	4	x	AM	7.25	H
B12	s	08	00	4	x	AM	7.75	V\C
B13	w	05	02	5	n	I\F	-1.25	V
B14	w	06	05	0	VC	M	-1.5	H\V
C11	s	07	04	1	n	A	0.0	H\V
C12	s	08	05	5	n	AW	-0.25	V
C13	s	05	06	5	n	x	0.0	V
J11	i	08	07	3	IR	I	-0.25	V\C
J12	s	08	09	2	n	AW	0.75	V
J13	s	08	08	6	n	x	0.0	V
K11	i	10	10	5	x	I	10.0	V
K12	w	05	03	1	V	I	5.25	C
K13	i	05	00	1	x	AM	8.75	C
K14	w	00	00	0	V	M	1.75	H
K15	s	02	04	7	VR	AM	8.75	H
K16	w	05	03	5	n	AM	1.92	C
M11	w	10	00	0	n	I\A	6.66	C
M12	s	00	00	0	x	F	xxxx	H
M13	w	00	00	1	x	I\A	0.33	C
M14	w	00	00	0	X	M\F	9.0	H
M15	w	00	I	5	V	F\AM	4.5	H
N11	w	10	05	0	n	AW	2.5	H
N12	i	00	02	4	n	F	-.25	V
R12	w	00	00	4	VR	I	0.06	C
S11	i	04	06	2	n	A\I	4.5	V\C
S12	w	00	02	0	n	A	5.0	H\V
S13	i	10	10	5	n	I	9.0	V\C
S15	w	01	01	3	n	I\A	3.3	V
S16	w	01	00	3	VR	M\I	4.25	V\C
S17	w	00	00	8	VI	F	3.63	H
S18	X	00	NA	0	VCR	I	8.5	C
S21	w	01	01	0	V	I\A	3.75	C
S22	w	02	04	1	n	M	6.66	H
S23	w	00	10	0	n	A	-1.88	H
S24	X	00	I	7	n	M	3.86	V\C
S25	s	01	07	10	V	AM	0.75	H
S26	i	09	06	3	VCR	I	1.66	V
S27	s	09	05	2	n	I	0.0	V
S28	w	00	03	5	V	I	9.5	H\C
S29	w	05	05	4	n	AM	-.13	V
S30	i	08	08	3	n	F\I	1.38	C
S31	w	01	00	1	V	AM	6.88	C
S32	w	02	02	0	V	AM	2.42	H
T11	w	00	04	7	VR	M	9.5	C
W11	NA	>>>>>		x	n	x	0.0	x
W12	NA	>>>>>		x	V	x	x.x	x
W13	NA	>>>>>		x	n	x	0.75	x
W14	NA	>>>>>		x	n	x	2.5	x
W15	NA	>>>>>		x	n	x	0.0	x
W16	NA	>>>>>		x	n	x	-3.5	x
W17	NA	>>>>>		x	V	x	-2.5	x
W18	NA	>>>>>		x	n	x	-3.5	x

Table Eleven

Effect of Frequency of Contact

No Contact

		Ha	He	Wb	Sc	Av
C11	(1)	05	01	00	- -	02.0
R14		03	00	01	03	0.15
K14		03	00	01	03	0.15
M11	(4)	00	10	10	- -	06.7
M12		- -	- -	- -	- -	- - - -
M14		10	10	08	08	09.0
M14		10	10	08	08	09.0
M15		05	03	05	05	04.5
N12		00	02	-02	00	-00.5
S12		10	00	05	- -	05.0
S12		10	00	05	- -	05.0
S17		-05	05	09	05	06.0
S17		00	00	05	10	03.8
S18		10	10	10	10	10.0
S18		10	10	00	05	06.3
S18		10	10	10	10	10.0
S18		10	10	00	05	06.3
S18		10	10	10	10	10.0
S21		00	05	05	05	03.8
S24		05	03	00	05	03.3
S24		07	03	04	- -	04.7
S28		10	10	08	10	09.5
T11		09	10	09	10	09.5
T11		10	09	09	10	09.5
Average		6.2	5.7	5.4	6.8	05.9

Less than eighteen times a year

	Ha	He	Wb	Sc	Av
K15	10	10	10	05	08.8
K15	10	10	10	05	08.8
M13	-03	00	00	00	-0.75
M13	-06	-05	07	08	01.0
S23	-05	05	-05	-08	-03.3
S23	-10	05	-05	-05	-03.8
S23	-05	05	-05	05	00.0
S31	05	04	10	10	07.3
S31	08	04	10	04	06.5
S32	05	00	08	00	03.3
S32	05	00	08	00	03.3
S32	08	00	-05	00	00.8
	1.8	3.2	3.6	2.0	02.8

Continued...

Table Eleven (Cont)

Eighteen to fifty-one times a year

B13		-05	00	00	00	-01.3
K13		10	10	05	10	08.8
K13		10	10	05	10	08.8
M11	(1)	00	10	10	- -	06.7
M11	(2)	00	10	10	- -	06.7
M11	(3)	00	10	10	- -	06.7
S15		05	00	05	- -	03.3
S29		-01	00	00	00	-00.3
S29		00	00	00	00	00.0
Average		2.1	5.6	5.0	4.0	04.4

Fifty-two to one hundred and three times a year

		Ha	He	Wb	Sc	Av
B14		00	-03	00	- -	-00.8
B14		- -	- -	- -	- -	- - - -
C12		00	00	00	00	00.0
C12		00	00	00	00	00.0
C12		-03	00	00	00	-00.8
J13		00	00	00	00	00.0
J13		00	00	00	00	00.0
N11		05	00	00	05	02.5
R12		02	02	02	05	02.8
R12		03	-02	03	05	02.3
R12		-05	00	-05	-05	-03.8
R12		02	-05	00	00	-00.8
S21		00	05	05	05	03.8
S22		10	10	00	—	06.8
S25		08	02	00	01	02.8
S25		-08	-04	-01	00	-03.3
Average		0.9	0.3	0.3	1.2	00.9

One hundred and four to two hundred and seven times a year

B11		05	10	08	06	07.3
B11		07	10	07	06	07.5
B11		05	10	06	05	06.5
C11	(2)	-03	00	-02	-01	-01.5
J12		-02	06	00	-01	-00.8
J12		-02	00	-02	04	00.0
K12		10	01	01	10	05.5
K12		08	01	01	10	05.5
K16		07	00	-02	00	01.3
K16		07	00	02	00	02.3
K16		07	00	02	00	02.3
S11		05	05	00	08	04.5
S16		03	05	00	05	03.3
S27		00	00	00	00	00.0
S30		01	02	03	05	02.8
Average		3.9	3.3	1.6	3.8	03.1

Continued...

Table Eleven (Cont)

Two hundred and eight times a year or more

B12	10	10	06	05	07.8
C13	00	00	00	- -	00.0
J11	-02	-01	00	02	-00.3
K11	10	10	10	10	10.0
K11	10	10	10	10	10.0
S13	10	10	06	10	09.0
S26	05	00	00	- -	01.7
Average	6.1	5.6	4.6	7.4	05.5

Widowers

	Ha	He	Wb	Sc	Av
W11	00	00	00	00	00.0
W11	00	00	00	00	00.0
W11	00	00	00	00	00.0
W12	- -	- -	- -	- -	- - - -
W13	05	-06	05	-07	-00.8
W13	05	-02	-06	00	-00.8
W14	05	00	00	05	02.5
W14	05	00	00	05	02.5
W15	00	00	00	00	00.0
W15	00	00	00	00	00.0
W15	00	00	00	00	00.0
W16	-10	-08	00	00	-04.5
W16	-05	00	-02	-03	-02.5
W17	-04	00	-05	-01	-02.5
W18	-08	00	00	-10	-04.5
W18	-05	00	-02	-01	-02.0
Average	-.8	-1	-.7	-.8	-00.8

Table Eleven Legend

Each of his children's happiness (Ha), health (He), behaviour (Wb) and performance at school (Sc) were assessed by the fathers compared to pre death or separation on a scale of -10 to +10.

The average score over all four is then shown.

The children are listed in the order given in table two.

In the two families in which children saw their mothers with different frequency the number in brackets indicates which child is referred to as enumerated in table two.

Table Twelve

Income Trends for Separated Lone Fathers

	Before	Adjust	Sep	Now	Dif	% Fall\Rise
B11	05.29	05.92	2.11	05.29	00.63	- 10.6
B13	14.80	15.69	1.07	11.00	04.69	- 33.5
B14	14.09	16.06	3.06	14.09	01.97	- 14.0
C11	15.00	15.00	0.0	12.59	03.41	- 22.7
C12	30.00	31.20	1.0	08.60	22.06	- 75.3
C13	07.86	09.36	5.0	05.82	03.54	- 45.0
J11	60.00	74.40	5.11	09.60	64.80	- 108.0
K11	07.80	09.67	6.0	07.80	01.87	- 24.0
K13	04.48	05.02	4.0	04.48	00.54	- 10.8
K14	18.00	20.16	4.0	05.30	14.86	- 82.6
K15	30.56	37.89	6.0	30.56	07.33	- 24.0
M11	07.80	08.89	4.06	06.03	02.86	- 36.7
M15	50.00	57.00	3.06	06.45	50.55	- 101.0
N11	30.00	33.90	4.02	15.00	18.90	- 63.0
R12	50.00	57.00	3.06	05.09	51.91	- 103.8
S11	06.50	07.87	5.03	04.22	03.65	- 56.2
S12	18.00	19.08	2.06	05.11	14.69	- 81.6
S15	10.92	11.90	1.08	11.96	+00.06	+ 00.5
S16	68.00	78.20	4.1	31.00	47.20	- 69.4
S17	14.80	16.28	2.08	04.50	13.78	- 93.1
S21	16.80	16.97	0.05	13.90	03.07	- 8.1
S22	05.00	05.65	4.03	05.00	00.65	- 13.0
S23	22.00	22.22	0.03	05.99	16.23	- 73.0
S25	22.60	24.40	2.0	05.40	19.01	- 84.1
S26	09.50	10.55	2.03	11.25	+00.70	+ 07.4
S27	27.00	29.16	2.01	22.80	06.36	- 23.6
S29	22.50	23.40	1.01	20.50	02.90	- 12.9
S32	10.00	12.40	5.11	06.93	05.47	- 54.7
Avg	21.39	22.74	3.03	10.58	-12.16	- 56.8
W12	10.00	11.20	3.0	04.28	07.92	- 79.2
W13	18.80	19.36	0.09	13.20	06.16	- 32.8
W14	14.00	10.70	1.08	06.91	03.79	- 37.9
W15	20.00	24.00	5.01	23.06	00.40	- 02.0
W16	15.07	17.93	4.08	20.05	+02.12	+ 14.0
W17	06.50	08.06	6.0	02.80*	06.26	- 96.0
W18	15.20	15.96	1.03	09.56	06.40	- 42.1
Avg	13.65	15.32	3.02	11.49	03.83	- 28.1

Table Twelve Legend

Respondents are those lone fathers who have been separated or bereaved for less than six years for whom full data is available.

Before = Net Income before break. Adjust = adjusted for inflation at 1% every complete three months. Sep = length of time since separation or bereavement. Now = net income now.
Dif = difference between income now and adjusted income before.
% Rise and Fall of difference to adjusted income before.

*Income of one respondent whose new mate gets a similar amount for the joint family.

Table Thirteen

Effect of Death or Separation of Father

	Ha	He	Wo	Av 1+2	Avg
B11	07	07	02	07.0	05.3
B12	07	08	06	07.5	07.0
B13	- 10	- 10	- 10	- 10.0	- 10
B14	- 10	- 05	- 05	- 07.5	- 06.7
C11	- 04	00	- 04	- 02.0	- 02.6
C12	05	00	- 05	02.5	00.0
C13	05	00	- 05	02.5	00.0
J11	- 03	- 03	- 08	- 03.0	- 04.7
J12	07	07	04	07.0	06.0
J13	- 05	- 05	- 05	- 05.0	- 05.0
K11	10	10	- 05	10.0	05.0
K12	05	00	- 10	02.5	- 01.7
K13	10	10	- 10	10.0	03.3
K14	10	00	- 10	05.0	00.0
R15	10	10	10	10.0	10.0
K16	10	00	- 10	05.0	00.0
N11	00	00	10	00.0	03.3
M12	- -	- -	- -	- - - -	- - - -
M13	- 02	- 02	- 10	- 02.0	04.7
M14	10	08	- 10	09.0	02.7
M15	- 06	03	- 06	01.5	- 03.0
N11	10	05	10	07.5	08.3
N12	10	00	10	05.0	06.7
R12	- 05	- 05	- 10	- 05.0	- 06.7
S11	05	09	- 10	07.0	01.3
S12	10	05	- 10	07.50	01.7
S13	10	- 05	10	02.5	05.0
S15	10	03	05	06.5	06.0
S16	09	- 05	- 08	02.0	- 01.3
S17	- 05	10	- 10	02.5	- 01.7
S18	- -	- -	- -	- - - -	- - - -
S21	- 05	- 05	05	- 05.0	- 01.7
S22	05	02	02	03.5	03.0
S23	- 10	10	07	00.0	02.3
S24	05	08	07	06.5	06.7
S25	- 04	- 02	- 08	- 03.0	- 04.7
S26	07	03	02	05.0	04.0
S27	06	00	02	03.0	02.7
S28	10	10	10	10.0	10.0
S29	- 10	- 05	- 10	- 07.5	- 08.3
S30	07	03	- 06	05.0	01.3
S31	05	03	- 08	04.0	00.0
S32	10	10	- 10	10.0	03.3
T11	10	10	- 10	10.0	03.3
Avg	3.5	2.2	- 1.6	01.1	03.1
W11	- 06	- 02	- 06	- 04.0	- 04.7
W12	- -	- -	- -	- - - -	- - - -
W13	- 08	- 08	02	- 08.0	- 04.7
W14	- 05	00	- 06	- 02.5	- 03.7
W15	- 02	00	00	- 01.0	- 00.7
W16	- 08	- 01	01	- 03.0	- 02.7
W17	- 01	00	- 10	- 05.0	- 03.7
W18	00	00	- 02	00.0	- 00.7
Avg	- 4.3	- 1.7	- 3.1	- 03.3	- 03.0

Table Thirteen Legend: Ha = Happiness; He = Health; Wo = How well off

Table Fourteen

Children's outcome\influences

Best Outcome	Ha	He	Wb	Sc	All	FH	Inc	Gy	Gm	Em	Cat	Sep	Ch	V	W
B12	10	10	06	05	7.3	07	8.2	10	09	E	Sk	??	G12		*
K11\1	10	10	10	10	10.0	10	7.8	10	10	E	Man	6.0	PB19		
K11\2	10	10	10	10	10.0	10	7.8	10	10	E	Man	6.0	G14		
K13\1	10	10	05	10	8.8	10	4.5	10	10	U	?	4.0	PB9		
K13\2	10	10	05	10	8.8	10	4.5	10	10	U	?	4.0	PB7		
K15\1	10	10	10	05	8.8	10	30.6	10	10	E	Pro	6.0	G20		*
K15\2	10	10	10	05	8.8	10	30.6	10	10	E	Pro	6.0	G17		*
M14\1	10	10	08	08	9.0	10	4.7	10	-10	U	Man	7.0	B8		*
M14\2	10	10	08	08	9.0	10	4.7	10	-10	U	Man	7.0	B10		*
S13	10	10	06	10	9.0	10	4.8	10	10	U	Man	6.0	B9		
S18\1	10	10	10	10	10.0	x	8.5	10	-10	E	Sk	6.5	G7	*	
S18\3	10	10	10	10	10.0	x	8.5	10	-10	E	Sk	6.5	G11	*	
S18\5	10	10	10	10	10.0	x	8.5	10	-10	E	Sk	6.5	G13	*	
S28	10	10	08	10	9.5	10	4.8	08	-10	E	Sk	9.8	G11	*	

Worst Outcome	Ha	He	Wb	Sc	All	FH	Inc	Gy	Gm	Em	Cat	Sep	Ch	V	W
B13	-5	0	0	0	-1.3	-10	11.0	0	0	E	Sk	1.7	G8		
B14\1	0	-3	0	ty	-1.0	-10	14.1	?	?	E	Pro	3.6	G7		*
C11\2	-3	0	-2	-1	-1.5	-04	12.6	2	?	E	Pro	0.11	B17		
C12\3	-3	0	0	0	-0.8	+05	8.6	6	1	S	Pro	1.0	G11		*
J11	-2	-1	0	+2	-0.3	-03	9.6	0	0	E	Pro	5.11	G11		*
J12\2	-2	0	-2	+4	0.0	+07	19.0	-2	-2	E	Pro	2.4	B16		*
N12	0	0	-2	0	-0.3	10	16.0	-2	-10	E	Sk	16.0	B18		
R12\3	-5	-5	0	-5	-3.8	-05	5.1	2	-2	U	Pro	3.6	B7	*	
R12\4	2	-5	0	0	-0.8	-05	5.1	0	0	U	Pro	3.6	B4	*	
S23\1	-5	5	-5	-8	-3.3	-10	6.0	5	-8	U	Sk	0.3	G9		
S23\2	-10	5	-5	-5	-3.3	-10	6.0	5	-9	U	Sk	0.3	B10		
S25\2	-8	4	-1	0	-1.3	-04	5.4	6	-1	U	SS	2.0	PB15	*	
W16\1	-10	-8	0	0	-4.5	-08	20.1	0	na	E	Pro	4.8	B11		
W16\2	-5	0	-2	-3	-2.5	-08	20.1	0	na	E	Pro	4.8	G8		
W17	-4	0	-5	-1	-2.5	-01	2.8	4	na	U	Sk	6.0	G8	*	
W18\1	-8	0	0	-10	-4.5	00	9.6	0	na	E	Sk	1.3	B18		
W18\2	-5	0	-2	-1	-2.0	00	9.6	0	na	E	Sk	1.3	G15		

Table Fourteen Legend

Ha, He, Wb, Sc children's score for happiness, health, behaviour and school performance on a scale -10 to 10. All = average.
FH = Father's happiness (-10 to 10) Inc = income. Gy = gets on with father, Gm = gets on with mother. Em, E = Employed,
U = Unemployed. Cat = employment category. Sep = time since separation or bereavement. Ch details of child(Table two)
V* = Violence. W* = Father thinks lone fathering worthwhile.

Figure One

Performances related to contact frequency with mother

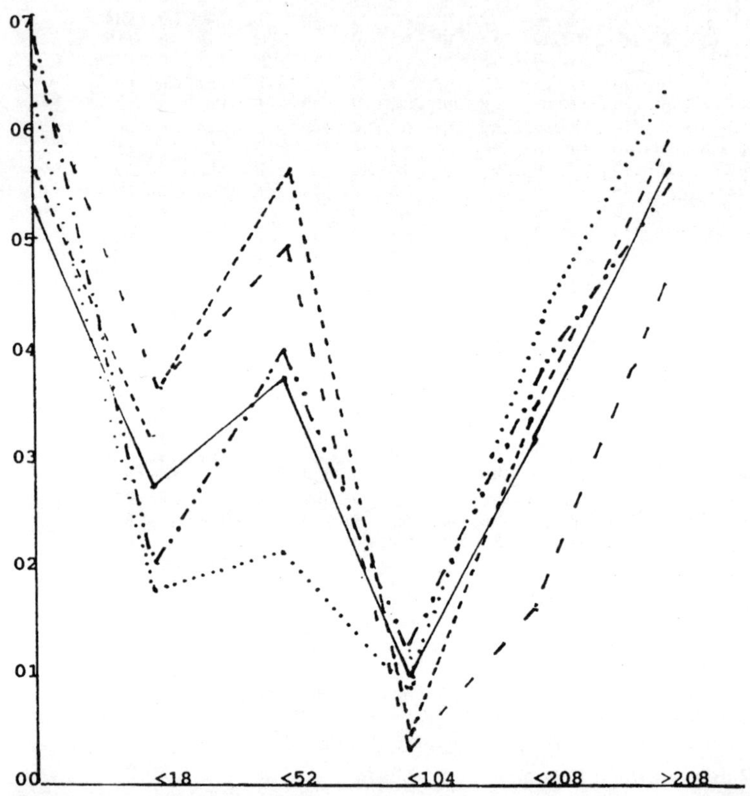

~1

Happiness = ...
Health = - - - - - - -
Behaviour = - - - - - -
School Performance = - . . - . . -
Overall = ————

Vertical axis indicates score on a scale -10 to 10 Horizontal axis indicates number of mother contacts a year. Widowers appear "below the line" as the scores were all negative.

Publications referred to in the text

B1 Breaking Even;Jacqueline Burgoyne. Penguin 84.
C1 Co-Parenting;Miriam Galper. Running Press.
C2 To and Fro Children;Jill Burrett.Thorsons 93.
C3 Children and Divorce. Kathleen Cox\Martin Desforges. Cox9 C3
C4 Interests of Children at Divorce. Richards Paper 94
C9 Running – The Risk.Frost\Rees\Stein. Childrens Soc Nov 94
D1 Divorce Matters;Burgoyne\Ormrod\Richards. Pelican 87.
D2 Disposable Parent,The;Mel Roman\William Haddad. Penguin 79.
F1 Fathering;Celeste Phillips\Joseph Anzalone.Mosby 82.
F3 Father Power;Henry Biller\Dennis Meredith. Anchor 87.
F4 Good Father,The;Peter Prince (fict) Cape 83.
F5 Father,The;David Lynn. Wadesworth USA 94
F6 Becoming a Father;Charlie Lewis. Open Univ 86.
F7 Divided Families;Frank Furstenberg\Andrew Cherlin. Harvard 91
F8 Fathers;ed Beial\McGuire. Junction 82
F9 Fathering;Ross Parke. Fontana 81
F10 Fathers;Ursula Owen. Virago 83
F11 Fathers' Role,The Cross Cultural Perspects. Ed Lamb. Erlbaum USA 87
F12 Fathers'Role,The Applied Perspectives. Ed Lamb. Wiley USA 86
F13 How to father;Fitzhugh Dodson. Signet 74
F14 Subversive Family,The;Ferdinand Mount. Unwin 82
F15 Step Families Talking;Elizabeth Hodder. Optima 89
F16 Lone Fatherhood;J Adams. Thesis Fen 93
F19 Family Therapy John Burnham. Routledge 96
F20 Goodbye Father;Maureen Green. Routledge 76
FF1 Frontiers of Family Law;ed Bainham & Pearl. Chancery 93
H1 Approaches History Western Families; M Anderson McMillan 80
LP1 Lone Parenthood & Family Disruption; Louie Burghes FPSC. 94
M1 Maternal Deprivation Reassessed; M Rutter. Penguin 72
M2 Motherless Families;Victor George\Paul Wilding. Routledge 72
M3 Remarriage;Helen Franks. Bodley Head 88
M4 Men on Divorce;Denise Winn. Piatkus 86
M5 Maintenance After Divorce;Eekelaar\Maclean.OUP86
MF1 Males and Females;Corinne Hatt. Penguin 72
MF2 Male and Female;Margaret Mead. Penguin 62
OPCS Office of Population, Census and Statistics
P1 How it Feels when Parents Divorce;Jill Krenentz. Gollancz 85
P2 Parenting Threads;Erica De'Ath\Dee Slater. Step Family 92
P3 Lone Parent Families in the UK; Bradshaw\Millar HMSO 93
R1 Reassessing Fatherhood;Charlie Lewis\Margaret O'Brien. Sage 87
R2 Richard Boynder in The Independent
R3 Cockett\Tripp Rowntree Social Policy Research Findings 45
St1 National Step Family Assoc Fact File July 94
St2 Step Family Fact Sheet July 95
WP When Parents Separate; Children's Legal Centre 94
YP1 Young People Under Stress; Sally Burningham. Virago 94

Silas Marner; George Eliot
The Kindness of Women; JG Ballard
Holy Deadlock; AP Herbert
Helping Children Cope with Divorce; Rosemary Wells Sheldon
Helping Children Cope with Grief; Rosemary Wells Sheldon